Changing
Colours

Changing Colours

The Irene van Dyk Story

RUSSELL GRAY

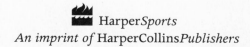

HarperSports
An imprint of HarperCollinsPublishers

National Library of New Zealand Cataloguing-in-Publication Data

Gray, Russell, 1943-
Changing colours : the Irene van Dyk story / Russell Gray.
ISBN: 1-86950-417-8
1. Van Dyk, Irene. 2. Netball—New Zealand. 3. Women basketball players—
South Africa—Biography. I. Title.
796.324092—dc 21

Harper*Sports*
An imprint of HarperCollins*Publishers*

First published 2002

HarperCollins*Publishers (New Zealand) Limited*
P.O. Box 1, Auckland

ISBN 1 86950 417 8

Designed and typeset by Chris O'Brien
Printed by Griffin Press, Australia on 80 gsm Ensobelle

Foreword

As a former shooter it is easy to appreciate the phenomenal talent of Irene van Dyk. Gifted with magnificent height, incredible athleticism and uncanny accuracy, Irene is one of the best shooters in the world, if not the best.

Like most top shooters, Irene spends hours each day practising shots, shooting perhaps 300, maybe more; firstly static, then moving; with a defender, then without one; with eyes open and then shut. It sounds exhausting and it is, but it's not unusual at international level. What sets Irene apart from other shooters, however, is her ability to shut out what is happening around her and almost routinely make the shot from anywhere in the circle, against any defender. She's the kind of player teams cry out for.

We all know netball is a team sport, but few would disagree that Irene single-handedly made South Africa competitive on their return to international netball. In those early days Irene, who was capped 72 times for South Africa, faced some of the toughest defenders in the world. Most times she came off best, but South Africa usually came off worst. That is until the 1995 world championships when the unexpected happened and South Africa seriously damaged New Zealand's hopes of world championship glory.

No one could believe what had happened, or how it had happened. But one thing is certain — had Irene van Dyk not been there it would not have happened. Irene's shooting prowess at that tournament turned her into a media darling. She topped the shooting statistics, and repeated the feat at the 1999 world championships in Christchurch.

Now an integral part of New Zealand netball, Irene has dominated the local scoreboards in both the Coca-Cola Cup and the National Provincial Championship, posting success rates of over 90 per cent. These days Irene is chasing the perfect game, the one where you finish with figures of 100 per cent, and she's not far away after being successful with 47 of her 49 attempts against Australia in 2001.

Few netballers have achieved the consistency and accuracy that makes them a super shooter. Picking the best is always tough. Perhaps it is Colleen McMarster, or maybe Mirth Solomon from the 1960s and 1970s. From more recent times Tracy Shortland can be regarded as New Zealand's most accurate. It is a tough call to make but one thing is certain, Irene van Dyk can be added to that list. For New Zealanders it is a blessing that she is now on our side and not South Africa's.

April Ieremia
January 2002

Contents

Acknowledgements

There were moments during the writing of this book when Christie van Dyk told me that I was spending more time with his wife than he was. Christie was correct. Irene and Christie were leading extremely busy lives, but Irene always managed to fit sessions for the book into her schedule. For that, and the way Irene, Christie and Bianca welcomed me into their home, I am grateful.

Thanks are also due to the players and coaches from New Zealand, Australia and South Africa who so willingly made themselves available for interviews.

Photographs are a vital part of any book and the cooperation of the *Dominion* newspaper, Ross Land at Fotopress and Andrew Cornega at Photosport is appreciated.

The team at HarperCollins, especially my editors Lorain Day and Sue Page, made the project enjoyable through their advice, encouragement and professionalism.

To my wife Barbara, thank you for the encouragement, help with proofreading and for putting up with me turning the dining room into a work station.

Introduction

It was early in 1995 that I first met Irene van Dyk. She was visiting New Zealand with the South African netball team and I had requested some time with her to prepare a feature story for Wellington's *Dominion* newspaper. What I didn't know at the time was that it was the first lengthy interview she had undertaken without being accompanied by captain Debbie Hamman or a member of the management team. It wasn't that they were concerned about what she would say, more Irene being worried that her command of the English language could lead her to say things out of context.

I remember the interview well. Irene laughed a lot and was open and forthcoming, which isn't always the case with leading sportspeople. While then virtually unknown in South Africa, where netball received little media attention, and able to walk unnoticed along the beach with her husband Christie and dog Adidas, Irene was attracting attention overseas. On South Africa's return to international netball Irene had made a strong impact with her skills and personality. Before long she was well known on three continents. It was in New Zealand, where netball is a major sport, that she was fêted most of all, and that undoubtedly helped pave the way for her to settle there with her family.

Irene's journey from carefree childhood days on the family farm in Meyerton on the outskirts of Johannesburg to the Lower Hutt suburb of Stokes Valley in New Zealand has been fun, but far from all plain sailing. This is Irene's story in her words, my observations and through the eyes of those who have been closest to her during that journey.

Russell Gray
March 2002

Chapter 1

A Star is Born

THE 1995 WORLD NETBALL CHAMPIONSHIPS in Birmingham, England, promised to be the biggest and best the sport had seen. Whether they lived up to that billing is open to question, but there is no doubt they were dramatic.

More teams than ever before were taking part in the tournament at the cavernous National Indoor Arena, and as players from 26 countries descended on the Midlands to join hosts England, most attention was focused on those who had travelled the farthest. The southern hemisphere trio of Australia, the defending champions; New Zealand, beaten finalists four years earlier; and South Africa, who had returned to the international fold from the netballing wilderness 12 months earlier for the first time since finishing third at the 1967 world tournament, were the names on everyone's lips. Of the three, New Zealand was probably the most bullish about their chances. Their supporters certainly were, along with the large media contingent that followed them across the world. Coach Leigh Gibbs and her players were more circumspect publicly, although privately there was a quiet confidence within the camp.

The optimism was understandable. Four years earlier the Silver Ferns had lost by a single goal to Australia in the Sydney world championship final. Since then Gibbs had taken over as coach from Lyn Parker. Gibbs had put the smile back on the face of New Zealand netball to such an extent that, in their last meeting before Birmingham, the Silver Ferns had beaten world champions Australia by four goals. On top of that there was the boost of knowing that Australia had recently been beaten three times by an Australian President's team. New Zealand had also beaten South Africa 67–49 in Auckland 19 weeks earlier, and made a clean sweep of a home test series against England.

It was in Auckland that the Silver Ferns got their first look at towering South African shooter Irene van Dyk. Impressive statistics of 40 goals from 46 attempts moved New Zealand goalkeep Bernice Mene to say that it was essential opposing teams stopped the ball getting to van Dyk or they would soon find themselves in serious trouble.

In Birmingham the draw, which was soon to be hotly debated, pitted New Zealand against Namibia first up. Predictably, they brushed aside the netball minnows with a hollow 87–22 win. At the same time South Africa opened their campaign by going close to breaking a world championship scoring record in beating the Cayman Islands 110–22, just short of Jamaica's record 114–23 win over Vanuatu in Sydney four years earlier. Irene van Dyk netted 90 of South Africa's goals.

New Zealand and South Africa easily got through their second games and on the third morning of the two-week tournament they met. Apart from the most fervent South African supporters, few gave the Proteas any chance of beating the Silver Ferns. Even the South African players viewed themselves as underdogs.

Whether the Silver Ferns had been lulled into a false sense of security by their easy win over South Africa in Auckland only those involved will know, but the match didn't go according to expectations. Rather than New Zealand being in control as they had at the last meeting, from the start it was a goal-for-goal encounter. Throughout the 60 minutes there were never more than two or three goals between the teams and in the final few minutes the tension was unbearable, on and off court.

As *The Times*' Louise Taylor wrote in her review of the game, spectators were left breathless by the pace, passion and panache on show, while a live television audience 12,000 miles away in New Zealand were kept on the edge of their seats as their favourites battled the unseeded South Africans.

With a minute left the score stood at 56–56. Three times in those last frenetic, nerve-racking 60 seconds the ball reached the safe hands of Irene van Dyk. Each time the South African shooter sent it arcing through the air and, inevitably, into the centre of the goal. The Ferns could manage only one goal in that last minute, and when the final whistle went South Africa had won 59–57. It was only then, as she saw team-mate Rese Hugo leap into the air with her arms raised, that Irene realised the Proteas had won.

When she talks about how the game unfolded Irene shakes her head as if, six years on, it is still hard to comprehend.

'As it got close to the end everyone was going ballistic around the court. Both benches were yelling at the teams and the spectators were going wild, but I didn't know whether we were winning or losing. For the only time in my career I didn't look at the scoreboard once during the game. I knew it was close because of the reactions of those around me on court, and the noise from the stands.

'Not looking was hard, but I managed to stay firm. Had I known the score I'm sure I would have missed some shots so I preferred not to know. What I did know was that everything was going our way. Every loose ball seemed to find its way into South African hands. Every time the whistle went it appeared to be in our favour. It didn't matter where I was in the circle when the ball arrived. Whether I was under the post or just inside the circle I 'd shoot and the ball would go through the net.

'For the Silver Ferns the opposite was happening. Nothing they tried seemed to come off. One of the wonderful things about sport is that on any given day something like that can happen. I always say that if things are going your way then milk the cow till it runs dry. That's what we did that day.'

As the South African players hugged each other courtside, and their small band of supporters cheered and waved the republic's national flag, there were mixed emotions among the other 99 per cent inside the stadium. Neutrals were still catching their breath after an exhilarating display from two southern hemisphere teams that put Britain's equivalent teams in the shade. Among the New Zealand supporters and media there was a feeling of stunned disbelief.

Most Kiwis were so confident of New Zealand making the final many Silver Ferns' supporters hadn't even arrived in Birmingham when the game was played. New Zealand fans were more interested in sightseeing than watching the early stages of the tournament. It was the business end of the championships they wanted to see. Now, thanks to the lopsided draw that meant none of the top five teams could afford to lose two matches if they were to make the final — a departure from previous tournaments, the Silver Ferns had to beat Australia 24 hours later or they would have no chance of reaching the final.

Irene took time out from celebrating with her team-mates to steal a glance along the court to where the New Zealand women were sitting. They were shattered. Some had their heads covered in towels, wanting to keep their emotions private; others just stared into space, probably contemplating the fact that the next day they would be up against their nemesis — Australia — when it would be win or bust.

While she was as delighted as anyone in the South African camp at what had just been achieved, Irene couldn't help feeling sorry for the Silver Ferns. She knew how they were feeling. While South Africa had successfully re-entered international netball 12 months earlier with a British tour that brought seven test wins, the harsh realities of how far they'd apparently been left behind during their isolation had been hammered home by both New Zealand and Australia earlier in the year.

As she watched the devastated Kiwis, not even in her wildest dreams could Irene have imagined that five years later, soon after more world championship heartbreak for New Zealand, she would swap the dark green uniform of South Africa for the black of the Silver Ferns.

'Happy as I was, I did feel for the Silver Ferns in those few minutes after the game when both teams were still courtside. They were smashed. After the way they'd beaten us earlier in the year they must have been absolutely certain they would easily account for us and go on to meet Australia for the world title.

'The result was so unexpected, not only by New Zealand, other teams and the supporters, but by the South African team as well. We were just as surprised as anyone that we'd beaten them. When we'd played Australia and New Zealand earlier in the year, the speed at which both countries played the game knocked the wind out of us. As the ball zipped all over the court, leaving us grasping at fresh air, I thought, "What the hell is this? It certainly isn't netball," and when we got off court I swear we were in shock.

'Looking back, those heavy losses helped us to produce that stunning upset at the world championships. Because of them no one expected anything from us. We were a minor irritant in New Zealand's way that would be easily brushed aside.'

While there was some tension in the Proteas camp the night before they played New Zealand, Irene was relaxed. Winning was more of an issue for the team's older players, because this would be their first and last world tournament for South Africa. They'd waited years for the chance to play on the world stage while the republic was in sporting isolation. When the next world championships came round in four years' time most would be too old.

It was a different story for Irene. She imagined she would be playing for South Africa for many years. She was determined to enjoy the moment; to savour the experience. She had a ball during the two weeks in Birmingham and enjoyed nothing more than the win over the Silver Ferns.

Australia beat New Zealand 45–44 the following day, ending the Silver Ferns' world title hopes. Instead it would be South Africa Australia played in the final. Had New Zealand beaten Australia, the defending champions would have been out of the running. No wonder the draw was being ridiculed. But while the draw was slammed by all and sundry, it was of no consolation to New Zealand that the format would never be used again. All the Silver Ferns had left to play for was third place, a position they achieved easily.

Thanks to their win over New Zealand the South Africans were looked at differently when they returned to the Chamberlain Hall hostel at the University of Birmingham, where all the teams were based. Suddenly there was a new-found respect from other competitors. Irene and her team-mates enjoyed life in the hostel, despite the rooms being basic and there being only one shower and four baths for every 20 people. With teams invariably wrapped up in their preparations for the following day's games there was little mingling among the players during the evenings. Going to the cafeteria for breakfast and lunch was fun, however — and a bit of an eye-opener for the South Africans.

They got along best with the Americans, partly because they were fascinated by their clothes. The South African women had led such sheltered lives through not being able to travel overseas with their sport that the mere mention of the United States conjured up wonderful visions of all that's supposed to be good in life. The Proteas thought America must be so cool, even at netball. In reality netball was bigger in South Africa than it will ever be in the United States.

There was also an affinity between South Africa and Canada because there were two South African women in the Canadian team, and, despite what happened on court, there was a bond between the Ferns and the Proteas. According to Irene, the New Zealanders always looked smart and were easy to talk to, ready to gossip about anything and everything.

'It was a different story with the Aussies. They didn't really talk to us, apart from Vicki Wilson, but then Vicki has always talked to everyone. She's a fabulous person. Since those days I've come to know Liz Ellis and Kathy Harby, both on and off the court, but at the time we were a bit scared to talk to the Australians because they looked arrogant.

'That's something you have to take into account in sport. A person can be completely different to the image they project on the netball court or rugby field. Liz and Kathy are ultra-competitive on court. But off it they are neat people.'

The South Africans thought they'd conquered the world with their win over New Zealand, and there was never a chance of them repeating the effort against Australia in the final. Irene says her team didn't focus properly on Australia because they were on such a high after the New Zealand game. As the final approached they became scared and nervous — the moment was too big for them.

Australia's experience of having been in such a situation previously counted for a lot, and the only positive thing South Africa could take from the 68–48 loss was that they improved on their efforts earlier in the year against the world champions. The closest they'd come in three games during February was 43 goals.

Irene had assumed that since South Africa were playing Australia, New Zealand's biggest rivals, the Silver Ferns would be supporting the Proteas in the final. She was wrong. Seeing the Ferns sitting high up in the stands, she was surprised to see they were cheering for Australia. Now she's a New Zealand resident van Dyk understands. While Kiwis and Aussies are passionately competitive on the court or field, when it comes to the rest of the world they pull together.

Australia may have left England with the world championship trophy again in their baggage, but it is fair to say that the person who made the biggest impression, both on and off court, was Irene van Dyk. It was no surprise when Irene was named the tournament's top shooter after scoring 543 goals in nine matches. Off court her height and good looks had reporters falling over themselves for interviews.

The tournament provided Louise Taylor, one of England's leading soccer writers, with a rare opportunity to focus on women's sport and she was just one of many to fall under van Dyk's spell.

'Those watching from the stands cannot fail to be impressed by her agile, on-court presence,' Taylor wrote. 'Rarely seen on court without a smile, van Dyk habitually hops from foot to foot, flicking her ponytail from side to side before peeling away from minders and shooting with unerring accuracy. A fair play paragon of apparently Corinthian proportions, she frequently applauds goals well taken by rival shooters.'

After meeting van Dyk off court Taylor seemed just as impressed, writing further: 'Despite possessing cover girl good looks, the primary school teacher from Vanderbijlltark remains shy, repeatedly lowering her huge Bambi-like eyes in a manner reminiscent of the young Lady Diana Spencer.'

Irene van Dyk was just the flag bearer South Africa needed for their return to the international arena. In return, the 1995 world tournament provided the stage for Irene to make her name throughout the growing netball world. It was probably all a bit much for the easy-going van Dyk but she coped remarkably well, making time for every interview and always stressing that, despite the attention she received, she was just another member of the South African team; that she couldn't shoot the goals if her team-mates didn't get the ball into the circle.

Considering all the attention Irene received at the world championships, it would have been easy for others in the team to resent her, to feel that she was hogging the limelight they should have been sharing. But talk to those in charge of the South African team in Birmingham and you soon realise that wasn't the case, though captain Debbie Hamman admits the other shooters in the team could have been a little put out. Used to being the golden girls in their own provinces, they now had to cope with everyone talking about another shooter.

'Even if they didn't really appreciate it, Irene is such a wonderful person they wouldn't have felt that way for long,' said Hamman, now a professor of law at the University of Western Cape. 'There was very little friction in the team. Most of us had been waiting for 10 or 12 years for the chance to play on the international stage and we didn't want anything to spoil it. Besides, we were all so bloody grateful that there was someone in the shooting circle we could throw the ball to and know it would be turned into a goal.

'Yes, the media did focus on Irene, but she's more astute than some people give her credit for. She handled it all extremely well and deflected the glory from herself on to the team. Everyone in the South African team accepted she was a unique player. We were a mature team in terms of age with four of us over 36. Irene was the youngest by far yet she made the biggest impact, but in doing so she was helping us achieve our goal.

'Life was blissful for Irene at that time. She had years of international netball ahead of her, while at least six of us knew that was our one and only chance of playing in a world championship. When I look back on that tournament I am very proud. History will show that, despite improved playing and training conditions, no South African team has reached the heights that we did.

'On leaving South Africa for Birmingham we were looking at a top five or six finish. That's not to say we didn't aim higher. We had a special piece of clothing made that we agreed to wear if we were playing for a medal. They were knickers with the South African flag embroidered on the back. Well we got to wear them in the final against Australia and I can tell you they scratched our backsides.'

Coach Marlene Wagner led South Africa back from the wilderness, and is proud of being the one who introduced Irene van Dyk to the world. Wagner played for South Africa at the first world tournament in 1963 and was in the team that finished third in 1967. That was the last time South Africa was allowed to play internationally until they were readmitted in 1994 following the abolition of apartheid.

Irene van Dyk came to Wagner's notice as a defender with the Western Transvaal — now North West Province — under-21 team. She was soon in the senior side and made an immediate impact as a shooter. Wagner says Irene was an inspiration to her team-mates, who never resented the attention she received. She always promoted the team and everyone connected with South African netball revelled in her achievements.

'The crowds might have been chanting "Irene, Irene", but it also meant the team was being noticed. On court the other players knew they just had to get the ball to Irene and it would be a goal. That meant she had to shoulder extra responsibility, but she handled it so well. It helped that Irene was new on the scene. She didn't care who she was up against because reputations meant nothing to her. Those marking her didn't know much about her either.

'In those two years back on the world scene we shared some very special moments and Irene will always have a special place in my heart.'

Despite losing to Australia, South Africa reaching the final made people back home take netball more seriously. On their return the Proteas received a warm welcome and had to attend a press conference, which was a novelty for them. There was a sizeable crowd waiting for them, although it was made up mainly of netball people rather than the public. It was a far cry from when South Africa won rugby's World Cup and the team rode through the city in an open-top bus.

But at least now South Africans knew their country had a netball team, and the netball world had discovered Irene van Dyk.

Chapter 2

Life on the Farm

ONE OF IRENE'S MOST TREASURED childhood memories is of sitting on the homestead porch with her father Herman, staring out into the pitch-black night listening to foxes howling.

It was on those balmy nights that Herman Viljoen helped develop the qualities that have played such a part in turning his daughter into a respected and loved sporting star in both South Africa and New Zealand.

The Viljoen family farm is, of course, a world away from Stokes Valley, a suburb of Wellington, New Zealand's capital city, where she has now settled with her husband Christie. But Irene and Christie dream of owning a small farm in New Zealand where they will be able to settle down at the end of a busy day, look out to the horizon and talk to their daughter Bianca in the same way Herman Viljoen passed on his views about life to his daughter. Such a dream is understandable. Irene and Christie both grew up on farms, and while they thoroughly enjoy the full life they now lead in New Zealand, it is only natural that they sometimes hanker for those carefree childhood days.

The fourth child of Irene and Herman Viljoen, Irene weighed in at 4.53 kg on 21 June 1972. As the youngest by five years she was always destined to be the baby of the family. Her brother Gerrit was 10 when Irene was born, her sister Janita 8, and Herman 5. The farm Irene grew up on and loved so much is in Meyerton, 30 kilometres out of Johannesburg. Horses, sheep, cows, pigs, chickens, rabbits . . . you name it, the Viljoen family had it.

While the farm was spread over a large area, it would be wrong to imagine it as palatial in the manner of American ranches seen in cowboy films. Situated on flat land with lots of trees, the farm was basically split into thirds. The first third, closest to the homestead, was devoted to corn. The second was all grass to cater for the cows and sheep, before again becoming corn for the final third.

The house was made of corrugated iron until, in 1984, Herman Viljoen moved the family into the town of Meyerton for two years while he rebuilt the homestead. A generator was needed to produce electricity, and most nights the family relaxed by candlelight. A torch was needed for visits to the outside toilet 50 metres away.

In summer the family would frolic in temperatures that could rise to 34°C, while in winter the temperature would sink as low as -4°C, although, as in the rest of the country, it didn't snow. It wasn't an economically productive farm as such because Irene's mother and father both had jobs. The milk, eggs and corn produced on the farm were for the family's consumption, though sometimes the neighbours would send over a two-litre jug that the Viljoens happily filled with milk. The farm was basically somewhere for them to get out of the city and relax.

'That was why I would get to sit on the porch with my father. My mother was matron at Vereening Hospital, which was about 35 km from the farm. She would work seven nights on and then have seven off. While she was working Mum would come home and sleep during the day.

'At the same time my brothers and sister were away studying at college so at night it was just Dad and myself at home. Once the chores were done I would pour him a drink, take his shoes off and settle down on the porch with him. We would look out into the dark and have daughter– father talks. I would tell him about my day and he would talk about what he'd done.

'There were some pretty rough kids at my school and I'd tell him what they'd been getting up to. Dad was a pretty wise guy and I'll never forget him telling me that it takes a lifetime to build your name, but only two lousy seconds to throw it away. Years later while at college I went out with several friends one night and some of them got drunk. They were doing really stupid things and I thought how ridiculous they looked. That was when I realised what my Dad had been talking about. I like a drink, but what I saw that night made me stop, look, and decide what's right and wrong.

'What Dad had told me also came in handy when it came to boys. At college a lot of my friends were boys, probably because I was a bit of a tomboy and played rugby and cricket with them. They seemed to think of me as one of their mates and would talk about all sorts of things. They would tell me which girls they'd slept with. They even had lists! Again I thought about what my father had said. It takes one night for a boy to ruin a girl's life.

'Living on a farm meant I didn't really go to pubs or clubs. I wasn't interested. I was more interested in getting on my horse and going for a ride.'

Such a pastime seemed unlikely at one time because while Irene eventually came to love riding, horses initially scared her and early attempts at riding hardly suggested she would become proficient.

'My brother's horse Florence was big and fat. Her back was so broad it was virtually impossible to fall off her but I managed it! I suppose I could use the excuse that because we didn't have saddles I had to ride bareback.

'Both my brothers broke horses in but I was scared to death of them in the beginning. Once I overcame the fear I loved riding and would spend so many happy hours riding round the farm.'

Like her brothers and sister, from the moment she could walk Irene had good ball skills and showed an aptitude for all sports. That was hardly surprising considering the family spent most of their time on the farm at weekends playing different sports. Other branches of the family would turn up from the city and they would all split up into teams led by Mum and Dad. Team numbers would swell when the neighbours turned up. They were not formally, or informally for that matter, invited. They would just pitch up. The kids would arrive on horseback while the adults would come in cars or on motorbikes.

The Viljoen's nearest neighbours were the Neethling and Schamagas families. In local terms they were relatively close, only a kilometre from the van Dyk's farm, but the next neighbours after that were another 30 kilometres away.

'It was a beautiful farm and we were always outside playing rugby, cricket, or whatever took our fancy. Being on a farm also toughened you up. At weekends we'd have to carry water cans from the well to the pigs and other animals. It was about 200 metres and they were heavy. My brothers had really good muscles and there was no gymnasium anywhere near the farm.'

The other side of farm life was doing the chores. There were usually three or four families living and working on the farm, but if the workers didn't front up for work it was up to the Viljoen children to get up and milk the cows at 5 a.m. before going to school. Primary school was 15 km away and the children needed to walk 2 km to the bus stop. Secondary school was in Meyerton. Again they travelled by bus, although when Irene was the only Viljoen attending her father would often take her in his truck.

Netball wasn't the first sport Irene stood out in. Athletics was then one of the biggest sporting pursuits in South African primary schools and Irene quickly came to the fore in sprinting, hurdling, high jump and long jump. According to her mother she also did well academically in primary school but later became lax in that area as she concentrated more and more on sport. She specialised in hurdling, but while she had a good technique there were problems with her start and, according to her mother, she wouldn't get into her full stride till about the sixth hurdle.

She also played cricket well. When bowling she could swing the ball, and she was the first girl to play cricket for the boys' team at her primary school.

'My female teachers didn't like it. Girls didn't play "boys" sport, full stop. Soccer was out and rugby definitely was. A girl didn't dare touch a rugby ball at school, yet at home I was playing rugby with my brothers all the time. I loved it.'

Irene's mother had been a provincial representative for the Vaal Triangle in korfball, which was played in South Africa before netball, so she was delighted when Irene took up netball in her last year at high school. There was no hint of what was to come when Irene first took to the netball court. Because she was small — yes, small — Irene began her career as a goal attack.

'She was small till the age of 16,' Irene Viljoen says of her daughter. 'Then she began growing quickly and didn't stop. As she got bigger she became a defender. While she played for her school at goalshoot, Irene played representative netball in defence and was named in the top 28 of all South Africa as a defender.

'In those days she never mentioned wanting to become a top netballer. I expected her to go on with the hurdles but things turned out for the best, didn't they?'

Athletics provided Irene with her first taste of serious competition. Schools would choose their best athletes to represent them in competition against other schools, and there would be heats to negotiate before the big day when the best athletes came up against each other in the finals. The last day would be huge, with every parent present to support their children.

'Athletics got really competitive from grade one which was when you were seven. You always wanted to be the best. That's how South Africans are. There's no room for it being about participation.'

There has been much debate in New Zealand in recent years about whether the country's netballers, cricketers and rugby players are hard enough. There is a feeling they have been softened up by the politically correct way certain factions want New Zealand sport run. Some sports administrators, including netball's, feel children shouldn't know the score of games they play. They don't want teams labelled A and B. 'Dolphins' and 'Penguins' are more apt, they say, so that children don't feel slighted by being in the B rather than the A team. It is a concept that's totally foreign to Irene van Dyk, and one she doesn't subscribe to.

'To say the kids shouldn't know the score of games they are playing in is ridiculous. The kids I coach want to know the score and there's nothing wrong with that whether they win or lose. A loss is not the end of the world. It's only a game, for goodness sake.

'It's just as important to learn how to handle a loss as it is to take part in the first place. Learning to win or lose with dignity is all part of growing up. My father said that if you gave your best right to the finish line and were able to say from the bottom of your heart that you had given everything you had then you were a winner wherever you finished. But you still wanted to finish first.

'At the 1989 national athletics championships I was competing in the 300-metre hurdles and I fell at the first hurdle in the final. As I hit the ground and rolled over I thought should I get up or just stay down and pretend I'm injured? The thought only went through my mind for a split second before I got up and finished the race, beating one runner to the line.

'My dad came running down from the stand where he'd watched the race, hugged me and said I'd just run my best ever race. He was so proud that I had given everything, even in adversity.

'If you have the drive to be the best as a child it helps you later in life. That's why I strongly believe competition is the best thing for kids.'

Athletics was one of the few things that could get Irene out of sedate Meyerton and into Johannesburg. The only tartan running track in the area was at Germiston, a Johannesburg suburb, and as a Transvaal representative hurdler that was where she had to go.

Farm people weren't keen to take chances in the city where there were all sorts of dangers lurking, real and imaginary. They preferred to patronise cafés — dairies to New Zealanders — for their groceries, or Checkers, a smaller version of Pak'N Save, in Meyerton.

It wasn't only the thought of how dangerous it was that kept Irene and her friends out of the city. It was simply too big for them. There was no danger of getting lost in Meyerton, which has only one main street. There are no traffic lights . . . but they do have tarsealed roads!

'That was also the thing about living on the farm. All my friends wanted to come to visit because it was safe — you can't get hit by a car because there are no cars — and we could do whatever we wanted. My mum and dad loved it because they thrived on having young people around.'

Herman and Irene Viljoen were more than parents to Irene. They were also friends, confidants and playmates to their daughter, who would otherwise have had no one to play with or confide in during the week, when siblings and friends were working or studying in the city.

Like many girls, Irene was particularly close to her father. When she talks about him her eyes sparkle more than usual. There are also moments of wistfulness, but the overall picture she paints of Herman Viljoen is of a strong, loud, caring, honest man.

'Dad seemed to know exactly what you were feeling at all times. I would be just about to say something when he would answer my unspoken question.

'When things might not have been going my way he would listen patiently before telling me not to worry. OK, he would say, perhaps you weren't good enough but you're going to have to live with it. In life you get ups and downs and there is nothing you can do to change that.

'There would be times when it seemed things couldn't get any worse — to a young girl anyway — and Dad would remind me that nothing was so bad that it couldn't be overcome.

'At the same time Mum would always look at the bigger picture. She would tell me not to focus on what had gone wrong, but to consider how whatever was happening at the time would affect people you love and care about.

'Because of the way Mum and Dad were we have always been a family that loves people. We have never been materialistic — worrying about furniture, jewellery and the like. Objects meant nothing.

'Dad was really down to earth — so much so that he would embarrass me terribly when he drove me to school. We would go in his truck, which would have the pig boxes on the back. Even though they would be empty when he dropped me off they were still so smelly. Imagine what it was like when he returned later in the day to take me home and they were full of food for the pigs. The food would be hanging over the side of the box, and the smell . . . whew!

'When I told him it was embarrassing for me in front of my friends he just looked at me and said, "But the pigs need food. Why is that embarrassing?"

'What he was basically saying is stuff what other people think. Our animals on the farm need feeding and it was up to us to take care of them. Dad was also like that with people, he'd think of others before himself. Not what they thought, but what their needs were.'

The children were all encouraged to play sport. There was no pushing them into any particular code, but once Gerrit, Janita, Herman junior and Irene had committed themselves to playing a sport they got all the support they could have asked for. While a lack of siblings to play with during the week might have seemed unfair at times to Irene, being the youngest had its advantages. By the time she was involved in athletics and, later netball, her parents had more time to support her since the other children were away studying. Both would be at every athletics meeting or netball match Irene was involved in. Her father would take days off work to be with her when she competed. As the matron of a hospital it wasn't as easy for her mother to do this, but she would often telephone the hospital and ask someone to cover for her as she would be a little late because she was still watching her daughter compete.

'Mum has always been amazing. She must have existed on four or five hours' sleep a night. When she was in New Zealand with me and Bianca while Christie was packing up back in South Africa ready to join us, I asked her how she managed on such little sleep and told her I'd never be able to. She just smiled and said I would if it was necessary.

'On the farm she'd come off night duty, sleep till 1 or 2 in the afternoon and then pick me up at the bus stop from school. She'd make me some food and then take me back to school for training, wait for me and then we'd go back home where she'd prepare dinner. Then she would go to work!

'While Dad was structured in everything he did, Mum took everything in her stride, just going with the flow.'

Irene needed her parents' love and understanding when, as a 14-year-old, athletics, which she had been so good at, suddenly became difficult.

'It was probably because my body had started growing. I actually shot up a couple of years later, but something must have been happening because I was suddenly so uncoordinated. I sucked at everything I did. I began finishing last in races I would normally have won or at least come second. That year and the following one were the only times I didn't represent my province. The way I was feeling it would have been easy to give it away, but Dad told me to just relax, keep training and it would come right. As usual he was correct.'

Gerrit, the eldest of the Viljoen children, was a distance runner and a top rugby player. A real leader, according to Irene. Herman played cricket, a game that suited his patient nature, while Janita played netball. Good enough to represent her college as goal attack at the South African championships, Janita would spend hours practising her goal shooting. Underneath the post would be little sister Irene catching the ball as it fell through the hoop and passing it back to Janita for the process to begin again.

It was during those sessions that Irene learnt to shoot goals through copying her big sister's style. The now familiar hands-above-the-head style that has taken Irene van Dyk to the top of world netball is how Janita shot.

Irene says being with and watching her brothers and sisters meant she picked up something from each of them. One day in particular sticks in her memory. It was while she was in primary school and her brother Gerrit was 18.

'Gerrit had prepared for this one particular race. He had put so much into his training preparing for it, but when the day came he wasn't quite right. Perhaps he was over-eager or too anxious, I don't really know.

'I think it was a six-lap race and after the first lap Dad could see Gerrit wasn't right. By the fourth lap he was holding his side and Dad said, "Gerrit is going to pull out of this race. Then I am going to kill him."

'As he was saying that Gerrit came into the straight and headed towards the side of the track, obviously intending to pull out. Before he could, Dad ran to the edge of the track and yelled, "What the hell do you think you're doing? You're going to finish this race!"

'The sight and sound of Dad had an amazing effect on Gerrit. He suddenly forgot about the pain, real or imagined, and set off in pursuit of those ahead of him. While everyone was looking at my dad, who knew what Gerrit had put into preparing for the race, my brother went on and won the race. Dad knew he had it in him. He just needed to be reminded. It was all part of the love and support we had from our parents.'

One thing Herman Viljoen had an aversion to was visiting the doctor. So when Irene, who was by now away at college, received a telephone call from her mother one Monday night in 1992 to say that her father was going to see a doctor the following day alarm bells began ringing in her mind.

'I was amazed. Dad must have been feeling really bad if he'd agreed to go to the doctor. When they went the next day the doctor sent him straight to hospital. On the night I received the call from Mum, I had a hole in my stomach and went cold all over. The thought kept going through my head that my dad wasn't going to make it.

'He needed a minor operation, but while under anaesthetic he had a heart attack and died. The operation hadn't even begun. I tried to put the thoughts out of my head on the Tuesday morning and convince myself that when I rang that night everything would be OK. When I was going back to my room, however, the hostel mother grabbed my arm and said she needed to talk to me. I knew what it was about.

'I was 20 when it happened. I thought I was too young to lose my dad, but then you're always too young to lose a parent aren't you?

'He died in February and in July I got my first national uniform from the netball team. It seemed so unfair that he couldn't have stayed alive another six months to see me wear that blazer. When I had first been chosen in South Africa's top 10 netballers he had been so proud. He would introduce me to people as "my Springbok daughter". I thought he was a bit pushy, but looking back it was just that he had so much faith in me. More than I had in myself.

'Making it worse for my mother was the fact that four days later they would have been celebrating their thirty-second wedding anniversary, and during that time they'd never been apart. In a way I was thankful it happened so quickly. He was such a happy person I couldn't have borne to watch him suffer.

'One of the few regrets was that he never got to meet Christie. Another is that we were never a family that took a lot of pictures at home so I have very few mementoes of him. Probably that's why Christie and I take pictures of everything that happens to us.'

In addition to having to adjust to the loss of her father, a lot was to happen to Irene on the netball front over the next two years.

Chapter 3

Netball, School and College

THOSE WHO HAVE AT TIMES SUGGESTED that Irene van Dyk is not mobile enough on the netball court will find it difficult to believe that when she began playing the game she moved around too much. Another surprising fact is an early dislike of the goalshoot position that would later propel her to international fame.

At the time Irene was a short-haired, skinny nine-year-old primary school pupil whose teacher-cum-coach was Ruth Van der Haar. Fortunately Van der Haar was a patient person, given the way her young charges raced around the court as little girls freed from the constraints of a classroom are wont to do. Keeping them in designated positions on the netball court was a nightmare. In fact it was impossible, as Van der Haar had undoubtedly come to accept during her teaching career.

None of her class was less disciplined than Irene. She was given the goal attack position simply because she was already able to shoot, thanks to the hours spent with her sister Janita under the goalpost her father had built on the farm. Getting her to play the position was another matter.

'Right from the start I thought I was the best player ever. Of course I wasn't, a few of my friends were already better than me, but that didn't stop me thinking it. I also wanted to do everything on court, including taking the centre pass. I couldn't understand why we needed seven players. I could do it all myself. Miss Van der Haar patiently explained to me that that wasn't possible, and quietly went about teaching me the basics.

'Really it was a very quiet beginning. Netball is a huge winter sport in South Africa, especially in schools. Boys played rugby, girls netball. Living outside the city meant the schools we attended were small so everyone participated. No excuses, you got out there and played. Everyone had to play or we wouldn't have had enough for a team to compete against other schools. That suited me. I loved it from the start.

'Gradually it dawned on me that netball was a team game. That other people were allowed to have the ball — so long as they passed it back to me, that is!'

There was nothing spectacular about Irene's primary school netball career, but when given the chance to play for the first team as a 13-year-old during her last year at primary school she wasn't happy because a change of position was involved.

'They switched me to goalshoot and that really upset me. I hated that position because you weren't allowed to move far. I told Dad what had happened. He suggested I talk to my teacher about it so I did, telling her I wasn't going to enjoy my netball if I was forced to play a position I didn't like. Very politely I asked if I could play goal attack.

'Looking back now I was being very selfish. I mean, what's going to happen if every child is allowed to dictate where she's going to play? You're going to have complete chaos. No one would want to be goalkeep or goalshoot. They would all want to be centre so they were involved in the game all the time.

'Anyway, the coach said I couldn't change my position. I either continued playing goalshoot for the first team or goal attack for the second team. The next week I was put back into the second team at goal attack. We were playing Suikerbos. The second team won their game but the first team lost. The next day at school I was called into the principal's office and told that if I didn't play goalshoot I wouldn't be playing netball. That left me with no choice. I enjoyed my netball too much to give it away so I swallowed my pride and played goalshoot.'

That wasn't the end of the matter so far as Irene was concerned, however. The following year at high school when she was asked what position she played the answer came quick as a shot, 'Goal attack.' It was at the much larger high school that Irene really found out about competitiveness in sport, thanks to three cousins of similar age who attended the same school. The Viljoen household Irene lived in wasn't overly competitive apart from the usual brother–sister type of one-upmanship. In contrast, her cousins' family was ultra-competitive.

In the beginning Irene wasn't seen as a threat by her cousins because she was in the under-16 team while they all played for the high school's first team. This didn't go down well with Irene, however, who felt she was just as good as they were, even though she now concedes perhaps she wasn't.

The under-16 side was the only age grade team at the school and once out of that the following year Irene had to play for either the fourth, third, second or first team. She had also continued with her athletics, at which she was showing real promise. The athletics season cut into netball's so that by the time Irene became available for netball the teams were well established. This meant she had to start wherever there was an opening. That turned out to be in the third team. One game was enough to convince those in charge that Irene was good enough for the second, so that's where she played the rest of the season while her ultra-competitive cousins were in the first team.

'I was very jealous of my cousins. How could they be good enough for the first team if I wasn't? It couldn't be right. I felt so hurt. The only consolation was that the second team I was playing for got to the regional finals and won the cup. Oh, and by that time I was playing goalshoot and starting to enjoy it.

'On the Saturday that we played the regional final there was a provincial schools selector called Gwen Fourie watching. The trials were to be played the following week and Gwen asked if I was going to be at them. I had to tell her I hadn't even thought about it because there was no way I would be allowed to go to the trials. I was in the second team. Trials were by invitation only. First team players from all schools were invited to the trials. That was all.

'Gwen said she wanted me there. I said no and so did Dad. He explained to her about my cousins being in the first team and me in the second. He said with all that had been going on I had been through enough for the year, and that now I was on a high after winning the cup I didn't need to be knocked down again.

'You should have seen Dad's face when Gwen told him she didn't give a hoot about what he thought. She wanted me at the trials. Not one to give up, she went to my mum and told her to make sure I was at the trials. Mum said it wasn't possible.

'Even then Gwen wouldn't take no for an answer and sent a note to the school principal. On the Monday I went to school wondering how the teacher that coached the first team would react to all this. She didn't say anything, and when I told her what had happened she didn't seem to believe me. However, after ringing the selector and having my story confirmed she said Mum had to take me because I wasn't part of her team.

'The situation had a really happy ending so far as Gwen and my mum were concerned. They eventually became great friends and travelled to Christchurch together to watch the 1999 world tournament.'

At the trials Irene couldn't play for her school team and finished up in a makeshift side. Playing alongside unfamiliar players obviously didn't handicap her, however, because when the Vaal Triangle team was named Irene was in it. The only other player from her school to make the representative team was defender Belinda Taljaard, and that was to have repercussions back at school.

'Our principal was amazed at what had happened. He didn't realise I was playing in the second team. He began to think something wasn't right when only two people were picked for the province and one of them couldn't get a place in the school first team.

'I, of course, was ecstatic. My cousins, however, were definitely not impressed and if I am honest that made it even more enjoyable. Dad said to me, "See, good things happen to people who wait for their chance." I said neither of us knew this was going to happen.'

The good news continued with Vaal Triangle reaching the semi-finals for the first time in its history with Irene playing goalkeep.

'Gwen turned me from a goalshoot to a goalkeep, which meant Belinda went into the province's second team and I finished up as the only representative from our school in the No. 1 side. At the end of the tournament I was included in the South African schools' top 28 players, which was fantastic.

'Part of my success at that tournament came because we had such a good attacking side which took some pressure off our defending. At that stage I was really quick and could adapt to different positions. Also I was eager to play wherever Gwen put me. After what she had done for me I would have done anything for her.

'The change came about because we swapped around one night so players could get a feel for how the person they would be playing against would react in certain situations. So the goalkeep went to goalshoot and vice versa.

'After a while I thought I was doing really well. This was the year when I was shooting up in height and being very tall helped with the defending. Next year, surprise, surprise, I was in the school's first team with my three cousins. Now we were on the same level we decided we could live with each other and all four of us got selected for the province.

'Two got chosen in the top 28 of South Africa, and I got selected in the top 10.'

Making the national top 10 as an 18-year-old capped what could only be described as a couple of strange years in the netballing life of Irene van Dyk. In retrospect, starting off playing for the school's second team may not have been a bad thing.

'While it was disappointing at first I enjoyed playing for the second team because we were a good side and we all got on well together. It makes a difference to your game when you're playing alongside people you enjoy being with. There were no pressures on us and we had a ball. Everyone expected things from the first team but not from us. The year taught me a lot.'

It was also Irene's first experience of netball politics. They were to play a bigger part in her life later, but even at school level she knew something wasn't quite right.

'I always thought that if the teacher liked me at all she would have at least put me on the bench for the first team. Unfortunately I don't think she liked me. I have a feeling it was personal because of something that had happened between her and someone in my family.'

Irene left high school in 1990 for college, where she earned a teaching diploma and continued her netballing education at the same time. Club netball didn't exist for college students. The only way into representative teams was by playing for a college, against club teams, at a tournament. Irene didn't play club netball until after she had made her international debut for South Africa.

Going to college was the first time Irene had been away from home. Having lived all her life on a farm, she had no idea what awaited her at Potchefstroom.

'It was scary because I was so innocent, having lived all those years in virtual isolation, really mixing only with family and close friends and neighbours. I hadn't got a clue what college life would be like. Everything was so new to me, but fortunately I soon had more than enough friends to show me the ropes!

'I had an absolute ball during college and came out with a teaching degree even though studying wasn't my strong point. My life was so full I didn't have much time for study. Well, that was my excuse anyway.

'I was more than happy to follow my brother's philosophy that 50 is a pass mark, so 51 is a waste of effort. Not that I wasted my time completely. I made sure I was steady and always did enough to get my symbols — As, Bs, Cs.'

It was at Potchefstroom that Irene met her future husband, Christie van Dyk, who was in the third year when she arrived. That meant a big gap between the pair at the start, even though they hit it off almost immediately.

The South African college system is completely different to New Zealand university life, and Irene had to treat Christie with respect.

'He was a third year and I was a first year, so he was my senior. When you're a first year student you must call your male seniors "Sir". Walking past him it is necessary to greet him with, "Good morning, sir," or "Good afternoon, sir."

'Even if I walk past him a zillion times a day I have to greet him a zillion times. It was so shocking. Not only did you have to greet them properly but you needed to know who they were. It was hard because as a first year you don't know anyone walking round campus.

'He and his friends would stop you and say "First year." You would jump to attention and reply, "Yes, sir." "What is my name?" "I don't know sir." "Are you going to ask?" "Sir, what is your name?" "Sir Christie." "Thank you, Sir Christie."

'Christie had about ten friends and I would go down all ten and be asked by everyone what their name was . . . and I could never remember.

'One day these guys went out to a dam for a barbecue — and a few beers — on the same day as some of us girls decided we would have two hours' sunbathing before going back to study. We got to the pool where Christie and his friends were having their barbecue and a beer. We were sunbathing and swimming. When I got back from a swim all my clothes were gone and I was left standing there in my togs.

'I was bigger than them so I went round shaking them. One had my shirt on, another my trousers, another my shoes. Christie was sitting there looking so innocent because he had none of my clothes. After that we played hand tennis and Christie asked me to be his partner. We smashed everyone. We just got on so well.

'The friendship improved even more when we began studying together after he said he would help me in a subject he turned out to be hopeless in. He was hopeless, and I mean hopeless, at English, but I didn't know that at the time. He asked what I was writing the next day and I said English. Christie said he would help me.

'You have English one, two, three and four for the years you're at college. I was in my first year. Christie was in his third year, but still doing first-year English. And HE was going to help ME!

'I had my books with me so we sat down and began to go through things together. I said, "This is what I'm writing tomorrow," and he said, "I know, I'm writing it too." "How can you be doing first-year English?" "Oh, I failed it the first two years so I'm doing English One again." So we studied together and the friendship firmed.

'At the time Christie had a girlfriend but I didn't know. Not that it mattered because we were just friends who seemed to do a lot of things together. I was 19 and he was 21.

'It was around that time Christie was diagnosed as a diabetic. I didn't know anything about diabetes so I rang my mother and she sent me the brochures about what diabetics are allowed to do and what they are not allowed to do. What they can eat and what they must not eat.

'Again it was just because we were such good friends. Then one day Christie told me he and his girlfriend had broken up because it hadn't been going well. That must have sparked something in our relationship because three months later we started going out together.

'Everything was going well, then she came to see me one night at the college. It threw me. I was so scared when it came over the intercom that someone called Tershia wanted to see me. It turned out that I had met her at the hospital when Christie was diagnosed with diabetes because all his friends would be there visiting.

'I needn't have worried. She was a really nice girl who wanted to tell me I had got a very special guy and I should look after him well. I said I would but really we were not that serious.'

Christie van Dyk was a good cricket player who would practise four hours a day. While he was practising Irene would be watching and eating, and eating, and eating. It didn't take long for her to put on 17 kg, thanks mainly to eating so much junk food on her first time away from home. In her second year at college she was eating breakfast, morning tea, a big lunch, a hot dog on the way to practice, dinner . . .

When her mother saw what was happening she put Irene on a strict diet, while Irene herself was watching how much Christie was practising and realised she needed to do the same thing. At the time she was playing for the college's first team and Christie began helping with her training. He has always been very good on the technical side of sport, and in those early days if Irene missed a shot he would inevitably be able to see why it had happened. Her elbow might have been turned out, her knee hadn't been bent, or her wrist was sloppy on the shot.

Christie quickly picked up the mechanics of the shooting motion, and having him around when she was practising became important to Irene. Even today she's still amazed at the way Christie can analyse different sports. When the pair watch rugby together he can't help but analyse what's happening. On one occasion when Andrew Mehrtens missed a kick Christie went back over the tape time and again just to work out the difference between that kick and the ones he had put over. Since those early days at college Irene has always had Christie at her side when she has practised netball drills away from a team environment.

Where they lived in South Africa there were no courts to practise on so all her training was done on the tar-sealed road outside the couple's house. Christie would make Irene jump on one leg and lift it high to get her bounding. Thinking back to those sessions now, Irene says the neighbours must have thought they were totally mad. The formula must have worked, however, because Irene was soon in the Western Transvaal team, and immediately made her mark at the national provincial tournament where she was chosen as goalshoot for the South African under-21 team.

It was a proud moment but, because South Africa was ostracised from the international netballing community, the under-21s didn't get to play as a team. The same applied to the senior South African side, which was frustrating for everyone concerned.

'It was shocking for people like Debbie [Hamman] and Rese [Hugo]. They waited so long for the opportunity to play international netball. They had one world championship in 1995 and then they were too old. If they could have played international netball when they were, say, 20, it would have made a huge difference not only to them but also to the development of South African netball.

'What they felt was brought home to me in 1992 when, after the national tournament, I was chosen for the South African senior team. You got selected but that was it. There was no one to play. There we were all dressed up and nowhere to go.

'Everyone would give it all they had during the tournament, then we would gather for the prizegiving. After the trophies were handed out the South African team would be announced. Of course you're delighted when your name is read out — it means you're one of the best players in the country — but it was tempered by the fact that you were never going to get to play with those who had been chosen alongside you.'

That was how Irene felt as she headed back to Potchefstroom College. She was now a senior netball international but no one in the world outside South Africa knew. Because of apartheid, South African sporting teams had nowhere outside the republic to play. Segregation of whites from blacks and coloureds had led to economic and sporting sanctions against the Republic.

Like others of her age, Irene was born into a society that accepted segregation on ethnic grounds as a way of life. As a child she was blissfully unaware of what was happening outside the calm, orderly life she led on the farm.

At the time of the Soweto uprising by black students on what started out as an ordinary Wednesday morning on 16 June 1976, Irene was five days short of her fourth birthday. She could have had no conception of the rest of the world's revulsion as 179 students were gunned down while singing protest songs and waving banners at lines of blue-shirted police seemingly more nervous than the schoolchildren, who were rebelling against a government decision that they would be taught in Afrikaans.

In reality, however, black and white was also an issue on the Viljoen farm, where the only child Irene had to play with during the day while her brothers and sisters were away at school was Gladys, the daughter of Mabel, the family's black maid.

'Gladys wasn't black to me, because she was my play friend, but her mother was. The workers had to do as they were told, and while it was never spelt out I knew intuitively that Mabel wasn't allowed to talk back to me.

'My dad was good to our workers. He made sure they had meat every day, food for their families and somewhere to live on the farm. In return they worked from six in the morning till eight at night. When I look back on it now it was so unfair, but at the time you just go with the flow. It was a way of life.

'One of the things I did notice as a little girl was that Mabel and the workers were given cups, plates and cutlery for their food that was different to the ones we used. You didn't question it. That was the way it was.

'As I got older and enrolled in school there would be talk about the sanctions on the news and that would lead to huge discussions in the classroom. Why were we being singled out? We thought all the other countries were wrong, because that's how we'd been brought up. It was totally insular.

'Two black students came to study with us at college and no one wanted to live on the same floor as them. That was a wake-up call for many of us and we began to think, rather than just accept what we'd grown up with. Who were we to judge? The only difference was the colour of their skin. They had hearts and lungs, desires and goals just like us.'

New Zealanders got a taste of South Africa's problems when the rugby Springboks toured New Zealand in 1981, playing games on fields surrounded by barbed wire and riot police, and beneath a light aircraft from which an anti-apartheid protester was dropping flour bombs. The tour caused big splits among New Zealanders, even dividing families, and that was the end of official rugby contact between the two countries for 11 years, though a New Zealand team calling itself the Cavaliers visited South Africa in 1986.

Change began on 2 February 1990 when President F.W. de Klerk lifted the ban on the ANC and other illegal organisations and announced the release of ANC leader Nelson Mandela after 26 years of imprisonment.

'When Nelson Mandela came to power he prepared the country for change and that's why it went so smoothly. There are still people who don't accept the new way of life but the majority have.'

Since the abolition of apartheid, pressure has been placed on sports to introduce quota systems to ensure mixed-race teams. When South Africa travelled to Birmingham for the 1995 world championships there were 12 white and two black players in the party. With international rules allowing only 12 players to be named for the tournament, the two black players took no part in the event. They were there because the government said they should be.

'It was cosmetic. Basically they were on holiday and I could never understand why they were with us. There were black players, such as Rosina Mogola and Manzo Machoga, who had international potential and could have learnt a lot by being with us, but instead it was decided to take two players for window-dressing who weren't up to it.

'Rosie and Manzo were among those chosen for the African Games in 1995 when five of our silver medal team were dropped and the players rebelled. I was delighted for Rosie and Manzo because they had terrific skills and deserved their places, but I was dead against quotas being placed on international teams.

'International teams should be selected solely on merit. No country should put itself in the position of playing with a second-best selection against another country's number one team. By all means put a quota system in place at club and provincial level because that will help players who have not previously had a chance to improve, but at international level . . . no way.'

On 15 August 1992 South Africa returned to international rugby when the Springboks lost 27–24 to the All Blacks at a seething Ellis Park. Netball followed two years later, and that meant the 1994 national championships took on a whole new meaning. Now the players really had something to play for. South Africa was back in the world netball fold and they were going to Britain for five tests against England as well as playing Wales and Ireland.

Chapter 4

The International Stage

THE SPORTS PAGES OF BRITISH NEWSPAPERS are, naturally, dominated by soccer, the national game. During winter the majority of column inches devoted to sport in New Zealand newspapers are filled with rugby news, though netball is recognised as a major sport along with cricket and rugby league. Netball is also the number one women's sport in New Zealand. Australia's world champion netballers have never been accorded the recognition they are due in their native land either in the written media or on television, and despite being accepted as the best, the Aussie players are still envious of the coverage the Silver Ferns receive in New Zealand.

So far as the South African media was concerned, before the 1995 world championships netball may as well not have existed, such was the scant mention the sport received in the newspapers. As for television . . . well, netball didn't exist.

It was against such a backdrop in 1994 that South Africa's netballing Springboks, accepted back into the international fold after the abolition of apartheid, were to make their first overseas tour in 27 years. On that trip to Britain they were going to fill more newspaper space than they could ever imagine, thanks mainly to one woman.

After spending so much time in netball's wilderness the South Africans didn't know what to expect on their return to the international arena. Their naivety quickly showed up with the naming of a 10-strong touring party when international rules specified 12 players. Fortunately for the red-faced officials 12 other players were named to train with the team and two extra players were quietly drafted into the team.

Traditionally South African national championships have always provided much more for the players than on-court competition where teams play two hour-long games a day, outside on concrete in searing heat and high winds. They are one big get-together where gossip is rife as players from different provinces take advantage of the once-a-year opportunity to mix and mingle, and find out what's been happening in other areas.

• One piece of gossip at the 1994 tournament was that Western Transvaal shooter Irene Viljoen, later that year to become Irene van Dyk, would be in the South African team to Britain. Through her performances in helping Western Transvaal reach the semi-finals Viljoen ensured the rumours would become fact. In the semis Viljoen and company came up against Western Province, who had six Springboks in their team — Rese Hugo, Debbie Hamman, Eleanor Melck, Benita van Zyl, Estelle Kruger and Lorrey Keevey. No one gave Western Transvaal a chance but they only went down narrowly, thanks to an outstanding shooting effort by Irene Viljoen.

Irene not only made the team, but was named Player of the Year. Not so lucky was long-time Springbok Elenza Bruwer who had played goalshoot for Western Transvaal with Irene at goal attack.

'This tour was what everyone had waited so long for, and you could understand the bitter disappointment among the older ones who missed out because they would probably never get another chance. Those chosen would also have the inside running for the 1995 world championships in Birmingham.

'I know it didn't go down well with Elenza when she was dropped to make way for me. It seemed as if she had been around for ever but I honestly felt I was playing better than Elenza and deserved to get in ahead of her. The rest of the women, who had been her fellow Springboks for years, were fine so they must have felt I deserved my place.'

As the only Western Transvaal representative in the touring team, Irene trained alone, spurred on by fiancé Christie van Dyk.

'Christie was my trainer. He was the one who made sure I was fit and sharp for what was going to be my biggest sporting moment. He has always believed in sportspeople working hard and there was no way Christie was going to allow me to slack with what was on the horizon.

'There were some days when Christie decided he was really going to work me. On those days we would end up not speaking. Glares would replace words, but he only wanted me to be as well prepared as possible.

'I admit there were times when I would have liked to do him a mischief but it was thanks to Christie that I, the baby of the team at 21, was ready to claim a place in the South African starting line-up on that historic tour.'

To say that those chosen to make the trip were excited would be an understatement. From the moment the team was announced for the November trip following the national championships in August, what lay ahead occupied the thoughts of those lucky enough to be going almost every waking hour and Irene was no different. After having hardly ventured outside the Vaal Triangle she was on the way to history-steeped Britain. Before that, however, there were training camps to attend, and that meant being coached by Marlene Wagner.

Wagner is a legend in South African netball, a brilliant international who played until 1982 before taking up coaching.

'She quickly became a very good coach because she knew the game so well and could evaluate it. Marlene knew what she wanted and could be very hard on the players but she always seemed to get the best out of them.

'The first time I went to a training camp I just couldn't take the pressure and burst into tears. Marlene was telling me to do all these different things and it got to the stage where I couldn't do any of them. I can tell you there was no pity from Marlene. She just looked at me and said "Get on with it." So that's what I had to do.

'No way would I have wanted the job Marlene had in getting us prepared for that first trip. It makes me smile now when I hear coaches lamenting the limited time they have to prepare teams for internationals. They're usually talking about having only four or five days together. Well, Marlene was trying to make up for 27 years out of international netball and had few opportunities to get her players together before going to Britain. How many coaches would have wanted to be in her shoes at that point?

'One thing Marlene did have in her favour was that she had this huge belief that any team she coached would do well. It wasn't egotistical. It was simply that she had great belief in those she picked. You always got the feeling that if Marlene picked you then you must be good enough. That makes a player believe in herself.

'Despite all that, Marlene had a very difficult job because we South Africans knew little about how far netball had developed outside the Republic. Marlene managed to collect a few tapes of other teams playing and I know she had contact with New Zealand's Lois Muir who she knew from her playing days. But really South Africa had arrived back on the international scene with no idea what to do or how to do it, apart, that is, from Marlene.

'She was really professional from the start, though the one thing that put fear into us all was her individual sessions with the players. They could be so traumatic that you would have a sleepless night beforehand. I think she deliberately heightened the tension by always telling a player at night that the session would be next day.

'I can still remember my first individual session with Marlene as if it was yesterday. No sooner had I sat down than she was telling me that I was totally unladylike. "You swear . . . ladies do not swear. You laugh very loudly . . . ladies do not laugh out loud." From then on whenever I laughed at a team function I would just know Marlene was looking at me.

'She would make sure she let you know about the things she considered good about you, but would then go on to say what was bad and how you needed to work on those areas.

'Marlene tried to make ladies out of us as well as making us better netballers. Her heart was in the right place and with the amount of work she put in she had the right to expect a player to give everything in return.

'For that tour South African officials had no idea what was needed. Unlike teams of today we'd no such thing as a nutritionist . . . we didn't even have a physiotherapist! Despite that they were really happy days. We had something special in that team, as the results on tour showed.'

It was while the team was preparing for the trip to Britain that a bond was forged between Irene and Marlene Wagner. The relationship was strengthened in 1996 when Irene went to play for Wagner at Western Province where the pair became firm friends as well as having a respectful player–coach relationship.

Few, if any, in South Africa possessed the netball knowledge of Wagner, but sometimes her people skills would let her down. In 1998, after South Africa hadn't played to its potential at the Kuala Lumpur Commonwealth Games, that led to player power rearing its ugly head and Wagner was dumped from the job she loved.

Regrets are few in the life of Irene van Dyk, but she would dearly love the opportunity to change what happened to Marlene Wagner and to take back the part she played in the coach's dismissal.

The team that went to Kuala Lumpur was a young one, with Dominique Haverson as captain, and most of the players didn't know how to handle Marlene. Wagner was undoubtedly missing former captain Debbie Hamman who, as skipper, had been the coach's confidante as well as a wonderful leader for the players and their go-between with the coach. There were many times during South African netball's emergence from the apartheid years that Hamman was called upon to calm troubled waters after the coach had created waves by perhaps not being as diplomatic as she could have been.

During the 1995 world championships, for instance, when journalists wanted to know why there were no black or coloured players in the team, Wagner would get uptight. The same thing happened when reporters asked about the black players who were accompanying the team but were not on the roster or staying with the squad. Each time, Hamman stepped in and, as only a lawyer can, talked for ten minutes, said nothing and then went on to the next subject. In the latter stages of the tournament Hamman would attend South African press conferences without the coach. For a journalist Hamman could be the most frustrating person to deal with, yet she was charming, articulate and, yes, a hell of a player.

During the Kuala Lumpur Commonwealth Games campaign, while other players struggled to come to terms with Wagner's ways it was different for Irene. She knew Wagner, knew how her mind worked, knew how much she cared about South Africa and the players who represented the Republic. She was, however, aware that several players were not impressed with the way Wagner prepared the team for Kuala Lumpur. Training was done for days on end under a burning sun in an effort to acclimatise the players for the hot and humid atmosphere they would encounter in Kuala Lumpur. Had South Africa performed to their potential at the Commonwealth Games what happened during the build-up may not have been questioned. When things didn't go well questions were immediately asked.

'When we were beaten by England Marlene had everyone in tears. She couldn't handle the loss. She knew we were a better team than England but that we'd not been able to put it together on court that day.

'We really sucked. The medical staff felt we were dehydrated and had been over-trained. They could have been right because Marlene is the type of person who will give you a certain task to perform and you will not be allowed to leave till you get it right, no matter how long it takes.

'After the England loss Marlene basically ignored us totally for three days. She didn't speak to us, didn't even look our way. That really got to the players and when we got back to South Africa Dominique and her husband Hugh drafted a letter saying that the players wanted her removed from the coaching panel.

'I think Letetia Vorster and myself were the only two players who didn't want to sign the letter. In the end, however, we did, and that's something I will always regret.

'It is not something I am proud of, and looking back, I am sure it was peer pressure. Everyone was phoning asking if I was going to sign the letter. It was shocking. I believe if Letetia and myself had lived in the same town then we wouldn't have signed it. We would have supported each other and stuck together.

'As it was Letetia was 1500 km away in Cape Town and we were not in contact with each other.

'The letter arrived with everyone's signature on it but mine and I agonised over what I should do. In the end I signed it, but if·I could have that one moment of my life back then I wouldn't have put my name to the letter.

'The pain we put that woman through I wouldn't wish on my worst enemy. Netball was Marlene Wagner's life. It was what she lived for. She had so much to give, and had given so much, yet what we put her through made her withdraw from almost everything. We not only hurt her netball career and her netball vision, we hurt her deeply personally. While she remained a selector for the national team she didn't speak to any of us. We had trials eight months later and she still wouldn't speak to us.

'That was worse for me than it was for the other players because Marlene and I had become so close. I couldn't handle the fact that Marlene was staying in the same building at the trials and wouldn't even look at me.

'The first time I saw her after the ordeal of the letter was at the trials and my mum was there. The players, those who had got her sacked and the newcomers, were all in the room when Marlene walked in and I remember my mother looking at me to see how I would react. I walked straight up to her, gave her a hug and said, "Hello kuchi," which was our nickname for her. She just looked at me and then turned away. That was the worst I have ever felt. I went across to my mum and cried.

'All the other players were watching because they knew if she wouldn't respond to me then she wouldn't respond to anyone. It was the worst time of my life. I hated every minute of it because that's not me. And nobody forced me to do it, that's the worst thing. I did it on my own and that's what I couldn't live with.

'After that I would phone Marlene and ask how she was. The only answer I would get was "fine." Then I would lose my nerve, say "Bye" and hang up.

'I think the only thing she wanted was for us to go and say sorry for what we'd done to her. Unfortunately no one did, apart from myself and Letetia. I suppose even I didn't say officially that I was sorry, I just worked my way back into her heart. It was after the 1998 tour to Jamaica, which was a disaster. When we got back to South Africa I phoned her and said we'd lost our games, which she already knew. I told her that I wished she had been there.

'Marlene said, "That's good news. So you missed me." From that point we gradually got back together but I really had to work on it.

'We hurt her far deeper than anyone thought because she's as human as the rest of us.'

But those traumatic events were a long way off when Irene, Marlene and the rest of the team set off on the tour to Britain. The team was given more press coverage than it would normally have received because of South Africa returning to international play. For the South Africans, England was a real eye-opener, especially the way they were treated by their hosts.

'With all the food we were given it was like being in heaven. Breakfast, morning tea, lunch, pre-match snack, after-match snack, after-match function . . . then dinner.

'I was getting married three weeks after the tour ended and I began to wonder how I was going to get into my dress.'

Arriving in Belfast for the game against Northern Ireland was a rude awakening for Irene, who thought Afrikaans was the language of the world.

'While I could read English I spoke very little and couldn't understand what people were saying. Imagine my fright on the second night when we went to a function and I was separated from my team-mates. There were 12 tables and one of our players had to sit at each.

'It was terrible. I was sitting there with all these people who rolled their Rs. I couldn't even tell them that I didn't understand what they were saying. I wanted to disappear into the floor.

'What I would have finished up like had Debbie Hamman not looked across and seen my predicament I don't know. Debbie realised how terrible I was feeling and came across to act as my interpreter. That was typical of Debbie. She was a brilliant captain. So articulate. She could say the same thing a million ways.

'Probably because of my height and through shooting the goals, the media all wanted to talk to me. I was so nervous about that I was freaking out. Debbie would tell me to take a deep breath and think English. I would say, "Debbie, I'm so freaked out I can't think South African." I couldn't understand half the questions and it didn't help that some of the reporters knew little about netball.

'There was one question to which my answer was, "Because of how they feed me." Well, everyone was hysterical. They thought I was talking about how they fed me food rather than how they fed me the ball in the circle. I was getting a lot more attention than I had bargained for and it was getting me all screwed up.'

Irene might have been finding it tough going off-court, but once on it the South Africans seemed more at home than their hosts, though the hours leading up to the historic first match against Northern Ireland on October 26 at Belfast's Maysfield Leisure Centre were tense.

'It wasn't too noticeable early in the day. During the morning Marlene gave us a good work-out on the match surface and we spent the rest of the day relaxing. On the way to the stadium, however, the atmosphere changed. Everyone went quiet. You could have heard a pin drop on the bus.

'I think everyone was starting to play the game in their mind and they were probably thinking that this was the beginning of a new era for South African netball. I know I was. It was an amazing feeling to be in the first line-up for the first game of your country's return to the international arena.

'We'd no idea how we would go, or how Ireland would play. We just went in and played the game.'

Irene lasted three-quarters of the game before rolling an ankle. With no physio on hand she spent the final quarter sitting with her foot in a chilly bin full of ice. It was so sore she was convinced there could be a real problem, but x-rays the following day showed no major damage.

A convincing win over Northern Ireland gave the rest of the world a first glimpse of Irene Viljoen, and those watching were impressed. English journalist Geoff Young recorded the historic moment:

Irene Viljoen shot South Africa to victory over Northern Ireland on their return to world netball in Belfast. The 6 ft 4 in shooter from Western Transvaal stood out like a beacon on the Maysfield court. Ninety-five per cent of South Africa's attacks ended with Viljoen and her accuracy was impressive. Poor Liz-Ann Walsh, the Northern Ireland goalkeeper who is herself 6 ft, could do little to stem the tide as Viljoen and South Africa dominated.

'The South Africans were largely an unknown quantity, having been out of the world scene for so long, and it took them some time to settle down after centre Rene Odendaal had passed off to signal their return.

'But the bigger, taller South Africans soon warmed to the task and Viljoen's radar worked overtime as Debbie Hamman, Rese Hugo and Odendaal sought her out.

Next morning the South Africans couldn't believe the amount of netball in the local newspaper, but it was something they, and Irene in particular, would get used to as the tour progressed. From Belfast the South Africans moved to Cardiff where they beat Wales. If they were taken aback by the welcome they received in Ireland then they were stunned at the reception in Cardiff.

'The thing that will always stick in my mind about playing Wales is the noise the crowd made. Few people turned up for netball games at home so the size of the crowd alone was a huge buzz but the noise they made . . . and they were not just shouting for Wales. I honestly believe they were cheering for netball. That's the kind of people they are.

'The newspaper was full of netball. Even in the street people were coming up and talking to us. It was unbelievable.

'Whenever we got back to the hotel there would be media people waiting for us and they all wanted to talk to me. I don't know how I would have coped without Debbie. It was so frustrating and I must have looked like a big idiot stood there with a grin on my face, not understanding what was going on.

'It was good in one way. I'd been thrown in the deep end and had to learn quickly. Speaking English was going to become a big part of my life over the next few years so I suppose it helped that I had no option but to work at it.'

The South Africans were a little surprised by their success in Ireland and Wales, since they'd thought the rest of the netball world may have left them well behind. After those first two wins Marlene Wagner convinced her players they were not that far off what was needed to win the five-test series against England.

'We knew the England series was going to be a biggie but it was also a great experience away from the netball court, because what the English are really good at is making muffins. I had never eaten a muffin before, but I must have eaten a million while I was there. All these people were dropping muffins off at the hotel for us and we seemed to be eating them all night long. England netball did a great job with the tour. Well, at least we thought they did. The English players were not as impressed.

'We weren't used to staying in hotels, getting so much attention and being recognised by strangers. So far as we were concerned the hotels we stayed at were really nice. The English girls thought they stank!

'It was probably a good job the people were so nice because England in November was a really depressing place to be. You can never see the sky because it's always cloudy and it gets dark so early. The one place that did impress me was Bath. It was one of the most beautiful places I have seen, even though the weather was miserable.

'London was too busy for my liking. There are so many people scurrying about. They're like ants. There was never any danger of me emigrating to England, that's for sure.'

If Irene found England depressing, the English found her to be a ray of sunshine in the middle of winter. To put it mildly, the English media took Irene to their hearts and most of it was so politically incorrect the feminists must have been choking on their cornflakes.

Chapter 5

Netballing Pin-up

If a modern female fantasy celebrates growing to Amazonian heights, then Irene Viljoen is one of the favoured few to have experienced this adventure twice.

The first time was when she was 16. Over a few, brief months, in awesome, jolting leaps she grew from class midget to towering above both sexes.

The second time was during the South African netball team's tour to England. When she first stepped on to the court she was 1.9 m (6 ft 3 in). As her awesome reputation as a phenomenal goal shooter grew (50 goals in one game alone) — so did her height in press reports. Towards the end of the tour she had reached a mythical 2.07 m (6 ft 8 in).

She is, in fact, 1.95 m (6 ft 4 in). This makes her the tallest — and youngest — member of the team that returned home last weekend with five test wins, making them our most successful side yet to move back into world sport.

To put it mildly, the South Africans surprised the English and Irene became the main attraction.

That was how South African journalist Janet Wilhelm introduced a profile on Irene when the team returned from their successful overseas venture. Wilhelm was spot on. Irene Viljoen was the main attraction for the English media who, unlike their New Zealand and Australian counterparts, were allowed free rein to wax lyrical about Irene's appearance. A little thing such as political correctness was irrelevant.

It wasn't only the male reporters who fell under Irene's spell. Louise Taylor, a talented English writer who spends more time looking at footballers' legs than netballers', was happy to comment on Irene's looks and graceful movement on court.

If there was one written piece that encapsulated the striking effect Irene had on those English males charged with covering the netball it was Paul Haigh's description of South Africa's 58–46 win over England in the third test at Gateshead, a result that put South Africa 3–0 ahead and clinched the series.

Here is Haigh's story, which appeared under the heading 'VILJOEN LOOKING GOOD IN THE DOMINANT ROLE'.

Is it sexist to refer to a female athlete's physical appearance? If so, too bad. Irene Viljoen is unusually beautiful, both in the sense of the rather hackneyed phrase and in the sense that she is beautiful in an unusual way.

The 22-year-old student teacher from Western Transvaal is goal shooter for the touring South African netball team who took a winning 3–0 lead over England in their five-match test series.

She is 6 ft 4 in tall and built in perfect proportion. She has the grace of a racehorse, the diffidence of a child, and legs that make Naomi Campbell look like Dawn French. The undoubted star of the side who clinched the series with a 58–46 win at Gateshead, she is also the possessor of that quality which defines excellence in any sport; time to play.

While colleagues and opponents bustle and scheme and scurry, Viljoen stands, hand resting nonchalantly on an elegantly elevated hip, and waits.

The ball comes in her general direction and she springs, or sometimes merely reaches up as though to a high shelf, catches it, pops it in the net, then turns, almost embarrassed, to applaud her team-mates for their ability to deliver what she needed in order to accomplish the inevitable.

Goalshooter is, of course, the glamour position in a sport in which players operate in pre-determined zones, but she brings a glamour to it that completely won over the crowd of fanatically supportive English fans who came to the Gateshead Leisure Centre.

Viljoen's height advantage is really only marginal. Natural coordination is what gives her the edge.

Afterwards it was round her that the supporters clustered like happy drones round an unassuming queen bee; on her that the cameras lingered; at her that the few males in the crowd gazed as though hypnotised.

It may well be politically incorrect to refer to her appearance, but it is not irrelevant. Netball is a sport which, in this country anyway, suffers from an image problem. It is part of the business of sexism to adopt a condescending manner to all women's sport.

Viljoen is the perfect antidote to that sort of attitude. If netball was more alert to her potential she would be a perfect recruiting poster for a sport that already claims one million schoolgirl players and 56,000 adults in Britain.

In Australia and New Zealand, during the years of South Africa's political isolation unquestionably the two strongest nations in the netball world, the sport is big on television and players are national celebrities. Its potential is only now dawning on television executives in Britain, and they are still not quite sure how they should project it.

Sky's attempt to sell it with dry ice and the now dismally clichéd 'Fanfare for the Common Man' are a bit of a joke.

The uncommon woman could be the answer which the television men are looking for. Viljoen's emergence — and her appearance — could be what the sport in Great Britain needs to lift it from its present relative obscurity to take in a wider audience.

Now that the series has been won, the South African coach, Marlene Wagner, is fielding some of the reserves in her squad in order to give them their own shot at stardom.

In fact, it may well be that there will only be one or two opportunities to see Viljoen in action again before the 28-nation World Cup gets underway in Birmingham next summer.

Is it sexist to suggest that, for anyone who saw her play on this tour, the wait will seem a long one?

Probably. Who cares?

It is a fact of life that good-looking, well-proportioned people, male or female, get more attention than the average man or woman, be it in sport, on television or just walking down the street.

Some years ago I was walking through the streets of Wellington in New Zealand with Argentinian tennis star Gabriela Sabatini and her Chilean coach, Señor Nunez. Numerous heads turned as we walked by, and it certainly wasn't me or Nunez they were swivelling to observe. Sabatini handled it all like the true professional she was, including signing grubby bits of paper that had been grabbed from the nearest source by enamoured young men.

It is not always easy to be so accommodating but Irene van Dyk will never turn away an autograph seeker, especially a child. Such arrogance is not part of her make-up. If she had ever felt that way inclined, a story of Christie's would have banished any such thoughts.

'It happened years ago when Christie was young but he still remembers it so clearly.

'He and his friends drove for about four or five hours to get to a rugby game in which one of his heroes, Naas Botha, was playing. After the game Christie handed Botha a ball and asked politely if he would autograph it for him. "I haven't got time. Go away," was Botha's response.

'I would never want to make anyone feel how Christie felt at being given the brush-off from one of his heroes. Rugby is so big in South Africa and for his role model to treat him like that was devastating for Christie. He has always encouraged me to sign everyone's autographs. He doesn't mind standing waiting for me because he knows what it means to the people asking.

'After playing for the Capital Shakers in a Coca-Cola Cup game against the Diamonds in Auckland one night I could see there were loads of kids wanting me to sign my name for them, but before I could oblige I was told I had to go for a drug test. I insisted I be given the chance to explain to them that I needed to go with the lady for a drug test, and that if they were still there when I got back I would sign it with love.

'Unfortunately it took me so long to produce the sample needed there was no one left when I got back to the court. Even though it couldn't be helped I still felt terrible about not being able to give those kids what they wanted. I hope they understood.'

Autographs are one thing, but what is it like for a leading sports-woman, especially one brought up in the quiet anonymity of a farm, to pick up a newspaper or magazine and find that her looks have been given as much prominence as her sporting attributes?

'It was totally overwhelming. Unbelievable really. While I was growing up no one had ever commented about my looks so it was amazing to think that these people thought I was pretty.

'During my schooldays there were all kinds of competitions, the type you have at a fair . . . prettiest girl, one with the most charisma. Well I was never considered as one of the prettiest but in my last year at school, at 18, I was chosen as Miss Charisma and that was nice. I thought, OK, you have charisma. But that was where it stopped.

'To be honest, when it all started on that tour to Britain I didn't pay much attention to what was being said and written. I just went with the flow. Looking back I think I tried to make out I didn't see it or hear it.'

Irene may have tried to ignore it but her team-mates didn't and, in the way that sports teams do, they made sure all the attention she was getting didn't go to her head — that she didn't rise above her station which was, after all, being the baby of the team.

'Yeah, they did give me a bit of a hard time. We had our initiation meeting and some of the girls would make their skirts really short. They would walk the way I did and ask "Who am I?" at which point all the other girls would shout, "You're Irene."

'At other times they would go and put loads of make-up on and ask "Who am I?" It felt pretty stink at first but I knew they were not doing it nastily.

'I got the make-up thing from Rese. She always looked beautiful. Whenever she was going out, whether it was shopping or to play net-ball, she would put her make-up on. Because Rese was my idol and also as I roomed with her it was something I started doing. Goodness knows why we did it before playing games because you sweat so much and it all gets ruined.

'Anyway, why wouldn't we want to look our best when we went to Britain? It was our first time on television playing netball . . . why not try and look beautiful? Those who thought I slapped loads of make-up on, however, are wrong. I only wore the amount I wear now when I am going to school or wherever. I must say, though, that I feel totally lost without my eyeliner.

'Another thing was that when we went training we wouldn't go back to the hotel before going shopping. So we wanted to look nice. It wasn't our intention to attract attention . . . but, hell, I'm so big people were going to notice me whether I wore make-up or not.

'My height obviously had a lot to do with all the attention I was getting. Several of the people who came to talk to me said they had a tall daughter who walked with her shoulders bent. How could they get her to walk up straight as I do? I could understand their concern. A tall person walking with a stoop looks a lot worse than a tall person walking tall.

'Being tall was never an issue with me because of my Dad. When we were walking if I was walking a little bent over he would slap me on the back and say "Up straight." Actually there are lots of girls who are not really tall — not like me anyway — but are self-conscious about how tall they are and so they walk with their shoulders rounded. It doesn't look good but it's only a habit and it can be broken.

'So much about posture depends on how parents treat their children during their formative years, and I'm not just talking about tall people. Today, because of the way they stand, many kids always seem to have big stomachs. That's only because they are not told to stand up straight. If they would stand up straight and pull in their tummy they would look so different.

'My schoolteachers would always make us sit up straight with our feet together. If you do it often enough it becomes second nature.'

Despite the mickey-taking she received from her team-mates because of the attention she was getting, the 1994 trip to Britain was an exciting time. Irene had never dreamt she would become an international netballer, considering such notions to be far-fetched. Even if she did achieve her ambition of winning national netball colours she could never have imagined how she would be fêted on the other side of the world. In South Africa netball was merely a game girls played. It was rarely written about in the newspapers and television coverage was non-existent.

When stardom arrived so unexpectedly on that 1994 tour of Britain it would have been easy for Irene to become carried away with her new-found celebrity. That didn't happen.

'When people began to recognise me, and things were written about me in the newspaper, Marlene Wagner said to me, "Remember, you're still Irene Viljoen." I knew that and had no intention of letting what was happening go to my head.

'I have never felt I am better than someone else. That's just the way I am. I am a normal human being who happens to have sporting talents and it is only those talents that make me different from another person. I will never ever think or say that I am better than anyone else as a person.

'You hear so many stories about people not wanting to mingle, they feel they are a different class to those they are being asked to meet. I believe everyone is the same and everyone should be treated in the same way. I don't want people calling me a friend just because I play netball. They should love me and know me for the person I am. Not the kind of netballer I am.

'One of our teachers at Fergusson Intermediate said I looked so down to earth that people feel they can come up and talk to me, whereas some leading sportspeople don't look approachable. I hope people will always feel that way about me.

'It is unfair, though, to judge someone on how they look. They may look unapproachable but actually be more than happy to talk to you. I always thought Australia's Liz Ellis was a bit stuck up, but once I got talking to her I found she was a lovely woman. She's so funny. She can take the mickey out of any situation.

'When I first came up against Fiji's Vilimaina Davu I thought she was the mother of all mothers. Again, appearance was deceiving. She has a big heart and is such a softy, though she wouldn't want opposing shoot-ers to realise that.

'What she's actually like is so different to what you see on court. The first time I came up against her at the 1999 world championships in the play-off for fifth and sixth I admit she totally rattled me. She was so hard and physical. After coming to New Zealand and joining the Capital Shak-ers, the first time we played the Canterbury Flames Tanya Cox said I must have played against Vilimaina Davu at the world champs but I had no idea who they were talking about.

'When the Flames arrived and Vili got out of the van I said, "Oh my goodness, I played against that woman at the world champs." Tanya just said, "I told you so." The minute I saw her I knew. I also knew what I was going to be up against that afternoon. I wasn't wrong. She knocked me about again that day.

'If someone doesn't know how to handle it Vili is the perfect person to rattle a shooter. The first time you come up against her, not knowing what to expect, she'll get the upper hand. Later in the Coca-Cola Cup I came up against her again but I wasn't intimidated because I knew what was coming. If you know that, you can prepare yourself.

'Vili is just as competitive in training but off the court she's hilarious and tells a great story.'

There are times, however, when first instincts are spot on. That was the case when Irene met Christie van Dyk, the man she was to marry at the end of 1994. The pair gelled right from the start, though outsiders watching them tease each other may have thought differently. Christie and Irene always enjoyed winding each other up, and nothing has changed over the years.

They'd been engaged for more than a year when, early in 1994, they set the wedding date for 10 December that year. Like any young couple, they looked forward to making the arrangements together, unaware of the possibility that the South African netball team would be going to Britain later in the year, and immediately before their big day.

Then came the news that the tour was on and, when Irene made the team for the historic trip, everything changed. It quickly became obvious that she wouldn't be on hand during the crucial weeks leading up to the wedding. She would be in Britain for seven weeks, arriving back in South Africa a week before she and Christie were to exchange their vows.

While British netball followers and media were getting their first look at Irene Viljoen, back home in South Africa Christie, his parents and Irene Viljoen senior were preparing for the wedding.

'They did basically everything while I was away enjoying myself playing netball and meeting new people. Quite fortuitous, wasn't it?

'I did feel a bit guilty because they had all the hassles while all I had to do was come back, go for a fitting of my dress and get married. Bonita, the wife of my younger brother Herman, was making the dress and before I left for Ireland she gave me strict instructions that I wasn't to gain weight. Even with all the food that was served up to us during our time in Britain I didn't put any weight on, much to Bonita's relief.

'The tour gave me so much to talk about with Christie and my family that the days flew past and before I knew it everyone was gathered in Meyerton's Dutch Reformed Church to watch us get married.

'Marrying Christie was the happiest day of my life, but it was also the saddest. I felt it was so unfair that my dad couldn't be there; that he couldn't see his daughter marry the man she loved.

'I thought of those wonderful nights we'd spent alone together staring out into the black of night talking about what he had done with his life, and sharing my hopes and dreams. In those dreams it was always Dad who would walk me down the aisle. Instead it was Dad's favourite brother, Nick, who gave me his arm as we walked into the church, and tears were streaming down both our faces as we walked towards where Christie was waiting. Uncle Nick was really cut up, knowing what the moment would have meant to his brother.

'The regrets didn't take anything away from what was a stunning day and I just wish it could have gone on forever. A wedding day is so special because you're making a commitment to the person you have chosen to spend your life with.'

An overseas honeymoon was out of the question, as was staying in a hotel, because Irene and Christie had no money. Christie had paid for half the wedding costs out of his teacher's salary and Irene had just got back from England where she had found everything very expensive. The newly-weds packed a tent and their bits and pieces and headed for Kroonpark, which was part of the Kroonstad holiday resort.

'It was a beautiful setting in which to start our married life. We had hot pools, which are rare in South Africa, to relax in and for three or four days we did absolutely nothing. It was wonderful.

'After a few days word got around that we'd just got married and for the rest of our time there we didn't have to cook a meal. We were invited to different caravans and tents for every meal.

'There are no regrets on my part that I couldn't have an expensive honeymoon. It was lovely just to get back to Christie after being away for almost two months. We wanted to make the most of being together; to have fun. That's what we did, and we met some great people while we were doing it.

'As we'd got married during the December school holidays we didn't have to go straight back to work. It gave us a chance to fix up the house we were renting and move my things from Mum's place to our house.'

The saying that opposites attract is certainly true of Irene and Christie. She's as carefree and happy-go-lucky as he is structured. It is Christie, not Irene, who ensures her netball things are in one drawer or cupboard, and his cricket equipment in another. Christie keeps the accounts and can produce a required invoice or receipt in seconds. Irene wouldn't know where to find them and cheerfully admits that while living in South Africa she wouldn't have known where to go to pay a bill.

'Mum had been just the same when Dad was alive. South Africa is very much male dominated. The men are in charge of everything, including money. When Dad died suddenly Mum had no idea where anything was, and that's quite normal in South Africa. When I came to New Zealand with Mum while Christie was still working in South Africa it took me time to come to terms with being responsible for what was happening. It was the first time in my life that I had needed to do things for myself.

'Because of the way things are in New Zealand women will find it hard to understand my situation. I even rang Christie in South Africa to find out how I went about getting the electricity turned on and how to get a telephone installed. Having to do things for myself, Mum and Bianca did change me, and when Christie joined us in New Zealand he found himself living with an independent woman for the first time.

'My becoming independent meant we basically had to get to know each other all over again. I still leave the money side of things to Christie, but I can assure you I am no longer as helpless as I was when I first came to live in New Zealand.'

Early in 1997 Irene and Christie decided it was time they started a family. If everything went according to plan the baby would be born in plenty of time for Irene to get back in training so that she could make the South African team that would be competing at a Commonwealth Games for the first time the following year in Kuala Lumpur.

'It sounded so easy, but that was far from the case. We tried — and I mean tried — for four months, but nothing happened, apart from us having fun that is!

'That year England were touring South Africa, with the last test being played in Cape Town. Christie and I had made lots of friends in Cape Town while working there the previous year so I suggested he fly down so we could spend the weekend with friends after the test. Perhaps it was because we were so relaxed, or perhaps the alcohol helped, but that was the weekend when it happened.

'Not that I knew I was pregnant for a while, but someone else did. That year's South African national championships were in September and on the Tuesday, I remember it so well, Rese Hugo told me that there was something different about me and that she was sure I was pregnant because she had had a dream that I was. I told her we'd been trying for a baby but nothing had happened. She simply repeated that I was pregnant; that I had a glow about me.

'When I got home on the Sunday Christie said he had a surprise for me. It was a do-it-yourself pregnancy test. Rese had phoned him from the tournament to tell him she was sure I was pregnant. We did the test and, sure enough, it said I was having a baby. I was stunned because I didn't feel any different. I rang Rese to tell her about the test but she wasn't in the least surprised. She just said, "I told you that you were pregnant." The next day I went to the doctor, who confirmed what the test had indicated. We were over the moon.'

Irene continued to play netball for the first six months of her pregnancy and was in the classroom teaching till a week before Bianca was born.

Just prior to the 2001 tri-nations series with New Zealand and South Africa, Netball Australia announced it wouldn't allow any pregnant woman to play the game, with officials citing legal ramifications should anything happen to the unborn child during a game. Their argument cut no ice with Irene. She insists that whether or not a pregnant woman plays should be a personal decision after consultation with doctors, not something dictated by officials.

'No woman would put what is inside her in danger once she knows that she's expecting a child. Doctors are qualified to give you an opinion on whether you should play or not, and it very much comes down to what you're comfortable with. The way we are created means the embryo is well protected.

'I was comfortable playing till late in the pregnancy because I was so small, just as [Silver Fern] Tania Dalton was when she played for Force in the [2001] Coca-Cola Cup. Some women may not feel it right to play netball or any other sport during a pregnancy. Fine. That's their choice and must be respected. But the decision of a woman who wants to continue should be treated the same way.

'I don't buy the Australian argument that they are concerned about the legal implications. The woman has made a choice and therefore has no right to seek redress if something happens. If I break my leg while playing for the Silver Ferns I'm not going to turn round and sue Netball New Zealand. It's the same thing.'

Irene thought she would 'blow up like a balloon' while she was expecting, but that didn't eventuate. After giving up netball she cycled and swam for the last three months of her pregnancy so that she would stay as fit as possible because she still had ambitions of playing in the Commonwealth Games at Kuala Lumpur. In this she had the support of her mother and Christie. In fact, one of the first things her mother asked when she was told that her daughter was pregnant was whether she would be back in action in time for the Commonwealth Games. Irene concedes that such sentiments might appear strange, but says the Games were a big thing for South Africa, since they were the first since the Republic was allowed back in international competition.

There were some worrying moments leading up to the birth. Christie spent eight days in hospital with a serious virus that could have been life-threatening, and was only discharged on the day Irene was admitted.

'I was two weeks overdue and at noon on the day I went into hospital the doctor decided to induce the baby. The contractions started and continued for the next nine hours. At about seven o'clock it became apparent to the doctors that something wasn't right. Every time I had a contraction the baby's heartbeat would miss, and they thought the cord might be round its neck.

'They were also concerned about the baby's size, which was more than 4.5 kg, and whether I would be able to cope. I said to do whatever was necessary and they decided I needed a caesarean. I went to theatre at 9.30 and Bianca was born at 10.03 on 21 April, 1998.

'I was oblivious to what was happening and Christie tells me he was holding our baby when I was wheeled past him out of the theatre. It was the next day before I saw Bianca. Mum, who had worked at the hospital for 32 years, wheeled her in and I just stared at her. She was the most beautiful thing, but so big. I wondered how she had fitted inside me. She must have been comfortable though because she stayed there two weeks longer than normal.'

It wasn't long before Irene was pestering the doctors to let her start training again. They'd originally told her that, because they'd cut through eight layers of muscles during the delivery, it would be at least eight weeks. No running or jumping, they decreed. Two weeks after the operation, however, the stitches were removed, and two weeks further on Irene was back training.

It was too late for her to make the team that would compete at the African Games in Zimbabwe during July but, curiously, coach Marlene Wagner selected only 11 players for that tournament rather than the usual 12.

'I honestly believe Marlene believed in me and that I would be ready to take my place at the Commonwealth Games; that she had left a place open for me. Not that she ever admitted that was the case. To the contrary, she made it clear to me that she felt there were other shooters as good as me and that I should take nothing for granted.

'Immediately after the African Games, trials were held for the Commonwealth Games team. I was fit again by then and did well enough to be selected.

'It meant leaving Bianca but I had no worries about her welfare. Mum and my maid Suzie, a fantastic person, looked after her as well as I could have done. That didn't mean I wasn't missing her, and I couldn't wait to hold her again.'

Chapter 6

Difficult Decisions

WINNING A SILVER MEDAL AT THE 1995 world championships breathed life into South African netball. Scoring 543 goals at the tournament launched Irene van Dyk to stardom. From being Player of the Year in South Africa, which no one outside the republic knew about, van Dyk was now the talk of world netball.

England, Ireland and Wales knew of her through the 1994 tour. Australia and New Zealand had been introduced to her brilliant shooting and off-court charm in the lead-up to Birmingham in 1995. The rest of the world discovered her at the world tournament.

Everything was rosy for van Dyk, but as a new year dawned the months ahead would provide her with two dilemmas that would mean making an agonising netball decision. One she knew about from the end of 1995, but there was no hint that the other was on the horizon.

Her life was also changing off the court. Irene had moved from Johannesburg to Cape Town; from the Western Transvaal team to Western Province, coached by Marlene Wagner. The move also necessitated a change of job — from kindergarten teacher to car salesperson. From teaching children to convincing a customer that a Nissan was the right car for them.

It wasn't long before Irene was yearning to deal with children again rather than adults as she struggled to come to grips with the male domination of South African society. While South Africa is gradually changing, it is doing so at a much slower pace than a country such as New Zealand. Things that women take for granted in New Zealand are often unheard of in the Republic. For instance, it wasn't until Irene emigrated to New Zealand and took up a teaching position with Fergusson Intermediate school in Upper Hutt, where Margaret Urlich was the principal, that she worked for a woman. In South Africa, school principals were men. Bosses in the private sector were men. When it came to buying cars the majority of men wanted to deal with one of their own, not a woman. What did a woman know about cars?

'It was the only job I could get. It turned out to be pretty interesting, though there were times when I wanted to scream. Some of the men who came into the showroom were not interested in talking to a woman about buying a car. They just didn't want to know. Fortunately the guys I worked with were not impressed with that attitude, and they didn't go out of their way to help someone who didn't want to deal with me. That was nice and something I appreciated.

'During the year I worked for the dealership in Bellville, apart from one month, I met my target of selling seven or eight cars a month. I must admit if a woman wanted a car then she came to me, but the guys didn't seem to mind that.

'Because I was an international netballer the company used me in promotions, along with the Western Province cricketers as both sports were involved in the same sponsorship. That gave me the chance to bowl to international cricketer Gary Kirsten during a sponsorship promotion and I don't think he was too impressed when I got him out twice.

'Despite my problems with sexist customers there were some good times and one of the guys I worked with, Wayne Zwicky, has become a great friend of ours. I saw him in Cape Town when I went back with the Silver Ferns in 2000. He told me that since I left South Africa Britney Spears had become his favourite woman, but now that I was there again I could win my place back.

'We became really good friends with Wayne and his fiancée Aretha. The night before we moved back to Johannesburg from Cape Town we stayed in their house. The next day all four of us had a good cry and then off we went.'

In netball a political row was brewing and, as was to happen again two years later, Irene found herself in the middle of it.

In the wake of the apartheid years South African netball, in common with other sports in the Republic, was going through turbulent times, although racial divisions were more prevalent among administrators than players. As an example, two of the seven players in the team van Dyk then played for, Vaal Triangle Technikon, were black. It didn't matter to Irene who she played alongside. All she wanted to do was play netball.

Unfortunately for South African netball, and the players who had brought honour to their country by reaching the world championship final the previous year, the administrators completely lost their way when it came to choosing a team to represent South Africa at the All Africa Games. Just weeks after South Africa, with an all-white team, had finished runner-up in the world championships, a team to play was named at the All Africa Games. It didn't include five of those who had played in Birmingham.

In contrast to the 1994 British tour and the 1995 world tournament, or even the days when teams were selected when there was nowhere to play, no trials were held. A team was simply announced, and while Irene van Dyk was included, five of the world tournament team were not.

Led by their articulate captain Debbie Hannam, the remainder of the successful 1995 team pulled out, an action that immediately led to them being labelled rebels. Along with her fellow 'rebels', Irene admitted there was nothing wrong with including five 'development players', as the newcomers were described, but felt that under those circumstances national colours should not be awarded to the team. It didn't matter to Irene that the five new players were black. She just felt they should have had to prove themselves in trials as she had done.

The players from the world tournament team felt so strongly about the situation that a stand-off arose which ended with the so-called rebels not going to the Games. They were replaced by seven white players, with the end result being that South Africa performed poorly and all the good work done in Birmingham was undone.

Most of those who pulled out were in the twilight of their netball careers, whereas Irene was only just starting out on a road that looked likely to take her to the top of the international scene. She was aware that by going along with her Birmingham team-mates she could be harming her future. There was even a veiled threat from coach Marlene Wagner that it could cost her dearly.

'It was probably irresponsible but I didn't care. Sticking with the rest of the girls was something I felt I had to do. I was part of them. They were part of me.

'The feeling in that 1995 team was incredible. I had never felt anything like it before and I didn't again till I went back to South Africa with New Zealand in 2000. That Silver Ferns team had the same feeling of togetherness that was prevalent in the 1995 South Africa team and it showed in our results, including the great win over Australia. We would have done anything for each other and that's why I went along with them.

'Debbie phoned everyone to find out what they thought about the team being chosen without trials and the fact that so many of the team that finished second had been left out. Everyone was behind her when she drew up a letter saying that if the five who had been dropped were not reinstated then the rest of us wouldn't go.

'Typically, Debbie was concerned for me. She said I was young and that I had a long career ahead of me whereas the others were nearing retirement. Debbie said no one in the team would think any the less of me if I looked after my future and went to the games. Other players were phoning me with the same message. Go, they said, don't worry about us. But how could I? As the baby of the team they'd looked after me. They'd taught me so much.

'When I told Marlene Wagner I was sticking with the other players she was spewing and tried to change my mind. That was when the veiled threat came in. Marlene told me no one was irreplaceable. She told me the same thing later when I was pregnant with Bianca. Marlene pushed me during my pregnancy. Told me to keep training. I said how could I when my stomach was so big, but it made me think and I began swimming to make sure I kept reasonably fit. That's the thing about Marlene, she knows that if she tells me something negative I will respond just to show her.

'When it came to me sticking by the team, though, she couldn't change my mind. Instead of just sitting back and letting things go I rang Florinda Brand, who was to captain the team, and suggested they should admit they weren't the best players available and that the best should represent South Africa. Florinda said it was an opportunity for others to prove themselves and they were going to take it.

'The tour turned into a disaster. Florinda, like me in 1994, couldn't communicate well apart from in Afrikaans and she didn't have someone like Debbie to help her. Consequently media relations were not good. There were also several injuries because the players weren't fit.

'While the argument was raging my mum thought I was wrong. Christie said he would back me whatever I decided, but I knew he felt the same as my mother. At the time it was something I felt I had to go through with, and, thankfully, it didn't cost me in the end.'

While all this was going on Irene was probably reflecting on the fact that had she taken up an offer to play in Australia, made to her after the world tournament, then she wouldn't have become involved in the 'rebel' furore.

Following the Silver Ferns' win over Australia in South Africa during the 2000 tri-series, Australian coach Jill McIntosh made the comment that 'it had taken a South African to enable New Zealand to beat her team.' Had things turned out differently at the start of 1996 Irene could just as easily have been playing for Australia instead of New Zealand in that test, though she now cringes at the prospect.

If Irene didn't realise the impact she had made during the world tournament, and in lead-up games in New Zealand and Australia, it was rammed home to her when Queensland approached her after the world championships and asked her to go to Australia. The initial contract was for one year, but Queensland made it clear that they wanted her to stay longer and that the contract could be renegotiated after the first year.

Queensland's interest had been whetted when they saw Irene playing in what could only be described as an average South African team against Australia in April 1995. The Queensland officials were impressed, and they became even more keen to get Irene after seeing her performances for the much improved Springboks in Birmingham. Their enthusiasm was also undoubtedly fired by the fact that their own great shooter, Vicki Wilson, had sustained a serious knee injury in Birmingham that necessitated a knee reconstruction.

'Queensland actually approached me during our first tour of Australia in 1995. I told them I wasn't interested but they asked me to think about it. That was pretty much it till after the world tournament. They came back to me again and what they told me made the move, if only for a year, seem so attractive.

'Within a few weeks they'd arranged jobs for myself and Christie. It was very tempting and I had definitely become interested. When I mentioned what was happening to Marlene Wagner she was horrified. Marlene said there was no way she would let me go, that she would pull out all the stops to keep me in South Africa where I belonged.

'Marlene couldn't have stopped me going because I wasn't under contract to South Africa. Contracts didn't exist at that time in South African netball. That didn't matter to Marlene. She was determined to use every argument at her disposal to keep me playing for her in South Africa.

'That she felt so strongly about me staying was a compliment. The fact that the compliment came from someone I respected so much did make me think about what I was doing. I was still enjoying playing netball in South Africa, though had I known then what was to happen with the South African team for the African games I might have gone so as to avoid the conflict.

'One of the big pluses so far as what Queensland were proposing for me and Christie was that Australia is such a beautiful country. It is so like South Africa, without the same level of crime. I have no doubts that I could have settled there quite easily and we came very close to going, so close that Queensland sent us our air tickets.

'We were scheduled to leave South Africa on 9 January 1996. Christie was raring to go. We had already packed our things. Then I began to have second thoughts about the whole thing. I started to think it wasn't the right thing to do, and two days before we were due to leave I called it off.

'The Queensland people had been great. They'd gone to so much trouble for us that I didn't want to pick up the telephone and make the call to tell them I wouldn't be arriving. It was fortunate that they'd kept my supposed arrival very quiet. There had been no media releases, which was just as well for both Queensland and myself.

'I still can't say for sure what changed my mind. Marlene probably played some part in it, but I think the main reason was that at that time I wasn't ready to leave my family and friends.

'Another reason was, and this will sound strange, that I didn't really want to go and play for a netball enemy. When it came to going to New Zealand four years later it felt completely different. Perhaps there was always a bit of Kiwi in me.

'Obviously Queensland were very disappointed but it was better to call it off then than go and not be happy. That wouldn't have been good for them or me. Had I known then what I know now I would still have made the same decision. I know now that I made the right decision.

'I am a great believer that your life is planned for you. You can't say what the future holds, but when I think back to that decision and how our lives have turned out since then I know there were good reasons for staying in South Africa at that time.

'Christie didn't think that he could ever settle permanently in a country where Afrikaans wasn't spoken. That might well have been the case had we tried to settle in Australia though we will never know for sure. Perhaps the jobs we were to get wouldn't have suited us. Had that been the case then either one or both of us could have become unhappy.

'Moving to another country is such a big thing. In either Australia or New Zealand we would be thousands of miles from our families and friends. In those circumstances, with no one close to talk things over with, small problems can become big ones.

'Christie has always said he would never stand in my way if I wanted to do something. That's the kind of man he is. Us moving to New Zealand proves Christie's words were not an empty gesture. Despite that, it wouldn't have been fair for me to ask him to live in another country if he wasn't going to be happy.

'I am sure he still had his reservations when we decided to live in New Zealand, but he was prepared to give it a go for the sake of myself and Bianca. Now Christie is so happy in New Zealand. He has a job he loves, coaching cricket with Wellington. We both have busy lives and while it means juggling our time we have so far managed it without too many problems.

'There are definitely no regrets about turning Australia down, though I have nothing, and never will, against Australia. Each time I have been to Australia everyone has been so kind to me.

'There are many twists and turns in life. So many things, big and small, influence the path you take. Had I taken up the offer from Queensland I possibly, in fact probably, wouldn't have ended up in New Zealand. Some things are just meant to be. Looking back on everything that has happened, my going to live in New Zealand with Christie and Bianca was meant to be.'

Chapter 7

Wellington Welcome

LATE IN 1997 NEW ZEALAND NETBALL'S domestic competitions underwent a facelift, with franchises replacing clubs in the Coca-Cola Cup competition.

Pacific Island Church — PIC — and Wellington East had been Wellington's perennial representatives in national competitions. Now it was a different ball game. Under the new format the Capital Shakers were born, and it was that franchise that was to bring Irene van Dyk to Wellington three years later.

The driving force behind the Shakers was Wellington legal executive Kathy Doyle, then president of Netball Wellington, and fellow board member Mary-Anne Edwards. While Doyle was chairperson of the franchise she was anything but a figurehead. Between them Doyle and Edwards turned their hands to almost anything within the franchise, from player recruitment to marketing, the latter being Edwards' speciality, as she was marketing manager for the Motor Trade Association at that time. It didn't stop there. The pair were just as adept at organising seating and it wasn't beneath them to deliver drinks to the makeshift corporate boxes in which they hosted the franchise's backers.

In those early days of the franchise Doyle and Edwards drew up a wish list and on it was South African super-shooter Irene van Dyk. From the moment Doyle set eyes on the tall shooter she was impressed, not just by her play on court but also her demeanour off it. To Doyle and Edwards van Dyk was just what the Shakers needed. In addition to improving the team she would also pull in the crowds.

Doyle's brother-in-law was a journalist in South Africa. She gave him the job of tracking down van Dyk so the Shakers could offer to bring her to New Zealand to play. Doyle offered her relative 'a great story' about van Dyk moving to Wellington but was told he wasn't interested. 'That type' of story wasn't printed. It was a measure of how the South African media rated netball.

When Doyle did get in touch with van Dyk the player was pregnant, so there was no way she could join the Shakers for the inaugural 1998 season. Pleased by the approach, however, van Dyk promised she would consider playing in the Coca-Cola Cup the following year. Unfortunately for the Shakers it was no go in 1999 as well. The timing of the Coca-Cola Cup clashed with South Africa's preparations for that year's world championships in Christchurch, which included a March tour to Jamaica.

Undaunted, Doyle looked further ahead. The 2000 season became her target to have van Dyk in the Shakers' line-up. She kept in touch with van Dyk, who by this time was extremely keen to join the Shakers, for a season at least. Once the idea had been floated Irene wanted to get things sorted out and couldn't wait to see Kathy Doyle, who would be at the world championships, when she got to Christchurch. Doyle's duties included meeting delegates at Christchurch Airport, so she was there when the South African team landed.

'Irene came straight over to me and I didn't know what to do,' Doyle says. 'It was quite embarrassing. I had to tell her that she was there to play for South Africa and we couldn't discuss anything else.

'During the tournament it was pretty hard for both of us. We wanted to talk about getting things moving so that Irene could come to New Zealand but it wasn't an appropriate setting to do that. I felt awful. At times I thought the South Africans were keeping an eye on me, so I didn't want to do anything to upset them. I did feel, however, at that time that Louise du Plessis, the coach, was quite happy for Irene to come and play for the Shakers.

'Once the tournament ended we were able to talk. When Irene got back to South Africa I telephoned her to confirm what we'd talked about and arranged for Irene and Christie to come to Wellington in December 1999 for a holiday.'

On Christie and Irene's first night in Wellington Kathy and her husband Paddy hosted a barbecue at their Karori home. Not surprisingly, Christie didn't seem as at ease as his wife, who knew many of the people there.

By this time Irene had started to think about living in New Zealand; about building a new life for herself, Christie and their daughter Bianca. Christie was thinking differently. While he was quite happy for Irene to play for the Shakers, he hadn't really considered moving to New Zealand permanently.

The first priority for everyone was finding a way for Irene to spend six months in Wellington playing for the Shakers.

'Every night we would talk about how it could be done,' Kathy Doyle remembers. 'It was always early morning when we eventually went to bed and Irene tells me that they would carry on talking once in bed.

'Christie suggested he could look after Bianca in South Africa while Irene played for the Shakers. I didn't like that idea because Irene would probably have ended up pining for her daughter and that would have affected her netball as well as upsetting her.

'It was Christie who came up with the idea that Irene's mother should come with her to look after Bianca for six months while he stayed in South Africa and worked. Knowing that Christie wasn't sold on the idea of living in New Zealand I admit there were a few nagging doubts when they went home after that holiday.

'In my heart I felt that Irene was sincere about coming to play, but seeing would be believing. Someone told me that she had pulled out of going to play in Australia at the last moment and that some of her South African team-mates couldn't see her moving to New Zealand. Despite that, I just had a good feeling about both of them. Christie is a very deep thinker who doesn't rush into things.'

After booking flights to New Zealand for Irene, her mother and Bianca, all Kathy Doyle could do was wait and trust that her instincts about Irene had been right. Imagine her feelings when she got a call from television journalist Maryanne Twentyman, who had been waiting to interview Irene at Auckland International Airport, saying that Irene hadn't got off the plane.

'My heart sank,' Doyle says. 'It turned out that, having arrived earlier than anticipated, Irene had switched to an earlier domestic flight from Auckland to Wellington and was already on the way. It had been a traumatic flight from South Africa with Bianca and she wanted to get it finished as quickly as possible.

'I managed to find out through Air New Zealand that she was arriving early and was there to meet her. I was over the moon when I saw her. There had always been a nagging doubt about whether she would actually arrive, but keeping me going was knowing that Irene is the type of person whose word is her bond.

'I felt a bit guilty about uprooting them. Seeing the family living apart with Irene and her mum in Upper Hutt and Christie back in South Africa . . . well, I felt responsible for it. Looking at the pair of them now, it has all been worthwhile.'

Irene smiles at the memories of her first few days in New Zealand with her mother and Bianca.

'Having Mum come with me was perfect. It served several purposes,' she says. 'It would have been impossible for me to cope with teaching, netball and looking after Bianca. No way could I have done it, no matter how much people wanted to help me.

'Besides the practicalities those six months I had with Mum in New Zealand meant a lot to me. While we'd been a close family I had never made a point of spending time with them after leaving home. When Dad died though I needed to make time for Mum. Our time together in New Zealand was great. She loved New Zealand, saying it was as close to heaven as you can get. She said it was so beautiful and clean — and safe.'

Ask Irene when she arrived in New Zealand and quick as a flash she says, 'January 25, three o'clock in the afternoon.

'We had such a terrible flight. Bianca was only 13 months old so we had only two seats and Bianca had to sit on my knee for 23 hours' flying time. The crew on the planes weren't very nice either so I was so happy when we finally touched down in Auckland. I must say that we were looked after much better on the flight from Auckland to Wellington.

'Kathy met us at Wellington airport and took me straight to Fergusson Intermediate School where I was going to be teaching. The next day there was a powhiri to welcome me. I must have looked awful because that was how I felt.'

The powhiri almost put a spanner in the works for Irene. Seeing a photograph of Irene and the Fergusson Intermediate children in the *Dominion* newspaper the following morning, Internal Affairs officials were quickly in touch with Doyle to point out that while van Dyk had a visa to play netball, it didn't allow her to teach.

'That caused a bit of a stir and we had to move quickly to make sure things were done properly,' says Doyle. 'We also wanted it done quietly so that the media didn't find out that there was a potential problem. Thankfully everything was sorted out quickly. Since we first set out to sign Irene I have found out more about visa applications than I thought possible.'

The powhiri was on Friday, the day after Irene arrived from South Africa. On Saturday she had to front up for trials and her first meeting with coach Lois Muir.

'The last thing I felt like was playing netball but in the end it probably did me good. It was a hard session and shook my body back into action.

'It was the first time I had met Lois and I found out immediately that she doesn't stand any nonsense. I told her I was very tired and she replied that she had no time for people who are tired and that I should just get on with it. Lisa Bogiwalu was the first player to talk to me. She asked how I was and I told her that I was tired but no one cared.

'Training is very different in New Zealand to what I was used to in

South Africa. In South Africa we would warm up with ball skills, play a game and that was it . . . end of story. South African teams have a coach. Full stop. At the Shakers there was a coach [Lois Muir], assistant coach [Tanya Cox], physiotherapist [Matt Wenham], a fitness trainer [Barbara Beable] who tries to kill you . . .

'I couldn't get used to it at first when after training players would go to Matt or Barbara to get niggling injuries seen to. I didn't go to them because I wasn't used to that sort of thing.

'Lois would take the shooters, then move on to the mid-court players, whereas in South Africa everyone worked together at the same time. Another difference is that in South Africa the coach has her view and that's it. There is definitely no player input. It was so refreshing that Lois and Tanya would ask how we felt about things. They actually listened to us.'

Away from netball Irene was about to get a taste of just how generous New Zealanders can be. Rana Te Maro, deputy principal at Fergusson Intermediate, moved out of his house so Irene and her mother would have somewhere to live. It was initially for two weeks, then became three, four . . .

'I said to Mum that we had to look for a house. She pointed out that I had no furniture but, what the heck, we needed a house. We got it on the Thursday and at morning assembly the following Monday Margaret Urlich told the kids that Miss van Dyk wants to move into a house but she has no furniture.

'Kathy organised beds for Mum, myself and Bianca but the parents of the kids at school were also fantastic. They arrived with tables, dining room sets, lounge suites, blankets, pillows . . . things you don't think about, such as cleaning materials and a bucket. It was unbelievable. Suddenly my house was furnished with other people's things.

'That tells you so much about how generous the people in New Zealand are. How helpful they are. I believe that's why New Zealand is such a dominant country in sport despite its size. New Zealanders do everything with passion. If they don't like you then they will never like you. But if they do like you they let nothing stand in their way to show you how they feel.'

When Irene first arrived in Wellington to join the Shakers she didn't intend to stay permanently. It was simply a six month visit to play netball. The thought of staying had, of course, crossed her mind, but that may have been it had it not been for her mother. It was she who planted the seed in her daughter's mind that New Zealand really could be the place for her. In the weeks ahead Irene senior nurtured that seed, giving it all the care and attention she would give a flower that was starting to bloom. That was the thing that struck her most. Her daughter really was blooming in the New Zealand environment.

For Irene's part she couldn't believe the difference in her own daughter, Bianca. She too was blossoming now she was away from the fears living in South Africa brought.

In South Africa the family had to be careful about whatever they did. Not because it was the family of Irene van Dyk, netball superstar — every family was in the same boat in Johannesburg. Simple things such as Irene senior being able to take her granddaughter to the park near their Upper Hutt house — unthinkable where they were living in Johannesburg — began to make Irene think about the future.

'Mum started it all by saying, "I wouldn't go back if I were you." I said, "Mum, don't even go there," but she was going to have her say in that lovely quiet way of hers. She pointed out what a bright future we could have. That Christie and I were still young and could make things work for ourselves.

'I think what made her start talking that way was the huge thing that had been made about me coming to play for the Shakers. She said these people really appreciated me. They appreciated my personality.

'It got me thinking deeply about what we were going to do and eventually I rang Christie to come over for a holiday in April. It didn't take him long to realise what was happening and that I didn't really want to go back to South Africa.

'If he had been adamant that we had to go back to South Africa, that there was no way we could emigrate to New Zealand . . . then I would have gone back at the end of the Coca-Cola Cup. But he wasn't too resistant. He kept saying, "Do you really want to stay here?" and I would tell him how much I loved living in New Zealand.

'One day he just said he should probably be getting back to South Africa to pack up our things and get them brought over to New Zealand. He went back earlier than planned to get everything organised, such as selling our cars. Within two months he was back in New Zealand and we were settling down.'

Once that decision was taken Irene had another to make — should she make herself available for the Silver Ferns? It was a question that didn't take long to answer. Irene loves her netball and she saw no reason not to play for New Zealand if, as was the case, she was eligible under international rules.

The news that van Dyk was switching her allegiance to New Zealand took the South African officials by surprise. Christie van Dyk rang new coach Elise Kortze while he was in Johannesburg packing the couple's belongings to say that the family would be living in New Zealand.

'It came as a surprise,' Kortze said at the time. 'Irene had applied at RAU University and Gauteng Region to play for them when she got back in June, so we all expected that she was coming back.

According to Kortze the public reaction in South Africa to the news was overwhelming.

'Irene is like a trade name in South Africa. She's a symbol of netball in South Africa and the people are most probably scared and thinking what is going to happen to netball now? There is a great feeling of loss, everyone is talking about it.'

Everyone in New Zealand was talking about it as well. It seemed the country was divided about whether she should be allowed to play for the Silver Ferns, and there were some hurtful things said. But a bewildered Irene van Dyk was just pleased to be settling down in her adopted country.

Chapter 8

A Different Lifestyle

IN NEW ZEALAND CRIMINALS LIVE BEHIND bars in prisons. In South Africa, especially in a city such as Johannesburg, ordinary people such as Christie and Irene van Dyk spend time behind bars every day. The difference is that in New Zealand the bars are to keep the criminals in, whereas in South Africa they are to keep them out of private homes.

Irene and Christie lived in the suburb of Vereeniging, 20 minutes out of Johannesburg, where the windows on all the houses were covered by bars out of necessity. There were security shields in front of every wooden door, and a steel door separated the bedroom from the rest of the house. That way the householders might lose all their possessions during a break-in while they sleep, but they will stay alive.

After living in such a security-conscious environment Irene and her mother found it difficult to adjust during their first few nights in Upper Hutt, a city on the outskirts of Wellington, New Zealand's capital city. Irene, of course, had visited New Zealand several times, but it was usually in a team situation and staying in hotels. That was a much different proposition to living in a house, especially one that had no bars on its windows.

While she can see the funny side of it now, for Irene and her mother that first night in New Zealand was no laughing matter.

'Had anyone been able to see us that first night they would have thought we were crazy. Mum was sitting looking out of the back window, while I was watching the front window, waiting for someone to come through them. We couldn't bring ourselves to go to bed that night and for the first few nights we didn't sleep well because we were not used to sleeping somewhere with no security.

'Security had been so much a part of our lives that we found it hard to get used to not having it. Even in South Africa where we had bars and security doors I didn't sleep well when Christie wasn't at home. I was scared to go to bed because I was aware that anything could happen.

'In New Zealand I have no problems sleeping when Christie is away.

Now that I have adjusted I sleep well every night, but to anyone who has not experienced such differing environments it would be hard to understand how scary it was for us not having bars on the windows.'

Christie and Irene taught in two contrasting schools in Vereeniging. Christie's school was in what could be described as a posh area. All the children on the school roll were white. The school where Irene taught was in a poorer area and the pupils were 95 per cent black and 5 per cent white.

New Zealand teachers can become cynical, having heard all kinds of excuses for lateness, but they probably won't have had a child telling them, truthfully, that they are not on time because their father has been hijacked.

'That did happen to people. In fact the principal of Christie's school was hijacked outside the family home. Those who attacked him threw him and his daughter out of the school van. The robbers took off in the van which contained his belongings, including all the keys to the school.

'It is that sort of incident which makes people drive round with a gun on their lap. Everyone walks around with guns. You're allowed to carry a gun to protect yourself. I carried a loaded gun. Most women have a gun in their handbag. You can hit people with the heavy handbag, or use the gun.

'At night you wouldn't dream of driving a car without having a gun handy. Whether I would have been able to use it is another matter. I grew up on a farm where we did some night hunting but I don't think I would have been able to use it on another human being, no matter what they'd done.

'It is a life. Unfortunately a lot of people in South Africa don't feel a life is worth much.'

Irene had that confirmed for her one day at school, where she taught nine-year-old children, 48 to a class.

'One day this little boy came up to me and said, "Miss van Dyk, I am going to kill my mother." Taken aback, I eventually asked why he would do that.

' "Because I don't like her." "Why don't you like your mother? She brings you to school every day, she looks after you, gives you food, she gives you love."

' "I don't like her. My dad doesn't like her either."

'I asked him how he was going to kill her and he said with a knife. A big knife.

' "Does your mother know about this?" "Yes." "When are you going to kill your mother?" "When I am 13."

'I said, "You must be joking," but he was serious.

'I got his mother to come in and see me. I asked if she realised what he was saying. That he was nine years old and was talking about killing her. She did, and said he probably would kill her. She said there was nothing she could do about it. It was like having a nightmare that you cannot do anything about, only I was wide awake.

'What happened with that boy can't be blamed on television, as is done so often these days, because he lived in a township where there is no electricity, never mind television. They just see what is happening around them.

'Christie taught at an Afrikaans school, whereas I taught at an English school. Christie as a teacher was treated like dirt, whereas a teacher at my school was looked upon as a goddess. Parents would thank us for educating their children. They were so thankful for what we did for their kids. I loved those kids just as much as I now love the kids at Fergusson Intermediate School.'

In November 1999, just prior to Irene and Christie's visit to New Zealand, an horrific incident occurred at Irene's school that still has her shaking her head in wonderment and sadness as she recalls it.

'It involved one of our kids, Petrus, who played cricket and was coached by Christie. Unbeknown to anyone he brought a gun to school. At two o'clock when school closed my friend and I were on duty outside to make sure the kids got onto the buses OK. We heard this shot, a huge bang.

'Our deputy principal ran to where the noise came from while we tried to stop the kids going to see what had happened. A boy, I think he was 16, was lying on the pavement with blood pumping out of his stomach and there was Petrus standing with the gun about ten metres away.

'I was hysterical but the kids just walked past all that blood as if nothing had happened. We phoned the police who came and took Petrus and the gun away. The boy who was shot was taken away in an ambulance. Thankfully he didn't die.

'The thing that really frightened me afterwards was that Petrus hated my friend Francien's guts. She was very strict with her pupils. Kids wouldn't dare to walk with their hands in their pockets or with their shoulders hunched. In her class pupils would sit up straight and keep their mouth shut. It was scary that Petrus had the gun in his case all day at school. He could easily have shot Francien because he would often abuse her, calling her names.

'The other worrying part was that at any time in the day one of the 7-year-olds — the school was for 7 to 13-year-olds — could have got the loaded gun out and shot someone while not realising what they were doing.

'He finished up shooting one of his friends. Petrus said he was only joking and that he didn't know the gun was loaded, but a boy of 13 knows whether a gun is loaded or not.'

Christie had his car stolen from outside their front door with the gates to the property locked. Irene's sister has had her house burgled so many times while she has been on holiday that she doesn't go on holiday any more. The house is alarmed and secured with barred windows, but who is going to go and investigate when an alarm goes off? No one, says Irene, because they don't want to be killed.

It was a way of life Irene and Christie had become accustomed to. That didn't mean they enjoyed having to be ever vigilant and security conscious. They simply made the best of it, going about their business in the same way as their friends even though Irene was now a star on the international netball scene.

Most of those who had taken Irene into their hearts overseas could never have imagined what life was like in South Africa for this ebullient young woman. Most probably thought she received the same treatment enjoyed by top sportspeople in New Zealand and Australia. One who saw the contrasts in 1999 was Maryanne Twentyman, then working for TV3 and now a producer on the TAB's *Trackside* programme.

A netball lover, Maryanne was eagerly awaiting the start of the world championships in Christchurch later that year, but she was becoming increasingly frustrated at seeing little lead-up material on television. She would have loved to have been out in the netball community generating stories to promote the upcoming championships, but it wasn't that simple. TV3's rival station TVNZ was the host broadcaster for the world tournament and therefore held the rights to the event. That didn't deter Maryanne, who wasn't a reporter but an assistant chief of staff. She suggested to her superior that TVNZ was missing some great opportunities and that TV3 should capitalise.

'Almost every night there were stories on the television news about this country or that country gearing up for rugby's World Cup, an event that was coming up *after* the netball tournament and wasn't being played in New Zealand,' Maryanne says. 'I didn't think netball was getting a fair go and I began thinking of stories that would be of interest to New Zealanders. Four countries were coming out of Africa for the world tournament. Some of their players had probably never been on a plane, never mind travelling across the world to New Zealand. That had the potential for some great human-interest stories.

'There was also the fact that South Africa were coming to New Zealand for a test series and would be playing a one-off international against Australia in Sydney on the way home. That provided an opportunity for a TV3 crew to accompany them.'

There was no budget for such a venture but, probably because he didn't think it had any chance of succeeding, Maryanne's boss gave her the green light to investigate ways of getting the trip sponsored and agreed that if she was successful then she should be the reporter. To Maryanne's delight, and the disbelief of senior reporters at the station, she pulled it off. When the Proteas left Auckland for Sydney Maryanne and her camera crew followed them.

Having been thrashed by Australia in what was shooting star Vicki Wilson's last international on home soil before the world championship and retirement, the despondent South African women were not very talkative when the plane left for Johannesburg on the last stage of the journey home. Maryanne had only spoken briefly to Irene in New Zealand and, being in the unfamiliar role of reporter, was nervous when she approached her during a two-hour stopover in Perth to discuss plans for visiting her home.

'I felt it was a big deal talking to this netball superstar, but what I found was the most effervescent, down-to-earth person. She's one awesome lady.'

Johannesburg Airport provided the first big surprise for Maryanne. After watching the players say their goodbyes in the baggage claim area, she walked out into the arrival hall alongside Irene and was stunned.

'I was expecting the media to be waiting for the players, but there wasn't one journalist or cameraperson there. Not one. I couldn't believe it. The netballers meant nothing to the public. The airport was packed but no one seemed to notice Irene, which was so different to when she had left Auckland and Sydney airports.'

Irene did have some profile, even if not to South African air travellers, because when Maryanne visited Irene and Christie's home there was a small hut behind the house which was virtually a netball shrine. On the wall were posters in which Irene was promoting orange juice, alongside all sorts of netball memorabilia including Bernice Mene's signed bib.

'Her profile was nothing like it was in New Zealand and Christie obviously didn't know just how highly she was regarded overseas. Christie was really cautious when talking to us; cautious about the whole New Zealand deal. He did ask questions though, and it became clear he was genuinely interested in learning more about New Zealand. Reading between the lines, however, it looked as if he felt he had been brainwashed by Irene about the concept of a new life in New Zealand. It was something he didn't seem to be able to get his head around because the South African way of life was all he knew. He couldn't work out how or why Irene's profile was so big in New Zealand. All he wanted to talk about were the likes of Jonah Lomu and Christian Cullen, and it was obvious he had a real passion for sport.'

After a night in a hotel, Maryanne and her crew set out for the suburb where Irene and Christie lived.

'The area they lived in reminded me of some sort of compound. We were driving round streets where the houses were behind 10- and 12-foot-high concrete walls topped with barbed wire. I was gobsmacked. It just didn't seem the right place for someone like Irene to be living.

'At the house we had to go through high metal gates that were quickly shut behind us, and to get inside you had to go through what I would describe as a cage, which was also locked, and then more bars. Had Irene not been so lovely and welcoming I could have imagined what it is like to go to prison. Even so, it was a shock to the system to see bars on every window of what was an average three-bedroom home.

'Irene practised her shooting with a goalpost at the back of the house and when I asked could we film it she said Christie would have to move the guard dogs first. When I suggested seeing the dogs Irene laughed and told me I couldn't go near them or I would be bitten. I looked through the barred window and didn't need telling twice. They were big, mean-looking animals.

'When we were leaving they were careful to give us precise instructions on how to get back to the hotel. Take a wrong turning and you could be in trouble, we were told. We had a rental car and were forever being warned to be careful. When we were leaving Johannesburg we had to go to the airport at five o'clock in the morning and it was stressed to us not to stop at traffic lights or we could be attacked. We had to try and gauge the lights by driving slowly.'

After South Africa the television crew went on to Botswana, Zambia and Malawi but, with Irene deciding to play for the Capital Shakers, it was the South African content that created most interest in New Zealand, though the footage almost didn't make the screen. The television crew's bags, including the tapes, were lost by South African Airways between Malawi and Sydney, leaving Maryanne feeling suicidal.

'I sat in Sydney Airport crying, thinking I hadn't only lost my footage but also my job and credibility as a journalist. It was embarrassing and I vomited all the way across the Tasman, knowing I had to tell them at work what had happened.'

Almost hourly calls to South African Airways and the baggage claim people in Johannesburg and Malawi brought no reward until two weeks later when Maryanne received a call from SAA saying the bags had been located. They'd been left on a baggage carousel at Johannesburg Airport and removed as a security precaution. To describe Maryanne as being relieved would be a massive understatement, and it was a travel lesson she would never forget.

Maryanne returned home convinced that Irene would be much better off living in New Zealand. While Irene ultimately took that course, and is now to all intents and purposes a Kiwi, it would be wrong to think that she dislikes the country in which she was born and bred. That's far from the case. She loves South Africa.

The carefree days growing up on the family farm, her college life and her early netball days all provide wonderful memories that will never dull. But as she grew older, had Bianca, and went to live in Johannesburg, the lack of safety became too much for her. In looking to New Zealand as a place to build a future, Irene was probably trying to rekindle those early days on the farm for herself, Christie and Bianca.

'New Zealanders take what they have for granted, as I suppose I did when I was growing up in a good family on a beautiful farm. Perhaps subconsciously when I first visited New Zealand I likened it to where I spent my childhood.

'Of course bad things happen in New Zealand, as they do all over the world, but they are minimal and so far removed from what I was used to in the last couple of years that I am glad to be out of it.

'I didn't really think I would emigrate. New Zealand was to be my home for six months, but it didn't take me long to fall in love with the place. Since Nelson Mandela became president things have changed a lot in South Africa, but there is so much still wrong with the country.

'Nelson Mandela is an amazing guy. The way he handled the country on becoming president was unbelievable. I do not believe any future president will be able to make the difference he did. I was privileged to meet him and was amazed at what a down-to-earth guy he is. He can talk to anybody.

'Of course he is old now. When you see someone like Nelson Mandela on television you don't realise how old they are. At the function where I met him he was walking really, really slowly. You could see it was an effort for him. We talked about sport, but he has such a huge general knowledge that he can talk to anybody for ages about anything.

'That night, which was for sporting awards, he had invited the South African paralympic team to the function. He made a point of greeting every single one of them. Whether someone was in a wheelchair or on crutches, or able-bodied, he would want to know all about them. One girl was blind and he spent a long time talking to her.

'Those are the moments you look back fondly on later in life. How many people get the chance to meet someone such as Nelson Mandela? The reason I got the opportunity came through playing netball for South Africa. Playing netball also gave me the chance to travel to places I would never have dreamt of going when I was growing up on the farm — Britain, Jamaica, Australia, New Zealand. Each of them attractive in their own way, but I am so pleased that the Capital Shakers brought me to New Zealand.'

Chapter 9

Becoming a Silver Fern

WHEN IRENE VAN DYK ARRIVED IN NEW ZEALAND to play for the Capital Shakers there was no hint of the controversy she would find herself the centre of three months later. The controversy, which divided the netball fraternity, was about whether van Dyk should be allowed to represent New Zealand and, if she was, would it be right for Silver Ferns coach Yvonne Willering to select her.

Playing for the Silver Ferns wasn't on van Dyk's agenda when she agreed to play for the Capital Shakers in the 2000 Coca-Cola Cup competition. While the Shakers had made it obvious they would like to see her stay permanently, Irene had committed herself for only one season. There is no doubt that she had thought about making New Zealand, and Wellington in particular, her home, but there were many things to consider, not least whether her husband Christie would want to make the move.

For the first couple of months getting used to new cultures, adapting to a different style of netball, learning a new teaching curriculum, and settling Bianca into a foreign environment was enough to keep Irene busy. During this time she was frequently asked whether she was considering switching her allegiance from the Proteas to the Silver Ferns, so it wasn't something she could simply ignore. But in those early days in New Zealand such questions drew a non-committal answer along the lines that she was in New Zealand to play one season for the Capital Shakers and that was it.

Van Dyk's presence in the Shakers line-up alongside England's Helen Lonsdale was welcomed, as was the appearance of Jamaican shooting star Elaine Davis for the Auckland Diamonds, and Vilimaina Davu in the Canterbury Flames' defence. Netball officials and critics agreed that having such international stars boosted the profile of the Coca-Cola Cup in particular, and New Zealand netball generally. The impact of van Dyk in Wellington was amazing. Twelve months earlier Wellingtonians couldn't be bothered going out to watch netball. In the 2000 season if they didn't get to Taita's Walter Nash Stadium early they wouldn't get a seat, with the full house signs out in front of the stadium at every game.

At the time New Zealand netball needed every boost it could get. The netball community was still down in the dumps after the Silver Ferns' dramatic one-goal loss to Australia in the world championship final the previous October in Christchurch. And it wasn't just netball followers who were smarting from the heart-breaking loss to Australia. The public, who had been lured in record numbers to watch the game on television by the hype surrounding the Silver Ferns, were convinced they would see a Kiwi win. When the Silver Ferns led by 6 goals going into the final 15 minutes those watching both in the stadium and on television were sure that at last the Australian bogey was about to be laid to rest, that New Zealand was about to be crowned world champion.

That scenario should have eventuated. That it didn't was because of an amazing turnaround during which the Silver Ferns lost their way and the Australians, sensing they were being let off the hook, found renewed faith in themselves. During the frenetic last few minutes of the game the respective coaches watched their teams' changing fortunes in a vastly contrasting manner. While Australia's Jill McIntosh sat quietly on the bench showing no emotion, even if her insides were churning, Yvonne Willering wore a tortured expression as she yelled and screamed at her players in a last desperate attempt to get them back on track.

Despite losing their way the Ferns still should have won the game as, with only seconds remaining and the scores level, goalshoot Donna Loffhagen lined up a shot at goal that she would sink with her eyes closed 99 times out of 100. This was the world championship final, however, and everyone's nerves were jangling. Loffhagen's shot hit the rim and, instead of dropping through the net, fell the other way. It was collected by a willing pair of Australian hands and transferred quickly through court to the opposite goal circle where Aussie goalshoot Sharelle McMahon slotted the winning goal.

Those watching at home, along with the 7000 inside the stadium, couldn't believe what they were seeing as the Australians celebrated wildly while the New Zealand women buried their heads in towels as if that could shut out what was happening around them.

As she had done four years earlier, Irene van Dyk felt for the New Zealand players. This time, unlike the game in Birmingham, she wasn't courtside but in the stand with her South African team-mates. That night Irene was reasonably sure she would be playing for the Shakers either alongside or against those whose despair she was watching. She couldn't have realised, however, the part some of those players would have in the controversy that would arise six months later.

Such is the contrasting profile of netball in the two countries that Irene has always been recognised more in New Zealand than in her South African homeland. That continued to be the case when she arrived in the Hutt Valley to play for the Capital Shakers, and she laughs about her first New Zealand shopping expedition with her mother.

'It was to Pak 'N Save and it took us ages to do our shopping. People were coming up asking, "Are you Irene van Dyk?" or just wanting to say hello. Mum asked me if I realised how popular I was in New Zealand.

'It is something you don't really think about. When I had been in New Zealand previously I was with the South African team and while I got a lot of attention I assumed it was because I was part of the Proteas.'

After two years in New Zealand the attention van Dyk receives has increased rather than diminished, especially after the leading role she played when New Zealand at last beat Australia in South Africa at the end of 2000, and again at the start of 2001. Irene takes it all in her stride.

'The attention has never bothered me at all. I find it quite nice. I like the people who have the guts to come up and talk to you rather than just stand and stare.

'I don't really notice people staring any more. One day I was going to a meeting in Naenae and gave one of our teachers a lift to the orthodontist. As I was dropping him off he said, "Do you realise how many people look at you as you drive past, how they turn their heads to see if it's really you?"

'I said I didn't really notice it any more, and anyway they must be looking at him!'

The Coca-Cola Cup started in April and that was when Irene and Christie decided they wanted to live in New Zealand.

In March every player taking part in the competition had been required to fill in a profile. Among the questions was 'Are you available for the Silver Ferns?' Given that she was only planning to stay for a few months Irene ticked the 'No' box. With the decision to live in New Zealand that situation had changed, and when Irene found herself sitting in front of Yvonne Willering on a flight to the South Island with the Shakers she took the opportunity to let the coach know her circumstances had altered.

'I turned to Yvonne and said she should change the tick to the "Yes" box.'

If Irene expected Willering to react enthusiastically she got a shock.

'Yvonne didn't seem that happy when I told her. She just said, "Are you going to stay then?" "Yes." "When did you decide?" "The April holidays." And that was it.

'I turned to Tanya [Cox] who was sitting next to me and said, "Has this woman got any feelings?" Tanya just laughed. Yvonne didn't even look interested. What I didn't know then was that Yvonne can put up a front so that people don't know what or how she's feeling. Obviously I have got to know her a lot better now, but there are still times when you don't know where you are with her.'

Two days after that conversation with Willering, Irene told Wellington's *Dominion* newspaper that she was available and would like to play for the Silver Ferns. Confirming that she had decided to settle in New Zealand, Irene said she wanted to play at the highest possible level. She was available for New Zealand and if selected for the Silver Ferns it would be great. If not, it would only make her more determined to be chosen in the next team. The fact that no one reacted to her comments made what happened a month later when she repeated them on television all the more surprising to Irene.

'On television I said the same thing I had told the *Dominion*. I said I would play to the best of my ability. If it was good enough to earn a place in the Silver Ferns, fine. If I didn't make it that year then I would keep on trying.

'The following day all hell broke loose and I couldn't understand what was going on. Four weeks earlier no one had said anything. When I look back now I believe it was some media people looking for some juicy action.

'They were asking if I had the right to play for New Zealand, and I admit that at the time I really didn't know how to handle what was happening. I had no idea that it would become such an issue because I had been told that under the rules I could make myself available to play for New Zealand. Had I not decided to make New Zealand my home then I wouldn't have done so. The crazy thing about the rules is that I could have played for New Zealand even if I only stayed a few months. It would just have meant that I couldn't have played for South Africa in the same year.

'Those were the rules. Had I not been eligible then Netball New Zealand would have told me so. The rules said that a player could play for only one country in a year. Had there been a stand-down period between playing for one country and another then I would have been quite happy to sit out that period while I continued to play for the Capital Shakers and Wellington.'

Rugby had previously gone down the path netball now found itself on. At one time it was commonplace for rugby players to play for Samoa, Tonga or the Cook Islands one year and New Zealand the next, or vice versa. It didn't take long for rugby to tighten the regulations to stop that happening, and a stand-down period was introduced to stop players swapping allegiances at the drop of a hat.

The transfer of players between countries was virgin territory for netball. Irene van Dyk, Elaine Davis, Vilimaina Davu and Helen Lonsdale were netballing trailblazers. The difference between van Dyk and the other three at the time — Davu is now resident in New Zealand and playing for the Silver Ferns — was that van Dyk had chosen to live in New Zealand.

Van Dyk admits she was delighted there was no stand-down period, but she believes the rules will be looked at in the light of what happened with her and with Davu in 2000. She also makes the point that had Bianca not been born then perhaps the van Dyks wouldn't have decided to live in New Zealand and she would still be a Protea.

'Everything changes when you have a child. You look out for them and basically you play second fiddle. If you go right to the bottom of it the reason we are in New Zealand is not myself or Christie, it is for Bianca.

'I watch her playing outside and she's so happy-go-lucky. She's free and has no reason to be scared. If we were still in South Africa she would never be allowed to play in the garden on her own. Christie or myself would have to be with her or she would have to play in her room.

'Coming to New Zealand wasn't easy for Bianca, and it would have been impossible for us had my mother not been staying with us for the first three months. The only language Bianca understood was Afrikaans so when we arrived in New Zealand she didn't have a clue what people were saying to her.

'It must have been very difficult for her. Had Mum not been with us it would have been worse because while I was at school or netball Bianca would have had to stay with someone who she couldn't communicate with. She's coming along fine now and often when we ask her a question in Afrikaans she answers in English.'

If Bianca found it difficult to understand what people were saying, so her mother found it hard to understand the fuss her availability for the Silver Ferns had caused. The row hotted up as the announcement of the New Zealand team to play Australia in Newcastle drew closer. The radio talkback shows had a field day, with opinions seemingly split 50–50 as to whether van Dyk should be in the team.

There were no question marks about her playing ability. The eligibility question, and the ridiculous rules that had never been thought through, were the main bones of contention. The pot was stirred when New Zealand players began expressing their opinions.

Given what had happened at the world championships, and the fact that it was her position that seemed likely to be under threat, it was no surprise that Donna Loffhagen's opinions were asked for and given prominence by the media. Some of what the straight-shooting Loffhagen said was taken out of context and blown up to suit the headline writers, but there was no doubt she didn't like the idea of an overseas player coming in and perhaps taking her spot or that of a team-mate. It was unfair that a player, she said, could switch from one country to another so easily, and so soon after playing at a world championship. The rules were wrong and needed looking at. She also questioned whether bringing overseas players into the Coca-Cola Cup was a good thing, and whether van Dyk's move would benefit world netball as her defection would weaken South Africa. Throughout the debate Loffhagen stressed the fact that she had nothing against van Dyk personally and said, prophetically, that she would even enjoy combining her talents with those of the former South African captain.

There were those who hit back at Loffhagen, saying that had van Dyk been playing for the Ferns at the world championship against Australia the outcome would have been different. This argument was ridiculous. The final wasn't lost because of one missed goal in the last seconds. It was thrown away by the whole team in the 15 minutes leading up to the dramatic finale.

The controversy was all getting too much for van Dyk. She's a person who loves life and likes to laugh a lot, but she didn't feel much like laughing during those turbulent times.

'There were times when some of the things being said hurt me a lot. Much of what was said was totally uncalled for. The situation wasn't helped by the media going to all and sundry asking whether I should be allowed to play for New Zealand. It wasn't so much what players like Donna were saying. It was the interpretation people were putting on what they said.

'To be honest, I probably would have felt the same way the New Zealand players felt. If I had been in Donna's or any other New Zealand shooter's shoes I would have thought, "Flip, this woman has been in New Zealand for six months and she gets to play for our country." The ultimate is to play for your country. It is a New Zealand girl's dream from an early age to be in the Silver Ferns.

'They probably had grounds for being upset and disappointed. I respected the way they felt, but I was doing nothing wrong. I wish they would have just taken a little time to understand my situation as well. I wasn't a netball mercenary coming in for a few months. I had made a lifetime decision and they knew that. The rules happened to be on my side and allowed me to play. I found it hard to cope with people taking pot shots at me. It all seemed so unnecessary.

'I am the last person to cause trouble. I want to live my life, play ball and go with the flow.'

During those tough times Irene was glad to have the support of her Shakers team-mates. And there were also words of encouragement from Yvonne Willering.

'When all this was going down Yvonne rang and told me to hang in and not let it get to me. That meant a lot to me at the time. When Yvonne was having problems later in the year and there was talk of a player revolt I knew how she felt having gone through my own troubles. I left a message on her phone telling her to hang in there. I hope that message helped a little.'

Despite all the flak she was getting, at no time did Irene think about changing her mind and withdrawing her availability.

'Hell no. If anything it just made me more determined. Had I not been picked for that team to Australia I would have just tried harder to make the team next time.'

In the period leading up to the announcement of the team to play Australia in Newcastle Irene tried to prepare herself mentally for rejection. While those close to her were saying she was a certainty for selection, Irene was frightened to believe them. There were no clues whenever she ran into Willering on her netballing travels.

'Yvonne is a closed book. You get no clues from her.

'There were so many people supporting me, telling me I would be in the team. They would say I had had a good Coca-Cola Cup and that the team was being picked on form from that competition. I wanted to believe them and I dreamt a lot at night. Had I not been selected then I would probably have cried. But I wouldn't have let anyone know.'

The moment Irene had been waiting for so anxiously came on the evening of 6 June 2000, when the telephone rang at her Upper Hutt home where she was enjoying a quiet evening with Christie, her mother and Bianca.

'It was Yvonne. She said, "Congratulations, you're in the Silver Ferns team."

'The moment she had finished saying it I think I shouted loud enough to let the whole of Upper Hutt know. That was when Yvonne said I wasn't allowed to tell anyone. I said it was too late so far as Christie and Mum went. They were in the same room. "Well make sure you don't talk to anyone else. You're flying to Auckland tomorrow morning." '

The moment Irene put the receiver down the celebrations started and there was little sleep for any of the family that night. They sat up talking till after midnight, and Christie and Irene continued the conversation when they went to bed. Early next morning Irene was on a plane to Auckland when she would rather have been sleeping. On the return flight to Wellington that evening she slept throughout the journey after the busiest day of her life.

'That was a whirlwind day. From the moment I was picked up at Auckland airport and taken to Netball New Zealand's offices I didn't have one moment to myself.

'It started out with me being measured up for my walking out clothes. The tailor was across the road from the netball office so I was back and forth there while alterations were made, which wasn't surprising as I am not exactly the usual size.

'There were so many people to meet and so many things to do I found it hard to catch my breath. I was so excited and everything was so overwhelming that it was all going past in a blur, as if I was watching myself from outside my body.'

It was while all this was going on that Irene met Yvonne Willering in the corridor at the netball office.

'Yvonne gave me a hug and again congratulated me on being chosen. I realised that she didn't look happy at all. In fact she was in a state. I asked if she was OK and she said not really. I asked what was wrong and she told me she had just had to tell an Auckland player that she hadn't made the team.

'I think it was Teresa Tairi, who was someone she had been close to. She had been to see her personally. I thought then that I wouldn't want to be a coach and have to tell someone I really liked that they'd not made the team. I wouldn't have the guts to do that.

'It also gave me an insight into the real Yvonne. She's not as tough and unfeeling as some people think. OK, she might put on a tough exterior but she has a lovely heart and is a very caring person with a good sense of humour.'

A sense of humour was something Irene was going to need during her first few hours as a Silver Fern.

Chapter 10

New Girl on the Block

IRENE VAN DYK OFFICIALLY BECAME a Silver Fern when the New Zealand team to play Australia in Newcastle was announced at a 7 June press conference in Auckland where Linda Vagana presented the former South African captain with her New Zealand uniform. It was an emotional moment for Irene. Not only would she be playing netball for a country other than the one in which she was born, it also confirmed to both countries that her decision to live in New Zealand was final.

As usual, Irene laughed her way through the press conference, only becoming serious when the question needed a serious answer. She was pleased that, this being netball, most of the questions carried no hidden barbs and were easily answered. But then this was a media briefing organised by Netball New Zealand — the tough questions were still to come in the many one-on-one interviews that would continue throughout the day.

In total Irene did 26 interviews that day. Some were easy, others needed negotiating with care as she recognised that some of the questions were designed to trip her up. It is part of Irene's make-up that she sees the best in everyone until they do something to prove her wrong. She was well acquainted with many of those wanting to talk to her that day, and she had a fair idea which ones needed to be treated with caution. The interviews she was most nervous about were those being done live on TV3 news and Television New Zealand's *Holmes*.

Fortunately for Irene she had the company of Bernice Mene throughout the day. Mene was also in the news after being appointed Silver Ferns captain in place of Belinda Colling, who had been dropped from the team. Reflecting on that day, Irene says she would have found it hard to get through without Mene's help.

'Bernie was awesome. Between interviews we would talk about what had happened and what was coming up. But most of all we just laughed. We had a great time together even though it was the most hectic day you could imagine.

'We were running from one interview to another. There were several newspaper reporters to talk to. There were visits to radio stations and television studios. No one in South Africa would believe that netball would be covered in such depth by all sections of the media. When a South African team was announced . . . well, it was . . . just announced.

'We had Kerry Manders' and Dean McLauchlan's mobiles with us and they were going so often it was hard to catch your breath. All of a sudden we both realised how hungry we were so we got some kebabs. It might sound strange, but out of all the things that happened to me that day one I remember most is Bernie and myself eating those kebabs on the way to the television studio.

'There was one really awkward moment when we went to the TVNZ studios. Yvonne went through the door first, but quickly turned round and suggested we go another way. It turned out that the New Zealand basketball team was in the reception area, including Donna Loffhagen and Belinda Colling. With what Donna had been quoted as saying about me playing for the Silver Ferns, and the fact that Belinda had been left out, Yvonne probably didn't know how they would react to me and wanted to avoid a confrontation. I was relieved that we went in another door. I am sure everything would have been fine, but at the time I was glad we took the easy way out and avoided them.

'During the interviews if someone asked me a question that sounded dodgy Bernie would jump in and answer for me. She never left my side all day. There were some awkward questions for Bernie as well since she had replaced Belinda as captain but she handled them so well. By the end of the day I felt I knew her dad Mene Mene because every show we were on asked about him.

'I was really nervous about doing *Holmes*. From what I had seen Paul Holmes can be really nice or awful to you. I didn't know what to expect or which side he would take in the discussion about whether I should be able to play for the Silver Ferns so soon after coming to live in New Zealand. As it turned out he was pro me playing for New Zealand, so it turned out to be really enjoyable.

'Being interviewed in a television studio is so different with the lights and make-up sessions. You would be amazed how much make-up they put on you before allowing you in front of the cameras. How you feel on television depends on how the host treats you. Paul Holmes was very relaxed that night, wanting to know how I felt and if I had settled in New Zealand. He made both myself and Bernie feel welcome.

'By the time the last interview was over and I was being driven to the airport for my flight home to Wellington where Christie, Mum and Bianca were waiting for me, I was feeling completely knackered.

'Whatever happens in the rest of my life, that's one day I will never forget. It was perfect and I suppose I didn't really want it to end because I would never get that feeling again. I wouldn't change one moment of what happened, but there is one small regret.

'If only it was possible to go through it all again; to appreciate what was happening to me. Everything was so hectic. It would have been nice to smell the roses along the way.

'Although in a way I did get to do just that because when I got home I sat down and told Christie and Mum what a wonderful day it had been. The next day the kids at school wanted to know why I had been away and wanted to hear about what I had been doing. Telling them helped me relive everything again.'

The excitement of selection had barely begun to fade before Irene had to get ready to go to Auckland again. This time it was to meet up with the Silver Ferns for four days of preparation before going to Newcastle in New South Wales for the Fisher and Paykel test against Australia.

Irene was, of course, a seasoned international. However that was with South Africa, and it didn't stop her feeling extremely apprehensive about how she would be received by her new team-mates. While she had been the baby of the team when she was selected for the South African tour to Britain and Ireland in 1994 she had at least known the players she was going with. Playing for New Zealand was a whole new ball game, especially as there had been so much controversy surrounding her selection.

'I had only met Bernie and Linda when I went to Auckland for the team announcement press conference. I didn't know how the rest of the team would react to me, or whether they would accept me. Everyone has had that feeling. Going to a new school or new job; joining a different sports club; even moving house and having to make new friends. You get that butterfly feeling in your stomach because you're not sure what will happen.

'I think I had a hundred butterflies in my stomach when I said goodbye to Christie, Mum and Bianca and set off for Auckland. During the flight I thought about a lot of things. What would the girls be like? Would they be nice to me? Would some of them resent me? I was getting myself really worked up. It was worse than preparing for a world championship final!

'I wound myself up something shocking but I needn't have worried at all. Everyone was great from the moment I walked into the motel.

'If I am honest, meeting Donna was probably what I was dreading. People had been making out she was a big, bad ogre. I know when I had been on the opposite side to her on the court she had always seemed so mean. There was also the fact that she and Belinda were big buddies through both being in the New Zealand basketball team. Now Belinda had been dropped and I was in the team.

'How wrong people can be about another person. Donna was really nice, and one of the first people to come up and ask me how I was feeling. Neither of us mentioned what had happened over the question of my availability and I was relieved about that. I had been picked for New Zealand and just wanted to get on with doing that. I am sure Donna felt the same way. It was in the past.'

If Irene needed confirmation that she was once again the new girl on the block it came during her first few hours with the New Zealand team.

The Silver Ferns have always been a close-knit group. The personnel does change, but not often. When it does it is usually only one or two players at a time. Those coming in have been playing alongside or against their new team-mates at club or inter-provincial level and know them well. Anna Veronese and Temepara George were first-time Silver Ferns but they'd known the rest of the team for years.

It was different for Irene. She had just finished her first Coca-Cola Cup season and the only players she knew well were her Capital Shakers team-mates. Unfortunately she was the only Shakers player in the New Zealand team.

'I sat there listening to all the players catch up on all the gossip. They were all talking about each other's partners, but I didn't know the people they were talking about. I was an outsider. No one was trying to make me feel that way because what they were doing was perfectly natural.

'Anyone who has gone to a new school or started a new job knows the feeling. Everyone is friendly to you and makes you feel welcome but they still have to go about their lives as they did before you arrived. It is their environment you're going into and it is up to you to fit in with them. A few months down the track when someone new is coming into the circle you're one of the old hands, but you don't really think back to what it was like when you arrived because you're now comfortable in your surroundings.

'For me the Silver Ferns really was unknown territory, and while I did feel like an outsider during those first couple of hours when each was catching up with what the others had been doing, they were not insensitive to what I was feeling. They pulled me in the whole time which made it easier for me to adjust. It is up to the person going into a new environment to make as much effort as those trying to help you fit in. You can't sit in a corner and expect them to do everything for you.'

Irene's introduction was helped through her being paired with Linda Vagana on the rooming list.

'Linda is such a caring person. When someone is down there is no better person than Linda to lift their spirit. She has the ability to make you feel better no matter how bad you're feeling.'

Linda Vagana remembers that day in the motel. As usual the players arrived one by one depending on where they were coming from.

'When I walked into the room Irene was just lying on the bed watching television. She looked OK but I had a feeling that she wouldn't be feeling that comfortable because not only was it her first time with the Silver Ferns but there had been the controversy over whether she should be selected so soon after moving to New Zealand from South Africa.

'I remembered my first time in the New Zealand team. It is not that easy to be yourself when you go into that environment. I wanted to help Irene feel comfortable and encouraged her to be herself. Like most people when they first go into a different environment she tried to please everyone.

'Irene is such an honest person who laughs at anything and everything . . . very loudly at times! You can't dislike her. Probably because there had been controversy over her selection it took her time to understand the dynamics of the personalities involved. She probably had preconceived ideas about some of the players she was getting to know for the first time, but what you hear from other people can sometimes be very misleading.

'I knew Irene pretty well from when we played against South Africa because she was down my end of the court. Irene can be a difficult person to play against, just because of her personality. You're trying to be serious while marking her and she's clapping when *we* score! You make an intercept to stop the ball reaching her and as you send it up court Irene turns to you and says, "That was a great intercept." As I said, you can't dislike her. She's a great person and a top sportswoman.'

Irene agrees with Linda Vagana that it took her time to work out the personalities of those she was teaming up with.

'I am a person who takes people as I find them. I don't know why, but I was a little wary of Anna Rowberry in the beginning. We got on OK but I was really pleased to be sharing a room with Linda because she made it so easy for me.

'I was also fortunate that when we got to Australia I roomed with Julie Seymour because she taught me some of the tricks of the trade you need when touring with a close-knit group like the Silver Ferns. One morning Julie asked if I would make her a cup of tea. I was happy to oblige and Julie said it was a lovely cup of tea. The only problem was, according to Julie, I shouldn't have made it so nice. The next day she asked Anna Veronese to make her a cup and Anna put salt in it rather than sugar. It was horrible. "See," said Julie, "I'll never ask Anna to make me another cup of tea."

'Getting to know the culture of any team is important. It becomes more so when it's a national team such as the Silver Ferns because you only get together every so often.

'On my first morning in camp we had a team-building session with [sports psychologist] Gilbert Enoka. One of the questions to be answered was what each individual wanted to get out of being there [in camp]. I think Anna, Temepara and myself, all the new ones, all said we wanted to be accepted and to be part of the team. It didn't take long for that to happen. By the second day I was starting to feel more comfortable. It helped that everyone was being positive so I started to relax. We went to a swimming session, which was enjoyable, then it was time for training and what a shock I got!

'When I first joined the Shakers I was surprised how fast and skilful the players were. That was nothing to what I was about to experience with the Ferns. It was a hell of a wake-up call for me. I remember one of our first drills so well. Julie Seymour was at centre, Anna Rowberry at wing attack, Adine Harper at goal attack and I was the shooter. The ball came flying at me harder and faster than anything I had ever experienced, and Julie hit the edge of the circle at the same time. I just stood there. Stunned. Julie whispered, "Irene, do something," so I took off. It was amazing.

'Even though I had often played against them I didn't realise how quick these girls are. How skilful they are. How much flair they have. Once again I stood admiring them just as I did when I was playing for South Africa. The only problem was, this time I was supposed to be doing the same things they were.

'It is very hard to explain how good the Silver Ferns are. They are simply breathtaking at times.'

Breathtaking to Irene they may have been, but the world champion Australian team didn't feel that way, as Irene and her new team-mates were about to find out.

Chapter 11

New Zealand Debut

AFTER FOUR DAYS IN CAMP WITH THE New Zealand team Irene was feeling much more comfortable about being a Silver Fern. The initial awkwardness she had felt in unfamiliar surroundings had almost worn off, thanks to the management and players making her feel at home.

Whether the New Zealand public, and netball followers in particular, had accepted her as one of their own as quickly as the players had was a question Irene still pondered over at night. Most of the time she was sure everything was going to be fine, but occasionally she would lie in bed contemplating some of the hurtful things that had been said when she made herself available for the Ferns.

In her worst moments Irene would find reassurance by thinking back to a radio talkback show she had appeared on. It hadn't been something she had really wanted to do, but if it helped people understand where she was coming from in wanting to play for her adopted country then she would go ahead with it. It didn't take long for Irene to relax, buoyed by the calls of support she was getting, and she felt much more optimistic after hearing several callers tell her to get on with the job and make the doubters eat their words.

Callers to sporting talkback shows are a rare breed. They are 'experts' in every sport and invariably critical. It is easy to bag someone to a third party, in this case the programme's host, but it is different when the person you're talking about is on the other end of the telephone line. Perhaps that's why 99 per cent of the calls Irene took that day were in favour of her changing colours from green to black. If that was indeed the case Irene couldn't have cared less. The support those callers offered made her feel better, and in darker moments their words were something to hang on to.

Her last lingering doubts were swept away when Irene walked into Auckland International Airport with the New Zealand team en route to a one-off test match against Australia in Newcastle. In contrast to when she had been in New Zealand with the South African team, Irene was no longer merely a curiosity who stood out from the crowd because of her height. She was now a Kiwi, and it seemed, much to her relief, that people were happy to see her in the Silver Fern uniform.

One after the other, people, mostly women, plucked up the courage to approach Irene and talk to her. What they said had nothing to do with whether she should be allowed to play for the Silver Ferns. All they were interested in was whether she was enjoying herself in New Zealand, and whether she and her team-mates were ready to kick some Aussie butt.

Answering in the affirmative to both, Irene kept to herself the fact that she almost didn't make the trip because of a bureaucratic oversight, with no one realising that, because she was still travelling on a South African passport, she required a visa to enter Australia. The fact that she needed a visa was only picked up 24 hours before the team was due to fly out of Auckland. Urgent steps were called for, and that was when Silver Ferns manager Sheryl Wells, known affectionately to the players as Ducky, showed her worth.

With any sports team, and doubly so with a high-profile national side, the coach and the players are the focus of most attention. A good manager, and Wells is definitely in that category, goes about the job almost anonymously, ensuring the coach and players can concentrate on training and playing with no distractions.

Wells had to move quickly if Irene was to travel, and the first port of call was Minister of Sport Trevor Mallard. At the time sport was just one of Mallard's portfolios in the Labour government, and undoubtedly one he loved. A member of the Parliamentary rugby team, Mallard didn't turn up at sports events through a sense of duty. It was pleasure rather than work, and netball appeared to be one of his favourite sports.

While Irene is unaware of the finer points of how she got the visa in time, Mallard undoubtedly pointed Wells in the right direction. It helps to have friends in the right places and, as the year wore on, Irene could claim the minister in that category after they'd met at several functions.

The visa wasn't the only thing Wells helped Irene with. One of her main missions on the trip appeared to be making sure that everything was well with the new recruit, and it seemed she was checking on Irene's welfare every few minutes. Small things that team regulars take for granted were new to Irene, and she couldn't believe what she was hearing when Wells said she should pack her team uniform, socks, knickers and court shoes in her hand luggage.

Those were the last things she would have considered carrying on the plane with her, but Wells patiently explained that unless she did that, should her checked luggage go missing she would have nothing to play in. Such things were never considered by the South African netball management.

Aware that controversy over her selection had drawn much comment on the other side of the Tasman, Irene spent much of the two and a half hour journey wondering what kind of reception awaited her in Sydney. Sure enough, the Australian journalists were keen to talk to Irene, but they had no joy. Yvonne Willering quickly let it be known that the only people in the party who would be doing any talking to the media would be herself and captain Bernice Mene. There would be no problems should a journalist want to talk to Irene after the game, she said, but in the lead-up she was off limits. Irene appreciated that line being taken. She was having enough trouble finding her feet on court without having to worry about interviews off it.

Back in New Zealand, and among the New Zealand journalists covering the game in Newcastle, most people expected Irene to be in the starting line-up. She had, after all, been the leading shooter at the last two world championships. Irene didn't share their certainty. In fact she would have been very surprised had Willering read out her name when the team was announced on the morning of the match following their final training session.

'I knew I wouldn't be in because it had become obvious during training that I wasn't ready to claim a place in the starting seven. The team wouldn't have benefited from having me in it.

'During training Donna Loffhagen and Adine Harper really connected. They were brilliant. They were combining so well that I would clap and shout "brilliant" when they did something special. It might have seemed brilliant to me but Yvonne told me to keep quiet.

'Rather than expecting to be in the team I was sitting there watching these awesome players and thinking how lucky I was to be a part of it. No way could Yvonne have preferred me to either Donna or Adine for the starting line-up that night. She knew I wasn't ready to cut the mustard just yet.

'I didn't mind sitting on the sideline. I knew I would be in the starting line-up one day, but at that moment it was good enough for me to be on the bench watching what was going on. Sitting on the bench can be frustrating, but it also hardens your resolve to get out on court and gives you something to work for.'

Irene may not have been in the starting line-up, but she was very much part of the team. Depending on how the game panned out, she was likely to get on court at some point.

It was while Yvonne Willering and the players were analysing how

Australia play that Irene experienced a familiar sinking feeling that she had felt while playing for South Africa. As Australia were dissected player by player, position by position, it became apparent that the emphasis was being put on how good the world champions were. There was hardly any mention of the Aussies' weaknesses. That was how the Proteas had prepared for games against New Zealand and Australia. They were almost in awe of the Silver Ferns and the Australians. They virtually accepted that they were going to lose. Even in that fateful 1995 world tournament game the South Africans had seen themselves as underdogs.

Listening to everyone around her talking about Australia's strengths, Irene wanted to scream. She wanted to jump to her feet and tell her new team-mates how good they were. The Proteas had always felt New Zealand was better than Australia, but obviously there was a lack of self-belief in the Kiwi camp. Being a newcomer to the team, Irene couldn't bring herself to tell the Ferns that they were doing themselves an injustice, that the Aussies should be the ones worrying about them, not the other way round. It was a shock to find the Silver Ferns seemingly had an inferiority complex when it came to playing Australia.

By game time Irene knew in her heart that the Silver Ferns were in the wrong frame of mind to take on the world champions. Australia had undergone changes since winning the world championship the previous year, and many thought they were ripe for the taking. Irene might have agreed had she thought the Ferns were emotionally up to the challenge.

On the night the Ferns either froze, or were simply outclassed. Whatever the reason, they suffered their biggest loss at the hands of the old enemy, going down 53–30 in front of a screaming packed house at the Newcastle Entertainment Centre. It wasn't just the New Zealanders in the crowd and on the press benches who had believed the Silver Ferns were capable of winning. The Australian media felt the same way. The only ones who didn't share that belief had been out on court wearing black uniforms.

Watching from the substitutes' bench, Irene was stunned. She couldn't believe what was happening as Australia sliced through the Ferns time and again, taking a lead that was never going to be pegged back.

She had expected to spend the whole game on the bench so she had to pinch herself when, during the second quarter, Willering tapped her on the shoulder and said, 'It's your turn. Off you go. Warm up.'

'There were so many emotions when that moment came. Part of me really wanted to get on court, but another was saying that I wasn't ready for it. A third said get out there and kick some butt.

'The start of the evening had been very emotional, especially when the New Zealand national anthem was played. I was desperate to get it right. I had watched other sports where the television cameras focus on a player during the national anthem and it is obvious they either do not know the words or are not prepared to sing them.

'I was proud to be chosen for New Zealand and determined to show those watching back in what was now my home that I could sing the anthem. I had practised so hard. Julie [Seymour] would say a word and I would have to recite the next four. I would get the Maori version a bit mixed up, but I was getting there and on the night I think I did OK.

'Once I got on court at the start of the third quarter my nerves soon went. There was no way we were going to come back from the deficit we had but I was determined to give it my best shot. That was all I could do really . . . give it my best.'

When the final whistle went the Australians, as had become the norm, were the ones celebrating. The New Zealand camp was funereal as the players gathered their things in stunned silence.

The black walking out uniforms seemed appropriate at that moment, and Irene couldn't help noticing that at the after-match function Trevor Mallard, who just happened to be in Sydney on government business, was dressed all in black, as was former New Zealand Rugby Union chief executive David Moffett who had recently switched to league and was based in Sydney.

It was a game everyone connected with New Zealand netball wanted to quickly forget. No one in the team had had a good game. No one, not even the normally inspirational Bernice Mene, could come up with the magic intercept that would have sparked the team into action. The loss probably didn't hit Irene as hard as it did most of her team-mates because it was balanced by the excitement of playing for New Zealand for the first time. Even though New Zealand lost it had been a wonderful experience to walk out on court wearing the silver fern.

On their return home the Silver Ferns were scheduled to play two games against Team Pasifika — made up of players from Samoa, the Cook Islands and Fiji — followed by a three-test series with a World Seven. On reflection Irene believes the Ferns should have played those series before facing the world champions. It is a theory Yvonne Willering espoused at the time, only to be seen by some as simply making excuses for her team's failure.

The New Zealanders were together for five days before the Australian game, but that's not the whole story. Had Willering been able to use the whole time for training and court work it would have been a little better, but the players have many commitments while in camp.

Without sponsors such as Vodafone and Fisher and Paykel there wouldn't be an international netball programme. Compared to the New Zealand Rugby Union, Netball New Zealand are paupers, but the players from both codes have to satisfy the corporate backers. The first day in camp for Irene and her team-mates involved being photographed, posing for posters, signing autographs and other sundry duties. It isn't too much of a chore because, as Irene points out, netballers can be quite at home in front of a camera. It is actually fun, but most of the time there is a fine line between organisation and chaos as players switch between playing uniforms, tracksuits and official walking out gear. Whether such things provide an ideal build-up to playing the world champions is questionable, but they have to be done.

On the flight back to Auckland Irene preferred to look ahead rather than back. She had played her first game for New Zealand; now it was time to build on that. Coming up were the two home series against Team Pasifika and a World Seven.

Australian coach Jill McIntosh had been asked to select and coach the World team. It was going to be interesting.

Chapter 12

Coaches

ONE OF THE PROBLEMS FACED BY NETBALL New Zealand and its Australian counterpart over the years has been the lack of competition available throughout the rest of the world. Only Jamaica, Trinidad and Tobago, England and South Africa have, at different times, offered the sport's big two any real challenge. Putting that scenario into perspective is the fact that South Africa's win over the Silver Ferns at the 1995 world tournament in Birmingham was considered the biggest upset in world netball.

Despite the lack of credible opposition, apart, of course, from Australia, netball has enjoyed substantial funding and media coverage in New Zealand through being regarded as one of the country's 'big four' sports along with rugby union, rugby league and cricket. The 'big four' have been paid substantial amounts of money by television companies eager to screen their games. Other sports, even high profile ones such as soccer, golf, hockey and basketball, have had to pay to get their games on television, and even then could often only get delayed coverage rather than live transmissions.

Looking to the future and to stimulate interest in the game, Netball New Zealand and Netball Australia have always been keen to help develop the sport in other countries. One way to do this was to loan coaches to developing netball nations to enable them to bring on their own coaches and, in turn, produce better players. That was how coach Yvonne Willering found herself in South Africa in 1994 watching Irene van Dyk who, six years later, she would select for New Zealand.

Willering's first visit to the republic was with the New Zealand under-21 team as an assistant coach, but her responsibilities on that trip were to help develop South African netball rather than work with the young New Zealanders. Back home New Zealanders had no problem with Willering helping another country develop its players, and it was the same story when she later went back to South Africa and toured that country giving advice to coaches. New Zealanders still had no qualms when Willering was asked to help South African coach Marlene Wagner prepare her team for the 1995 world championships.

'What you have to appreciate is that the South Africans were going into that tournament cold after being on the outer for so long,' Willering says. 'Because they were so enthusiastic they were always going to improve quickly. There was plenty of raw talent there but they needed to be more disciplined and a structure had to be put in place.

'They wanted me on board because I had been to several world championships and they felt the experience I had gained at the tournaments would be valuable to them. I enjoyed watching them improve with every coaching session.'

Everything was fine until South Africa beat New Zealand. Suddenly Willering's loyalty to New Zealand was being questioned. How dare she help another country beat the Silver Ferns? Callers to talkback radio stations and writers of letters to newspapers seemed to be blaming Willering rather than the New Zealand players.

Willering didn't enjoy seeing New Zealand beaten. A former Silver Fern, she knew how those wearing the black uniforms were feeling when the final whistle went and they were two goals in arrears. Making it worse was the fact that Willering was helping commentate the game for South African television. While she had to remain neutral and explain to viewers what was happening, her pounding heart was with the Silver Ferns. When it was all over and she could reflect on what had happened, Willering heard about reaction back in New Zealand.

'I found it very interesting,' she says. 'They want to help develop other countries, but seemingly only to a certain point where there is no threat to New Zealand. When it hurts us it's suddenly a different matter.

'I wasn't responsible for South Africa winning that game. They'd nothing to lose and went for it. New Zealand played badly on the day.'

In describing public reaction as 'interesting' Willering is understating how she felt, because it undoubtedly hurt her more than she admitted. Willering tends to come across as intense and serious, especially when the television cameras focus on her during international games. Away from netball, Yvonne Willering is very different to the image perceived by outsiders who only see her in a coaching role. Those who know her well talk of a fun-loving woman with repartee a comedian would be proud of. Even some journalists, who wondered what they were in for when this stern-looking woman took over the Silver Ferns, will attest to Willering differing from her public persona.

The Silver Ferns job was one Willering had coveted throughout the coaching career she moved into after playing her last game for the Silver

Ferns in 1983, but one she seemed destined never to achieve after being knocked back several times. That made her wary, particularly of the media. Once a journalist gains Willering's trust she's more forthcoming, but heaven help any reporter who misquotes her.

Unlike some coaches, she doesn't expect reporters to always portray the squeaky clean image administrators would prefer. A column that's critical of Willering is accepted as part of the job, providing it's the journalist's honest belief.

Friends will also tell you that Willering is a sensitive person, a softy at heart even. That should be no surprise when you consider that the menagerie that inhabits her Auckland home includes four rabbits, two dogs, four cats, guinea pigs, a donkey and two dogs, many adopted after being abandoned.

That's why Willering would have been more upset than she let on by what was said about her helping South Africa. She would also have been disappointed at anyone questioning her loyalty to New Zealand. Although Willering was born in the Netherlands and moved to New Zealand as an eight-year-old in 1958 with her parents Johanna and Peter and older brother Robert, there is no prouder Kiwi than her.

During her time with the South African team in the lead-up to the world tournament, Willering had been keeping an interested eye on the tall goalshoot who was to have such an impact when the Proteas returned to the international fold.

Willering's philosophy is that international coaches have a responsibility not to force change on other countries. It is important, she believes, that those who are trying to help should work on the particular country's strengths. In South Africa's case a major strength was the long ball into the circle for Irene van Dyk. Playing a lot of aerial ball was a successful tactic for them in 1995, but since then they have moved away from that style and attempted to copy the way Australia and New Zealand play. It hasn't worked.

While Willering didn't work individually with van Dyk, she had seen enough of her to know that when South Africa arrived in New Zealand early in 1999 for a three-test series against the Silver Ferns, a team Willering now coached, stopping van Dyk was the key to success.

'As she became known in world netball the expectations on Irene grew. If she missed a goal people were surprised. Irene was expected to always have shooting statistics in the nineties.

'Of course we focused on Irene when we played South Africa because they were so reliant on her. We would double team her or look for the pass going to her because we knew it was going to happen.

'Making it harder for Irene was the fact that they often didn't feed her good ball. When I look back on those games she took some amazing ball considering the standard of pass she was given.'

At that time Willering's focus was the 1999 world tournament in Christchurch. All New Zealand was hoping that on home soil the Silver Ferns would gain revenge for what had happened four years earlier when losses on successive days to South Africa and Australia put them out of final contention early in the piece. South Africa presented no problem but Australia smashed the Ferns' title dreams in dramatic fashion.

Soon after the Christchurch event, which was an outstanding success despite the end result, Willering heard that van Dyk planned to play for the Capital Shakers in the 2000 Coca-Cola Cup. The news meant little to her at the time and, from a New Zealand coach's perspective, there was definitely no immediate thought about the possibility of her becoming a Silver Fern. Willering felt that van Dyk playing in New Zealand had nothing to do with her. In all probability the imposing South African would play for the duration of the competition and then return home. That's what had happened with the Shakers' English imports, Amanda Newton and Olivia Murphy, the previous year.

Everything changed, however, when Willering heard that van Dyk intended not only to stay on after the Coca-Cola Cup, but was applying for New Zealand residency.

'Once I realised she was intending to stay, at least for a year, then I kept in touch with her franchise. I didn't talk to her personally about it at that stage because I don't do that with any player. To me Irene was then just another potential Silver Fern. When it got nearer to the time that a New Zealand team was going to be selected, and she was in our reckoning, I did ring to talk about her plans.

'I needed to hear from her that she was going to become a New Zealand resident, that she was available for the Silver Ferns and that she was going to commit herself for the whole year. Under international rules she was eligible for New Zealand anyway, but I wanted to see her make a commitment.'

Willering rejects the argument that van Dyk should not have been selected for the New Zealand team because she was keeping out a home-grown player.

'Irene got in on her own worth. The selectors picked what they believed to be the best players and most balanced team. It wasn't as if she had just made herself available either. She had indicated publicly several weeks earlier that she was available, but people had only taken notice after she repeated it on television.

'Those watching her play in the Coca-Cola Cup who realised she was available for New Zealand wouldn't have been surprised that she was picked.'

Willering says she felt no pressure either in the lead-up to the team announcement, or in the aftermath.

'I had no problems with any of it. It was within the rules and I am fair with my selections so it didn't bother me at all. Once she was selected I was prepared to ride everything with her.

'It wasn't as if we were bringing in overseas players just to beat Australia. I don't buy that, and if you look at what happened it took Irene a little time to settle in. New Zealand netball is multicultural anyway. There have always been Samoans and Cook Islanders involved and now there is also a Fijian. At all times those chosen have made a commitment to New Zealand.

'I also believe that there was a time factor in the controversy over Irene. We were playing internationals so early in the year after the world championships had been held late the previous year. Had the internationals come up late in the year I am sure there would have been no problems. You also have to understand that she was a key player and had a very high profile internationally. Had it been one of the English girls who had been with the Shakers previously there wouldn't have been anywhere near the same interest.'

Willering smiles when she thinks back to van Dyk's early Ferns training sessions and how the international star struggled to come to terms with the talents of those around her.

'The speed of the ball just got her. I looked at what was happening and could see that either we would have to change our complete game plan, and work round her, or that we should just take some time with her. It was better that we take the time. People asked why I didn't start off with Irene against Australia in Newcastle. Well that was one of the reasons. You cannot change six players to accommodate one. We do have a set style of play, though we can change so that we play to each player's strengths. It was just a matter of bringing her into our style gradually.

'I'm sure it was a great learning curve for her, and I enjoyed the challenge. She's a delightful player to work with and if you look at it now our feeders have learnt how best to feed her so that we can utilise her strengths. There is no point putting low ball into a shooter of that height.'

So how did the other Silver Ferns feel about having to make changes?

'Some handled it better than others, but at international level you have to be adaptable.'

Clockwise from top left: Irene and her mother at Irene's grandparents' home.
Her father was impressed when Irene whistled for the first time in front of the family.
Irene at 12 during her last year at primary school.
In 1997 Irene received this trophy for best netballer in the Vaal Triangle. Her sister, Janita, received the same award ten years earlier.
Irene welcomes brother Herman home after his first day at school.

Playing for South Africa in Auckland in 1995, Irene played against Bernice Mene for the first time.

Irene is all concentration while playing for South Africa against New Zealand in 1995.

The happiest day of Irene's life, leaving the church with Christie.

Photosport

Beating Linda Vagana, who was to be the first person she roomed with on joining the Silver Ferns, during a 1999 Fisher and Paykel test in Wellington.

Christie and Irene with 12-hour-old Bianca in Vaal Park Hospital, Sasolburg. Both parents were on intravenous drips, Christie after a serious viral infection.

Bianca, aged three months, at her christening.

Irene and Christie arrive at Wellington Airport for a holiday in December 1999. It was Christie's first visit to New Zealand.

Fergusson Intermediate pupils welcomed their new teacher with a powhiri on 26 January 2000.

DOMINION/ANTHONY PHELPS

In action for the Capital Shakers against the Canterbury Flames. At right is team-mate Helen Lonsdale, while left is Canterbury's Anna Veronese with Belinda Charteris behind.

Hanna Howard

Irene takes the ball under pressure while playing for the Shakers against Western Flyers.

Picking a winner — Irene with Michael Walker, New Zealand's top apprentice jockey and Wellington Cup winner Smiling Like.

Bernice Mene helps Irene to relax at her first press conference after being named in the Silver Ferns.

Donna Loffhagen getting a point across to Irene, during a break in play.

FOTOPRESS/PHIL WALTER

Irene lines up a shot while being challenged by World Seven goalkeep Leana du Plooy, also from South Africa.

'Don't pass one handed,' is the message from coach Yvonne Willering during a Silver Ferns training session.

FOTOPRESS/DAVID HALLETT

Showing her athleticism, Irene makes sure she stays in court, while playing for the Capital Shakers.

FOTOPRESS/MICHAEL BRADLEY

Rough and tumble: Irene hits the deck after a clash with Australia's Liz Ellis.

England defender Naomi Siddall tries to block Irene's shot.

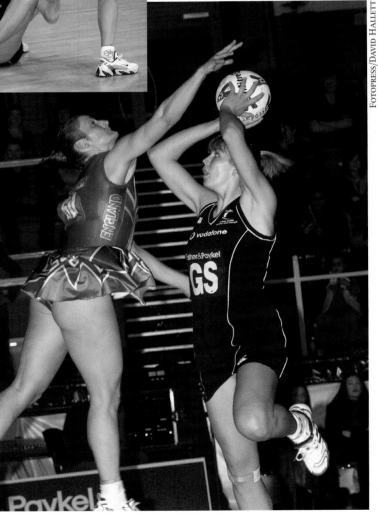

FOTOPRESS/DAVID HALLETT

FOTOPRESS/DAVID HALLETT

Irene pulls in the ball during a 2001 test match against England in Palmerston North, watched by 16-year-old England goalkeep, Geva Mentor, who was making her international debut.

With Bernice Mene at Silver Ferns' training.

Unfortunately, Willering didn't have time on her side with only five days in camp before playing Australia. Consequently, the coach had no intention of throwing van Dyk in the deep end and watching her struggle. Irene was improving day by day, however, and Willering says she always intended putting her on at some point. With the way the game went, it became a matter of when, rather than if, van Dyk would take the court.

Reflecting on that day, Willering says it was a shame they had to play Australia first up, and that it should have been van Dyk's debut game. Playing at international level at any time is tough, but to go from a practice situation into a game with a new team and be up against the pairing of Liz Ellis and Kathryn Harby was asking more than usual.

It wasn't only Irene who found the situation difficult. Those feeding her were also having to adjust. Had it not been Irene, but any other new shooter, Willering said it would still have taken time for the feeders to adjust, and time is something you do not have on court when you're playing the world champions.

Since that day Willering has watched van Dyk grow in stature as a player. While the team has had to make some changes in the way it plays to accommodate her, Irene has added much to her netballing repertoire as she has adapted to suit her adopted country's style. It's not just the way she has improved on the court that has impressed Willering and confirmed to her that she did the right thing in selecting van Dyk and backing her through the controversy.

Willering was disappointed at the way van Dyk's selection was greeted in some quarters, feeling that it could have taken off some of the gloss for a player who was so excited about joining the team.

'She was so proud to be in the team. When I told her she had been selected her reaction was just wonderful, and it was terrific to have such bubbly enthusiasm as part of the team. It was a pity there was so much negativity. I take great pride in the Silver Ferns and believe everyone should get a huge thrill when they are selected for the team, whether it's the first time or the fiftieth.

'It is no one's right to assume they are in the team. If players expect to be in the team then they should look at themselves. I did wonder if some people were getting like that at that time.'

As soon as Irene joined the Silver Ferns it was apparent to the coach that she wasn't selfish, that she cared about all the players around her. Willering can understand how Irene felt when she became one of the Ferns and found that they didn't have enough belief in themselves, that they didn't appear to know how good they were.

Come the end-of-year tour to South Africa, where the Australians were well beaten, the attitude within the New Zealand team had changed. Everyone believed in themselves, in each other and, just as importantly, in the coach. Willering says acceptance of her as coach, just as much as the acceptance of any new player, was important in the development that occurred during 2000. To Willering, Irene was a pleasure to coach. From the start she was impressed by her attitude and her sheer enthusiasm for everything that was happening around her.

'I enjoyed coaching her because she's prepared to try anything. You also get feedback from her. There was one game where at quarter time she was one of the few players I didn't speak to. After the game she came up and asked why I hadn't spoken to her. It was because she was playing well, but she still needed, or wanted, some communication from me. At least she came and talked to me about it. Whether she's playing well or not she always wants to do better.'

While valuing Irene for the tremendous team person that she is, Willering wouldn't like a whole team full of players with her character. She jokes that if that was the case the whole team would be clapping each time the opposition scored a goal. When she first came on the international scene van Dyk would applaud every goal, whether it was scored by her team or the opposition.

'I don't ever want Irene to stop acknowledging play that goes on around her, but it had to be toned down. The focus has to be on us, not the opposition. When she came into the Silver Ferns she was admiring all those around her at training rather than doing her own job. At one point I had to tell her to shut up because she was shouting "brilliant" after a move I wasn't happy with and wanted repeating.

'Like clapping the opposition, Irene had to be toned down at training. She was so loud at times. That's the way she is, but sometimes you want the intensity and that's something she has never really had before she came to New Zealand.

'There was one session where she and Linda Vagana collided and ended up on the floor together. They were still laughing a couple of minutes later. I would have preferred ten seconds then back to business. Having said all that, I wouldn't want to stop her totally because that's Irene. It is important to her that she enjoys herself.

'What I really like about Irene is that what you see is what you get. She's very open and honest. That has helped her settle into life in New Zealand. For a newcomer to New Zealand netball she has had a lot of responsibility on her shoulders. People look up to her, literally and figuratively. She's the kids' favourite and their role model.

'While she was still coming to terms with what was required of her in the Silver Ferns she had lots of extra things to cope with. I think she has done a great job.'

Ask Jill McIntosh, who has coached Australia to two world championship titles, what she thought on first seeing Irene van Dyk and she laughs.

'It was early in 1999 and she was certainly different. We'd never encountered a shooter with such height, mobility and athleticism. It is one thing to come up against a very tall shooter, but it makes it very difficult when the player also has those other qualities.

'South Africa were using her well, and marking her proved to be a big challenge for Liz Ellis, Kathy Harby and Janine Ilitch. We had to rethink our whole defensive strategy, which was a compliment to Irene and her team-mates.

'Just how well using Irene as they did worked for South Africa is borne out by them reaching the final in 1995. Much of the credit for them getting to that final must go to Irene for the way she finished it off every time the ball reached her.

'When South Africa played New Zealand in Birmingham we were due to play the loser the following day and I admit that we'd expected it to be South Africa. When it went South Africa's way, thanks in the main to Irene's coolness under pressure, I had to go home to the hostel and rethink our strategy.'

McIntosh believes that Irene van Dyk arrived on the international scene at just the right time. A player of her ability, who also had a great personality both on and off the court, was the type of injection world netball needed at a time when Australia and New Zealand were clearly dominant.

While there were players with better skills at the 1995 world tournament, none was more popular than the South African shooter and McIntosh found it hard to comprehend that such a big woman could be such a terrific athlete. The Australian coach was also impressed by the way she conducted herself.

'Irene is a vibrant woman. She's a great advert for netball. Off-court she's obliging to the media, and she has a lovely disposition on-court. That's why fans outside South Africa have warmed to her from the start. There would be few sportspeople as popular, if not more so, in other countries than their own. I hope she never changes.'

By 1999, McIntosh says, van Dyk didn't pose the threat she had four years earlier because South Africa had changed their style of play. Rather than stick to what worked for them, South Africa had started trying to play like Australia and New Zealand. They'd put too much speed into their game and, consequently, had less control of the ball. That meant van Dyk wasn't getting the type of ball into the circle that she needed.

At a time when New Zealanders were debating the rights and wrongs of Irene's move to New Zealand and her selection for the Silver Ferns, McIntosh was one person who took it in her stride even though the shooter's change of colours would probably make life harder for Australia when they played New Zealand. McIntosh could have been in the same position as Willering — deciding whether to select van Dyk — had Irene and Christie gone ahead with the proposed move to Queensland.

'Who knows whether Irene would have settled in Australia as well as she has done in New Zealand,' McIntosh says. 'So far as playing for the Ferns is concerned, Irene and her husband made a family decision and moved to New Zealand for personal reasons. You can't hold that against her.

'Once she decided to make New Zealand her home it was only natural Irene should be eligible for the Silver Ferns. Under the rules she was eligible even if she didn't settle, though I'm sure Yvonne wouldn't have chosen her had that been the scenario.

'I do know that it would have been a terrible loss to netball had Irene settled in a country that didn't want her to play for them, even though she wasn't going to play for South Africa.'

McIntosh was surprised that van Dyk wasn't in the starting seven for the game in Newcastle. On reflection, however, she can see why Willering chose not to put her in.

'Her style of play with South Africa had been so different to the way New Zealand play. It did take her almost 12 months to settle in, but I never had any doubts she would.'

While Capital Shakers coach Tanya Dearns (née Cox) may not yet have the international coaching experience of Yvonne Willering or Jill McIntosh, the former Silver Ferns defender has had a unique insight into Irene van Dyk's development. In addition to coaching the former South African shooting star, Dearns has also played against her competitively.

The on-court clash came at Wellington's Queen's Wharf Events Centre during the Proteas' 1996 New Zealand tour. Much of the pre-match hype centred on the duel between Wellington captain Dearns, a no-holds-barred goalkeep, and the woman being hailed as one of the world's best shooters alongside Australia's Vicki Wilson. There was no shortage of people telling Irene what she would be up against, while Cox, who was in the twilight of her playing career, was eagerly anticipating a marking job she knew would be challenging.

Fittingly, the game was played in front of what was at the time a New Zealand record netball crowd of 3351 — 99 more than the previous best, recorded at Palmerston North — and there was plenty for them to shout about. The home fans roared their approval during a frenetic last quarter in which Wellington turned a 6-goal deficit into a 7-goal advantage and a 58–51 win over the international side.

It was all too much for the relatively inexperienced South Africans who panicked and eventually fell apart under the onslaught of noise and the brilliant attacking play of Wellington. Not even Irene's mercurial shooting skills could stem the tide, and while she netted 43 times there were also 9 misses which was one of her least productive returns since arriving on the international scene.

The clash between the two netball giants lived up to expectations. It ended with honours shared and the protagonists extolling each other's ability. Irene had been warned to expect a bruising encounter, but she left the court with a smile on her face despite the result.

'Tanya was great to play against, but I expected someone totally different after what I had been told. We had a real battle, but it was played in the right spirit.'

Dearns was also full of praise for Irene, saying she was strong and clever. 'She uses her body really well. I made sure she knew I was always on her shoulder and thoroughly enjoyed playing against her.'

Five years on, and having coached Irene for two years, Dearns smiles as she recalls Wellington's game against South Africa.

'Irene didn't know who I was and I think some people were trying to scare her with tales of what an ogre I was. I had the advantage of having seen her play, but the first time you come up against her Irene is very difficult to mark.

'She takes the ball at the weirdest angles. You don't think she's going to reach the ball, but suddenly she stretches those long arms and pulls it in.'

While Dearns enjoyed that encounter with Irene she says she wouldn't like to mark her now.

'Irene has improved out of sight since she came to New Zealand to live. In South Africa she had never done much work on the basics such as footwork and body balance. She was reliant on her height and ability to shoot.

'In New Zealand she was up against quicker and bigger defenders than she was used to and they quickly learned how to play her. It is to Irene's credit that she has worked so hard to add new dimensions to her game. She's getting better all the time. In the [2001] series against

Australia she showed things she hadn't done for the Shakers.

'Irene is a perfectionist and becomes annoyed with herself when she can't get things right. From a coaching point of view she's a dream to work with because she gives it everything and wants to give a coach what they are looking for.

'Shooting practice can become totally boring but that doesn't stop her spending an amazing amount of time on what is a major part of her game. I understand the sacrifices she has made because I was a shooter in my early netball days and played for the New Zealand under-21 team in that position. My dad used to make me put up 200 shots each night, even if it meant doing it in the dark with only the porch light showing me the target. If you want to be a consistent shooter that's what you have to do. Irene accepts it as part of her job. There is still much she can work on so that she doesn't revert back to her old habits when the pressure goes on.'

Much has been made about the battering Irene has taken from Aussies Liz Ellis and Kathryn Harby-Williams since she became a Silver Fern. Dearns says Irene can look after herself.

'She's not quite the "butter wouldn't melt in her mouth" player some people make her out to be. Irene can hold her own, as I'm sure the Aussies will testify. The Australians do hit you late and that can be annoying. It is more mental than physical. To get hit late every time you go for the ball wears you down mentally.'

Always a world-class shooter, Irene has improved markedly as a player since moving to New Zealand and Dearns is happy to have played a part in that development.

'I'm just pleased she chose to live in Wellington.'

Chapter 13

Taking on the World

NO NATIONAL SPORTING BODY TRIES TO DO more for its players, sponsors and those who follow the game than Netball New Zealand. Those who run the organisation pride themselves on running professionally what is essentially an amateur sport.

Chief executive Alistair Snell and his successor, Shelley McMeeken, have endeavoured to follow the example of the New Zealand Rugby Union in running their sport as a business but, unlike rugby, they have retained a strong link with the grass roots of the game.

One of the most important things for Netball New Zealand is keeping its sport in the public eye. To that end it ensures there is a home international series every year. Sponsored by Fisher and Paykel, the international games are played throughout the country. Dunedin, Palmerston North and Auckland were the favoured venues during the 1990s but by 2000 Wellington, Christchurch and Hamilton had begun to take over the big games thanks to new indoor stadiums being built. In 2001 Invercargill's Stadium Southland was up and running and New Zealand's southernmost city was added to the roster.

For the 2000 season Netball New Zealand had hoped to have Fiji playing two tests against the Silver Ferns, in Auckland and Palmerston North, followed by a three-test series against Jamaica, a country that, through its flair, had captured hearts at the 1999 world tournament in Christchurch. The unavailability of key players saw Jamaica pull out of the proposed tour and Netball New Zealand moved quickly to fill the gap with a 'rest of the world' team under the World Seven banner. It was an innovative move that could be used more often in the future in different countries, but at the time those who run netball in New Zealand were just keen to keep faith with their sponsors, players and supporters.

The second masterstroke was to invite Jill McIntosh, who had led Australia to the previous two world titles, to coach the team. McIntosh's involvement was two-fold. Not only was she undoubtedly the best person to take players who played different styles of netball with their countries and blend them into a competitive unit, McIntosh's presence would also ensure world champions Australia would be well represented in the World team. That was essential if the series was to be taken seriously by the knowledgeable New Zealand netball fraternity.

Just when everything was in place for the World Seven series, Netball New Zealand suffered another setback with Fiji pulling out of its proposed series because of a coup against the government. Undaunted, a two-test series was swiftly arranged against Team Pasifika, a side made up of Pacific Island players, most of whom were playing their netball in New Zealand.

Donna Loffhagen wasn't available for the New Zealand team to play Team Pasifika and the World Seven, the shooter preferring, not surprisingly, to concentrate on basketball, in which she was to represent New Zealand at the Sydney Olympic Games.

That Team Pasifika would pose little threat to the Silver Ferns was confirmed in the first test in Auckland as New Zealand crushed the Pacific Island players 77–35. One journalist's report on the game said it proved two things: that Adine Harper and Irene van Dyk, who teamed up in attack, should have been the favoured combination against Australia the previous week, and that the Silver Ferns had been seriously underdone when they crossed the Tasman and got a drubbing from the world champions.

The two-test series should, the reporter said, have been played before the trip to Australia. Yvonne Willering must have smiled if she read those words because that's what she had been saying all along. In fact Willering would also have preferred to have the World Seven series under her belt before facing Australia.

Irene will tell you, however, that the reporter was wrong on the first count. She and Harper were definitely not the best combination available against Australia, though things were starting to change.

Harper and van Dyk were together again for the second test against Team Pasifika, in which the Silver Ferns were just as convincing in winning 64–38. Harper, who the following month was to captain the New Zealand under-21 team at the World Youth Championships, stole the show that night, displaying lovely ball skills and outstanding vision. With the opposition defence often double-marking van Dyk, Harper relished the space she was given and stamped herself a star of the future.

Van Dyk, who scored from 39 of her 49 attempts at goal, was still not quite the dominant shooter she had been with South Africa, but it was obvious she was gaining confidence all the time, benefiting from the work she was doing with Willering.

'The Pasifika and World Seven games, along with all the training we did while playing them, provided me with the chance to settle into the team and get to know the players,' Irene says. 'With Donna's withdrawal I was number one for the first time and that meant Yvonne began working more and more with me and those who were feeding the ball into the circle.

'We, myself and those I was now playing with, were used to completely different styles of play. You cannot change overnight everything you have been used to for years. Yvonne had given everything she had at training before we went to Australia but she just didn't have enough time.

'Had we played Pasifika and the World before Australia I know it would have been a lot different. I still might not have been in the starting line-up but everyone would have been more confident with whatever combinations were used.

'Once back in New Zealand and preparing for the Pasifika games I began to settle into the team and started to get to know the players. Getting to know those you're playing with is so important. Sure, I had spent time with the New Zealand players but I didn't really know them. Jill McIntosh always says a team is seven players performing as one. She's right. You need to know those you're playing with and be able to instinctively trust them whatever situation you find yourself in.

'Getting to know the Silver Ferns was a lovely period of my life. It is not simply a matter of being chosen, going into camp and then going on court. There is so much more to it than that. Anyone who has played sport will know what I mean about a team being like a second family. You go to training and catch up on what has been happening to everyone since the last game or training session. You develop relationships that can continue long after you have finished playing sport. There are times when someone can feel easier talking to a team-mate than a family member if something is troubling them.

'When you're training week-in, week-out with the same people it's easy to forge bonds. With a national team, however, you only get together every so often and that's why it can take longer to build up friendships and become comfortable in your surroundings. It is quite intimidating when you first assemble. You know the players but you're not part of their circle. They try to help and encourage you to join in but it takes time for a newcomer to feel comfortable. When we'd finished playing Pasifika and the World team I felt at home with my new family.'

The World Seven, which is a misnomer in that while only 7 players can take the court at one time the squad always consisted of 11 or 12,

were about to forge some bonds of their own. Under the astute steward-
ship of McIntosh, players from several countries would come together,
get to know each other, learn from each other, and attempt to beat world
silver medallists New Zealand on their home soil.

Could McIntosh turn a collection of individuals, albeit talented ones,
into a combination good enough to beat the Silver Ferns? If anyone could
it was McIntosh. When it came to coaching international netball teams
McIntosh was, well, simply the best. The record books — two world
championship titles, the gold medal from netball's inaugural Commonwealth Games, and a 96 per cent success rate in test matches — told that
tale, as did those who had played for her.

Until Netball New Zealand came up with the idea of a 'rest of the
world' team we had to take the word of Australia's top netballers that
McIntosh was the best. Now elite players from other countries had the
chance to sample her methods.

Jamaica's Elaine Davis had always wondered what McIntosh was really like. After four days she gave her verdict.

'I would see her sitting there watching Australia play and her demeanour would never change, whatever the state of the game,' Davis
says. 'Not smiling, not getting angry . . . just sitting there. I wondered
what she was really like under that exterior. Well, now I know. She's
awesome. Her coaching is simple and compact. Nothing extravagant. She's
one good coach.'

Given what had happened over the previous five years, it was hard
to believe that when McIntosh took over as Australian coach from Joyce
Brown late in 1994 she was more apprehensive about the team than the
team was about her. When she took the reins McIntosh had seven months
to prepare Australia for the world championships. It was going to be a
huge learning curve for her and she was understandably feeling a little
unsure about dealing with players who were well established on the international scene. It was a long way from her first netball steps, taken as
an eight-year-old in a Perth primary school where she missed out on the
top side and had to make do with a place in the B team.

Her journey to the top as a netball player was via the West Australian
State team, and at the conclusion of the 1974 national championships
McIntosh was chosen for Australia. The only problem was that there
were no games for the Australian team that year, and it wasn't until 1980
that she was again picked, making her debut in 1981 in a triangular
series with England and New Zealand.

Coaching was always on McIntosh's mind and when she left the international scene as a player in 1986 she became player-coach of Western

Australia for five years before being given charge of the Australian under-21 team in 1990. That meant a three-month stint at the Australian Institute of Sport — three months that had been extended to almost ten years when she was asked to coach the World team.

Asked the night before her World Seven played New Zealand at Wellington's Queen's Wharf Events Centre how the team would go, McIntosh held up crossed fingers. 'We will be competitive . . . I hope.'

McIntosh was actually in a win-win situation. Because of the circumstances her coaching reputation wouldn't suffer if the World team was beaten. If they could win, her stock would soar higher still.

There was an added incentive for McIntosh. She wanted to see the World concept adopted as part of the international calendar, with a 'rest of the world' team regularly playing test series against other top countries, including Australia. She was hopeful the public would embrace the format if it was competitive. If the games were one-sided they wouldn't.

On 1 July 2000 a World team played together for the first time, and what a star-studded line-up it was. Australia's Kathryn Harby was captaining the team and she was joined by compatriots Liz Ellis, Sharelle McMahon and Shelley O'Donnell. Elaine Davis and Nadine Bryan came from Jamaica. South Africa provided Rosina Magola and Leana Du Plooy, while towering goalshoot Alex Astle, Helen Lonsdale and Olivia Murphy came from England.

The teams had widely differing build-ups to a game that was played in front of a sell-out 3400 spectators. While the Silver Ferns, who had trained and played three games together over the previous ten days, were enjoying their pre-match meal, World goal attack Sharelle McMahon was still on a flight across the Tasman. Within three hours of arriving at the team's hotel McMahon was on court partnering Elaine Davis, who she had never played or trained with. That didn't stop the attacking duo slicing through the New Zealand defence time and again in a first half, during which the World Seven eased out to a 30–22 lead.

They were helped by the Silver Ferns carelessly throwing away possession, especially in the midcourt. Wing attack Temepara George threw three successive passes to the opposition and her second-quarter replacement, Anna Rowberry, was just as guilty.

With a foundation laid by that solid first-half effort the World Seven held out against a strong late rally from the home team to win 51–47, leaving the Wellington netball public torn between being disappointed at the loss and happy at seeing so many international stars on court at one time. New Zealand put up six more shots than their opponents, but the World's brilliant defensive duo of Harby and Ellis made Adine Harper and Irene van Dyk shoot from difficult positions. In contrast, at the other end of the court Ferns defenders Bernice Mene and Belinda Charteris, who was replaced by Linda Vagana at half-time, were dragged around by McMahon and Davis. An excited Davis shot 100 per cent for the first time in her career by sinking all 35 of her shots, while McMahon scored 16 from 20.

It all added up to more pressure on New Zealand coach Yvonne Willering. While her job appeared safe for the time being there were murmurings that unless improved results were obtained in the next two games that situation could change.

Losing to the World Seven, so soon after being mauled in Australia, meant the Silver Ferns were again being criticised in the media. While some players prefer to ignore what is said about them, claiming not to read newspapers or listen to the radio, Irene was fascinated by what was happening. It was completely new to her because in South Africa the media didn't really care about netball. If the Proteas won or lost it was simply recorded, unlike the in-depth analysis of the Silver Ferns that she was now reading.

'I was interested in everything that was written about the team, whether it was good or bad. Overall, the people who are writing the articles know what they are talking about. There are some who don't, but you soon catch on to that and don't bother reading what they write.

'I found interesting the points of view offered by those who knew netball. So many times they hit the nail on the spot, but there are players who are scared to accept it.

'Of course there are times when you do not play well. When that happens it is the job of those reporting the games to point that out. If you cannot accept a writer's criticism then you should not accept that person's praise because you're saying it means nothing.

'Much of the criticism levelled at us after that first game against the World Seven was fair, but what some people failed to recognise or point out was that our opposition contained the best players in the world outside New Zealand. OK, they'd not played together before, and didn't have a lot of time to practise. On the other hand they had no pressure on them and were doing what came naturally.

'When I was reading what the critics had to say I took those things into account and then decided we deserved some of the stick we were getting. I try to look at criticism from a positive point of view. We all knew there were things that were not right and seeing it written in the papers reinforced it. Let's face it, everyone knew it wasn't working and that we'd better do something about it quickly.'

Because of the short notice at which the series was put in place, players were coming and going from the World Team camp. Liz Ellis had returned to Australia after the first test and been replaced by Vilimaina Davu who had played a leading role with the Canterbury Flames earlier in the year, helping them reach the Coca-Cola Cup final.

In an intriguing turn of events, Davu had made herself available for the Silver Ferns in the wake of the Coca-Cola Cup. Overlooked when Yvonne Willering selected the team, Davu played for Team Pasifika and had now joined the World Seven. In the lead-up to the second test, Davu was coy about her prospects of playing for New Zealand, saying she was concentrating on playing for the World as it was a dream come true for her. Davu also said her netball had improved markedly during her time with Canterbury and she was now learning a lot more from the world-class players she was training with and, of course, Jill McIntosh.

The second test, in Christchurch's WestpacTrust Stadium, began in the same way as the first with New Zealand slow to get going and finding themselves 6–1 down within minutes. So quiet were the 4720-strong crowd it seemed they feared the worst, but by the end of the first quarter the Silver Ferns were back on even terms at 12–12 and there was a more optimistic feel among their fans. By half-time the crowd were feeling even better with New Zealand having eased out to a 31–24 advantage after a second 15 minutes during which they took control in midcourt and defended superbly.

McIntosh tried to upset the Ferns' rhythm during the half-time break by introducing three new players, and it worked wonders in the early stages of the third quarter as her team scored ten goals to the Ferns' two and turned a seven-goal deficit into a one-goal lead.

Van Dyk had got the better of Davu during the first half but the introduction of South Africa's Leana Du Plooy, who is about the same height as Irene, helped the World defence. At three-quarter time the World Seven still held their one-goal lead at 40–39 but there was a more resolute look about the New Zealanders than had been evident in Wellington four days earlier. Willering reintroduced Temepara George and that switch paid dividends as the diminutive wing attack used her flair to find openings in the World defence.

The service to van Dyk improved and her accurate shooting saw New Zealand through in a tense finale to a 52–51 win. Van Dyk was back to the shooting machine that had served South Africa so well, netting 47 goals from 55 shots.

The venue was, of course, the same one where the Silver Ferns had

Changing Colours

suffered a one-goal world championship final loss eight months earlier.
That probably accounted for the fact that there was surprisingly little
elation from the Kiwi players at the final whistle — more relief that they'd
laid to rest their WestpacTrust Stadium nightmare.

Willering admitted the result was a relief. Everyone had been screaming for a result, she said, and the players had felt the pressure. There was
still one test to go, however, and the series was level.

The vital third test which, crazy as it may seem, could decide
Willering's tenure as New Zealand coach was held at Hamilton's superb
Mystery Creek Stadium. There were two defining moments in the hours
leading up to the game. On the one hand was the disjointed preparation
of McIntosh's World Seven. On the other was a television comment Irene
heard just before leaving the team's hotel, a comment she took to heart.

Amid the many comings and goings from the World team, Australian
midcourter Shelley O'Donnell in particular had what could only be described as the preparation from hell. After playing in the Christchurch
game on Wednesday, with the after-match obligations not finishing till
close on midnight, O'Donnell had to fly back to Australia on the Thursday morning. On arrival she caught a flight from Melbourne to Brisbane
with her national league team, played there Friday night, and jetted back
to New Zealand on Saturday morning to rejoin the World Seven for the
final test that night.

Making things worse was the fact that O'Donnell and fellow Aussie
Sharon Finnan were caught up in a traffic snarl-up caused by a horror
accident south of Auckland. The pair only joined their team at a hotel
near the venue 90 minutes before the third test started. That both players performed well drew praise from McIntosh.

'They had a half hour to say hi, then we were off to the game. It was
a really remarkable effort from both players to play as well as they did.'

While all this was happening Irene was watching the television news
with Adine Harper. The question was posed: 'Is Irene the problem, or is
it the feeding?'

'While I don't mind people having their say, I just felt that particular
comment was a bit negative and it made me want to show them what I
could do. Adine said we only had to click and that would shut them up.'

Click they did. Not only that but wing attack Temepara George had a
brilliant game. George's feeding into the circle was outstanding and, getting the best service she had received in six Silver Ferns appearances,
Irene made sure it wasn't wasted.

Sinking shots from all ranges — she even had one goal cancelled out
through an umpire ruling she had shot from outside the circle — Irene

scored 55 goals from 63 attempts in a decisive 60–47 win.

It was no surprise that Irene won the Player of the Game award, but it was far from a one-woman show. The feeding of Temepara George and Julie Seymour made her shooting performance possible, while Linda Vagana and Bernice Mene were towers of strength in defence. Vagana had another outstanding game, and won a $30,000 Hyundai car as Player of the Series.

McIntosh pronounced the concept of the world selection a winner, but called for more notice next time so players could organise time off work. She was sure that if she could have kept the same 12 players together for the whole series the crowd would have seen a more spectacular finale.

Willering was delighted to win the game and the series with a result that would keep at bay those advocating a change of coach.

Irene went back to Christie and Bianca in Wellington a much happier woman than she had been a month earlier on making her debut.

But then everyone connected with the Silver Ferns felt it was a long way from that miserable night in Newcastle.

Chapter 14

Return to the Republic

FROM THE MOMENT YVONNE WILLERING announced the New Zealand team to visit South Africa late in 2000, to play two tests against the Republic and one against world champions Australia, Irene had mixed emotions about what lay ahead. No one was surprised that Irene was among the 12 chosen after her performances during the year, and those close to the national netball scene expected former Fijian international Vilimaina Davu to be included. Those thoughts proved to be spot on.

The team Willering chose reflected the changing face of netball. The Silver Ferns would be going to South Africa with a team that contained players of New Zealand, Samoan, Fijian and South African heritage. There was nothing mercenary about those with ties to other countries, however. Sheryl Clarke had captained Samoa, but at a time when there was swapping and changing of players between New Zealand and Pacific Island nations. Those involved lived and played in New Zealand. Indeed, many were born there, but if a player was surplus to New Zealand's requirements for a world tournament then it made sense for her to revert to her country of origin. Why rob the tournament of an international-class player unnecessarily and in the process deny that player a place on the world stage?

Irene van Dyk had, of course, captained South Africa, and Vilimaina Davu had led Fiji at the 1999 world championships. Like Irene, Vilimaina had immigrated to New Zealand for lifestyle reasons, though her decision, and her subsequent elevation to the Silver Ferns, caused barely a ripple and was far removed from the storm that greeted Irene's availability for New Zealand's national team.

Controversy over Irene's Silver Ferns selection had dissipated in New Zealand, but she was unsure how her donning the black uniform was perceived in South Africa, and how she would be treated on her return. While she was eagerly anticipating seeing her family and friends again, those thoughts were offset by an uncertainty about the reception she might get. Irene was still irked by some of the comments that had emanated from

South Africa in the wake of her going to play for the Capital Shakers in the 2000 Coca-Cola Cup.

'I kept hearing stories that people such as Ntambi Ravele, [president of Netball South Africa] and Louise du Plessis and Benny Saayman [co-coaches of the Proteas] had no idea where I was and what I was doing.

'That was just rubbish. I had telephoned Ntambi in November after we got back from the world championships to say I was going to New Zealand to play and she said it was fine. Christie later rang her to confirm that we'd decided to live in New Zealand and they had a long conversation about it.

'Louise and Benny knew while we were in Christchurch that I intended playing for the Shakers so I couldn't understand what was going on. Looking back what I should have done is put out a press release detailing my plans, but then the South African media hadn't shown a lot of interest in netball in the past.'

Christie was also concerned about her return to South Africa in New Zealand colours. He would have loved to have been there alongside his wife, but that wasn't possible. Instead he set out to prepare her for any abuse she might receive from the crowd during games. During their training sessions together he would hurl insults at Irene. As she was about to shoot a goal he would yell: 'You suck, you're hopeless, you're fat.' Christie was so convincing that Irene admitted at the time she was hurt by what he was shouting at her.

When reports about Irene's concerns reached South Africa the reaction was predictably scornful. There would be no problem, netball officials promised. Those sentiments didn't exactly make Irene feel any easier. It was OK people saying everything would be all right, but they weren't the ones in the firing line.

Making Irene and Christie more apprehensive were memories of an incident that had happened during England's 1997 visit to South Africa in which police had to intervene when Irene was threatened with a knife. South Africa had just beaten England by two goals in Cape Town's Good Hope centre in front of a thousand fans, and Irene was signing autographs courtside when she suddenly found three policemen between her and the fans.

'I told them to chill out, that I was just signing autographs, but then I looked beyond them and saw this woman waving a knife and shouting at me. "Why are you so selfish and shoot all the goals? Why do you not pass to your goal attack and let her score some?"

'The police, who must have been really alert, moved in and took her away. It was as if everything was happening in slow motion. It was unbelievable. Next minute Christie, who had seen it all unfold from up in the stand, was by my side.

'He had seen the woman, a knife and me. He realised what could have happened and it shattered him. That was one of the reasons we were both so worried about me going back. That had happened while I was playing *for* South Africa. What would it be like now I would be playing *against* South Africa?'

Irene wouldn't admit it at the time because there was no way she was about to give up the place she had earned in the Silver Ferns, but she thought perhaps it was a little too early to be going back to the Republic. It was, after all, only 13 months since she had played the last of her 72 tests for South Africa.

In the lead-up to the trip Yvonne Willering was well aware of how Irene was feeling and went out of her way to reassure her that every precaution would be taken to ensure her safety. At no time would Irene be isolated from her team-mates.

On board the aircraft carrying the Silver Ferns to South Africa Irene couldn't relax, continually asking herself if she was doing the right thing. There were no regrets about playing for New Zealand because that was where her future lay. She just wondered if it wouldn't have been better to wait a while longer before returning.

Those thoughts quickly vanished when the plane landed at Johannesburg where the team would have a 90-minute stopover, which included a press conference, before heading on to Cape Town where the first tests in the tri-nations series would be held.

'My mother, sister, brothers and cousins were all there, along with several people from Gauteng netball. I was so happy to see everyone and was crying my eyes out when I looked back and saw that all my team-mates also had tears in their eyes. It was at that moment I realised there was something really special about this team and the bond between us.

'Everyone wanted to know how I was and what had been happening to me. The Gauteng people were so friendly that relief flooded over me. It felt as if a mountain had been taken off my shoulders.

'The only sour note so far as I was concerned was when Ntambi Ravele came over and gave me a big hug. After what had been happening it was really two-faced of her and done just for the media. Sure enough, that was the picture the newspapers used next morning.

'A room had been set aside at the airport for a press conference and I was shocked to find about ten reporters waiting for us. I had never seen so many South African media people interested in netball. It was so different to when we returned to South Africa after finishing second in the world championships and no one was interested.'

This lack of media interest is surprising given that netball is the biggest participant sport in South Africa, outnumbering rugby, cricket and soccer. Unfortunately there is little promotion of the game and those charged with running it do not help themselves, adopting an insular attitude that prevents them seeking advice and help from elsewhere. During the tri-nations, games involving South Africa, who were getting hammered by record scores, were televised live, yet the biggest game of the series between New Zealand and Australia wasn't screened.

'That's a ridiculous attitude. New Zealand–Australia games provide the best netball in the world. Surely that's what netball officials should have been using to whet the public's appetite and get them interested in the sport.

'They need to make netball interesting, more vibrant and appealing to the public. Because they don't do that they are in a catch-22 situation. When sponsors are approached to put money into the game they ask about the coverage they will get. Those who can provide coverage aren't enticed to promote the game.

'Netball in South Africa is not marketed at all. It is in dire need of a competition along the lines of New Zealand's Coca-Cola Cup or Australia's Commonwealth Bank series. All it has at the moment is the national championships where three people turning up at a game is a crowd.

'A Coca-Cola Cup could be scheduled away from New Zealand and Australia's main competitions so there would be a chance to get loan players to lift the standard, but I can't see that ever happening. Those running South African netball live in the past and carry on the way they did thirty years ago.

'They are frozen in time because they don't want to ask for help, which is really sad. That's why South African netball now sucks, and has wasted the opportunities that came through the second placing at the 1995 world tournament.

'Netball New Zealand is run by young people with fresh ideas. [Chief executive] Shelley McMeeken is progressive and open-minded. She wants to make netball sexy and appealing. Those running South African netball don't want to hand over the reins to people such as Debbie Hamman, Rese Hugo and Elize Kotze who have good ideas and training programmes that would take the game forward. Until they let some of the young, bright people have a say they will never get back to where they were in 1995.

'To come out of isolation and finish second in the world was a fantastic achievement but without a change of attitude such heights will never be reached again.'

The Johannesburg press conference provided further relief for Irene, with those asking the questions providing a warm reception with hardly a trace of negativity, and she was in a much better frame of mind when she boarded the flight to Cape Town with a bunch of bubbling team-mates.

'The girls were so excited. I think only Linda Vagana, with the under-21s, had been to South Africa before and they were full of questions. The weather was beautiful. It was typical summer with 30-degree temperatures, sun and no wind. The Ferns loved that. Cape Town is a beautiful city, hilly, with the sea on one side and mountains on the other. Very green, just like New Zealand. I lived in Cape Town for a year and loved it.

'There wasn't much time for sight-seeing but we did manage to get up Table Mountain which was great for the girls who enjoyed the scenery from the cable car that took us up.'

As is normal when sports teams visit South Africa there was a noticeable police presence when the New Zealanders arrived in Cape Town, and the young officers were suitably impressed by the young female athletes they would be protecting. They were oblivious to the presence of an Afrikaans-speaking woman amongst them and Irene smiled to herself as they helped move the team's luggage.

'I listened to them talking about the girls. As they put faces to baggage tags they would be talking about one girl being beautiful, another gorgeous. I thought typical men, so hungry. I couldn't resist wandering over to them and saying, in Afrikaans, that before they embarrassed themselves they should know that I could understand everything they were saying. There were a few red faces amongst them.'

While in Cape Town the Silver Ferns conducted several coaching clinics. One in particular, in the Kayalitza township, brings back pleasant memories for Irene.

'There were kids there who had never seen a ball, never mind played netball, and after watching what some of them could do Yvonne Willering was moved to say that if this was the first time they'd played with a ball South Africa was going to have a hell of a netball team one day.

'The township was a real eye-opener for the New Zealand women who would never have seen people living with no toilets, no electricity or running water. People would have to walk 400 or 500 metres to a water point, fill a bucket and walk back with it on their head.

'They also couldn't get over the fact that there were kids running around everywhere, even though it was a school day. They talked to some of the kids who told them they'd never been to school and had no intention of ever going. There is no law in South Africa that says a child has to go to school.

'All the players had fun at the coaching clinics and that day in Kayalitza the children thanked us for coming by singing in their language. We didn't understand a word but their singing was so beautiful it brought tears to our eyes.'

Irene speaking Afrikaans came in useful on the way back from training one day when one of the policemen's radios burst into life and he was told, in Afrikaans, that there had been trouble with people being shot randomly in their cars in Delft, which was where the Ferns were to conduct a coaching clinic the following day. The policeman didn't realise Irene was South African but the look on the van driver's face gave the game away and eventually it dawned on him that she had understood everything that was said.

'I don't know whether they would have told us about it had I not understood what was going on, but I told him he had to talk to Yvonne or Sheryl Wells about it. He did that and clearance was given for six girls to go to Delft the next day. When Yvonne and the girls set off for the clinic their van was surrounded by police. There were police in front, behind and at the side but they were not needed and everything went off smoothly.'

The Cape Town games were being played at the Bellville facility which had been run by Christie in 1996, and many of those who had worked for him turned up at New Zealand training to ask Irene how he was.

First up in the series was South Africa against Australia. It was an early test of Irene's emotions as she stood in the stand alongside her teammates while the South African national anthem was played. Tears rolled down her cheeks but, in retrospect, it was good to get this moment out of the way while she was in the crowd rather than out on court with television cameras in her face, as would have been the case had the Ferns been involved in the first game.

It was a painful night for the Proteas as they suffered a 73–33 hammering at the hands of the world champion Australians. Irene didn't enjoy watching the humiliation, but her mind was already on New Zealand's game against South Africa 24 hours later. While she felt no extra pressure in the hours leading up to the test, subconsciously the significance of the occasion must have been preying on her mind if the warm-up was anything to go by.

'Before a game the shooters go out and have a practice. It is usually pretty relaxed which means most of the shots go straight through the hoop. That night I missed every one, which was something that had never happened to me before. Belinda [Colling] told me to relax, that it would be OK, but Yvonne motioned for me to go back to the bench. As I got close to her I said, "I missed every one of my shots," to which Yvonne replied, "Don't tell me, I saw you".

'It was a relief to get out on court and, thanks to Bernie, I got through the national anthems without a problem. Whether Bernie had planned it I don't know, but just as the South African anthem started she quietly said something that made me smile. She was trying to put me at ease, to tell me that the team were there for me. Bernie was terrific and I was fine.

'As we moved into position I asked Belinda to get the ball to me as close to the post as possible for my first shot, because if I was going to play well I knew in my heart that the first shot had to be successful. Typical of Belinda she put me in right under the post for the first one; it went in and I was OK. It was the first time Belinda and I had played together but Bill has such amazing talents she made it easy. She knows when and how to pass. I know I am not good at taking a bounce pass because it takes me so long to get down, but it's not a problem for Belinda. She bounces it under the defender's hands and straight up into mine.

'I enjoy playing with both Belinda and Donna because they are totally different. Donna is a shooter and will take a shot from wherever she is, while Belinda is more of a feeder.'

Sheryl Clarke, Vilimaina Davu and Canterbury's Anna Veronese made their international debuts in a record 88–34 win for New Zealand, while Belinda Colling was playing her first test in more than a year. Irene, playing her seventh test for the Ferns, had probably her best game since donning the black uniform as she sank all but 5 of her 69 attempts on goal. The big win was satisfying, but everyone in the New Zealand party was aware that the big test would come in Pietermaritzburg four days later against Australia.

Irene couldn't understand why Pietermaritzburg was chosen to host games in the series. Close to the sea, but more humid than Cape Town, Pietermaritzburg is not recognised as a netball area and the facilities are primitive by international standards.

Players from the world's top two netball nations faced off in the Pietermaritzburg Girls High School gymnasium with around a quarter of the two hundred temporary seats installed for the big occasion unoccupied. Used to playing in modern stadiums on sprung floors, they were back in the Dark Ages on concrete.

Off the court conditions weren't what the Kiwis and Aussies were used to either. In Cape Town they'd been housed in a brand spanking new hostel, in stark contrast to the dingy establishment they found themselves in at Pietermaritzburg. Neither set of players was impressed but while the Australians moaned, the New Zealanders laughed, accepted what was happening and did as manager Sheryl Wells suggested, going with the flow.

In the lead-up to the game the Silver Ferns were constantly reminded by the media about the last time they'd played Australia four months earlier and been trounced by 23 goals. 'Are you up for the challenge?' was the question most often posed to the New Zealanders.

'We didn't need reminding about Newcastle, but what outsiders couldn't appreciate was that there was a completely different feel about the team this time. The other difference was that, unlike before Newcastle, Yvonne had time to prepare us and she did a great job.

'At breakfast on game morning I asked Linda if she was ready and she said, "You bet." That summed it up for everyone. Throughout the day everyone had the belief that this was to be our time; that we were going to kick some Aussie butt. I spoke to my mum during the day and told her that there was something really special about this team; a chemistry that meant everyone connected. The comfortable feeling continued when Yvonne was so relaxed in her team talk. She said we'd done the work and that we should go out and enjoy it for once against Australia.

'From the first pass I just knew it was going to be our moment and I always felt we were in control. I think the best feeling I had during the game was watching Liz Ellis and Kathy Harby trying to bring the ball through and having no one in space to give it to. You could see the fear on their faces as they got a taste of what it had been like for other teams for so long playing against them.

'Usually so cool and calm, the Aussies were now yelling at each other. That was a good feeling.'

It was a classy performance from a New Zealand team that had been battered unmercifully after the Newcastle debacle, and they saved the best till after the final whistle.

'When Australia win they always go ballistic, and we'd joked among ourselves that when it was our turn we would jump all over each other, take our tops off and run naked round the stadium.

'Yvonne told us to accept victory gracefully, but really it was something we didn't need reminding about. With Bernie as captain New Zealand will always win or lose with dignity. She always has the right word for the moment.

'It was hard for us to contain ourselves though. The win meant so much. Yvonne enjoyed the moment but she must have been absolutely bubbling inside after what she had been through in the previous 12 months.

'When we got back to the dressing room it was time to let loose with our emotions and there was a bit of singing in the shower. In the hotel later we shared two bottles of red wine so we could make a toast, which was simply, "We did it."

'It was great having my family there. Mum and Janita had driven 16 hours to Cape Town for the first test and then 9 hours back to Pietermaritzburg for the next two. My brothers came to Pietermaritzburg on the day of the game, along with some of my old school friends. With training, coaching clinics and games I didn't get to see them that often but just having them close to me was enough.'

The win over Australia wasn't only vindication for the players but also for Yvonne Willering and Netball New Zealand, which stood by Willering when some players were allegedly trying to get her sacked. Close friends will tell you there were times when Willering wondered if it was worth staying on when such things were happening around her. In the end, her love of netball, and the job she had waited so long for, won the day. In Pietermaritzburg she got her reward.

Perhaps the stirring that went on after the 23-goal loss to Australia in June, along with the stuttering 2–1 series win over a World Seven, had changed Willering as a coach. Once perceived as conservative, Willering chanced her arm by going for the flair of Adine Harper, Temepara George and Belinda Colling in attack and it paid handsome dividends.

New Zealand duly put the seal on a successful tri-nations with a comprehensive 81–35 win over South Africa in the tour finale then it was time to go home, but not before Irene experienced the only really negative moment of the tour.

'I was kneeling by my bag in the airport when a pair of men's shoes came into my vision. I looked up and this guy was staring at me. He said, "You're a traitor," and then turned to his wife, pointed at me and said, "Look, this is the traitor." I looked around to see if anyone had heard what was going on but nobody was nearby, apart from Yvonne who was reading a newspaper.

'It took me completely by surprise and all I could think of to say was, "Yes, I am living in New Zealand, and I love it." His wife looked at me as if I didn't exist before they walked off, turning round every few seconds to glare at me.'

It was a moment Irene could have done without, but it didn't worry her unduly. It might have been a different story had the encounter happened at the beginning rather than the end of the tour. At that point, however, Irene wasn't going to let one boorish individual spoil a trip that had turned out to be far more enjoyable than she had dared hope.

Chapter 15

Christie van Dyk

PICKING OUT CHRISTIE VAN DYK IN A packed stadium where his wife Irene is playing netball is easy. While all around him are cheering and shouting, Christie will be the one with his eyes fixed firmly on the court and a serious look on his face.

Whenever the ball reaches Irene there is an involuntary tightening of Christie's muscles, but they immediately relax again once the ball goes arcing through the air and into the hoop. Should the shot miss its target Christie will file away in his mind the reason it didn't find the net. Maybe her elbow was in the wrong position, or she didn't bend her knee. Whatever the reason Christie will know, often before the shot is completed. Through watching Irene for so long, training alongside her and helping her with her shooting technique, he can sense when she's going to miss.

No sporting partner gets more involved with the game than Christie. He feels part of it, despite being just a face in the crowd along with several thousand others. It is through being in such situations that Christie has had to learn to control his emotions and reactions. Those sitting close by have no reason to know he is Irene's husband and therefore see no reason to hold back their feelings, whatever they are — though knowing Kiwis it wouldn't deter them even if he was recognisable.

Usually what is being said is positive and supportive of Irene and her team, be it the Silver Ferns or the Capital Shakers. Sometimes, however, the comments are negative and that's when Christie has to bite his tongue. No husband or wife likes to hear their partner criticised, even if they are seen to be public property through the sporting role they play.

Dealing with negativity towards Irene is something Christie has learnt over time. There was a time when he would turn and glare at those making the comments, but even then he knew better than to get involved in a slanging match. If that were to happen there would be only one loser and that's Irene.

At the final whistle, as the teams warm down and children surround the court awaiting an opportunity to get the players' autographs, Christie will make his way out of the stadium to wait for Irene. This is her time, when she belongs to the netball fraternity. Later Irene and Christie will close the door in their Stokes Valley home, play with Bianca, and talk about the game.

Because of Christie's passion for coaching, and the support he gives to Irene, they can talk for hours about the game, good and bad parts alike. He is the first to congratulate her on the good things, but he is not afraid to go down the negative path if he has seen something he thinks could have been improved upon. Irene listens patiently and evaluates what her husband is saying. Sometimes she feels he goes too far, but she knows he means well. Christie for his part accepts that sometimes he is too hard on Irene; that she's only human and, like everyone, will make mistakes.

There are times when Christie wishes he could get closer to the court and pass on some of the things he has seen during a game. Of course that's impossible, and he must wait until they are alone before he can pass on what he has gleaned from watching.

In one game during the 2001 Coca-Cola Cup competition Irene wasn't receiving enough quality ball in the circle. She appeared to be moving into space well enough, and many in the crowd would have been blaming those whose job it was to feed her. Not Christie. Yes, she was moving well into space, he said, but her head was down. How could a player throw to a team-mate who wasn't looking? A small thing, perhaps, but Irene took it on board and endeavoured to make sure the same thing didn't happen next time she took the court.

While Christie is a development coach with the Wellington Cricket Association and coach of the province's under-19 side, he does not restrict his analysis of players to netball and cricket. Whatever the game he is watching, either live or on television, he is thinking all the time. Why is this player good? What made that guy miss those kicks at goal? Since Christie began to get serious about cricket coaching he has spent hours analysing people in all sports, and he wishes he had time to do more.

Christie was the first child of Eric and Annette van Dyk, who lived around 30 km away from the Viljoen family. Three years later his sister Yolande was born, and another three years on Eric and Annette had another daughter, Tanya.

It was while he was at primary school that Christie became infatuated with cricket, South Africa's national summer game. Unfortunately no cricket was played at his school. Instead he and his mates headed for the park where they played the game under their own rules. If anything, in the early stages at least, that was better than having to abide by the same rules as the rest of the world. At least that's how it seemed to them at the time.

It must have worked for Christie. When he got to High School as a 14-year-old he was considered good enough to play in the under-18 and under-19 teams. Those were idyllic times for the young van Dyk, although he was frustrated that he didn't get the technical help he needed from the school's cricket coaches. Perhaps that's one of the things that later guided him down the coaching path. Instead of being helped he was left to improve his own cricketing skills through reading books and studying the action of the great South African fast bowler Allan Donald.

Like all South African boys Christie also loved rugby, but by the time he arrived at Teacher's College as a 19-year-old his involvement with the national winter game was restricted by a knee injury. Rather than bemoan the fact that he couldn't play much rugby, Christie preferred to dwell on the positive, saying it saved him having to decide which of the two sports to concentrate his efforts on. Cricket would be his game.

'My parents brought me up to believe that to achieve anything in life you have to work hard, to put the effort in. That was what I was doing with my cricket in those days.

'I would bowl on my own for two hours every day, trying to correct my technique, which I knew needed changing. Practising and training on your own can be thankless. It can also be very rewarding when what you're trying to improve suddenly happens. There is a great feeling of achievement.

'During my four years at teacher's college I was always pushing myself at cricket. Perhaps I should have put the same energy into my studies! On reflection, I have probably been so hard on Irene during our training sessions together because of what I had been doing to myself at that time.'

Christie played for the national Teacher's College team during his last two years at college, and he also played five times for North West Province. After graduating Christie began teaching, while also representing the Vaal Triangle. But playing cricket is time consuming, and before long his principal told Christie he had to put more time in at school, even if it did interfere with his sporting pursuits.

While he was disappointed at this edict, in hindsight it came at the right time. Injuries were beginning to affect Christie's cricket but, more importantly, he was by then involved with Irene. His love of cricket was still strong and the game had given him lots of enjoyment. Coaching offered him a way of staying involved while not being as time consuming as playing. He realised that being a good player didn't necessarily make a good coach, but he was prepared to give it a go, and besides, there were other things on the horizon.

'Watching Irene play and practise netball I felt that she could go a long way in the game. She was young and needed support. I was young and frightened of losing her, of us going our different ways if I carried on playing cricket and she pursued her netball.

'From the moment we met, Irene has been so important to me, but I was silly enough not to do anything about it at first. Girls were OK but sport was my number one interest, and whenever I became friendly with a girl I would start to find fault with her.

'My friends used to tell me that I would never get married because I wanted a perfect woman. When Irene and I got together I was still like that, and even though she was undoubtedly different to anyone I had been involved with previously I fought my feelings.

'One day we were playing hand tennis against a friend of mine and his girlfriend and I suddenly thought what a good team we made. Still I didn't do anything about it. Then I saw that other guys were getting interested in Irene and everything changed. Before anyone could move in between us I let Irene know how I felt about her and we have been together ever since.

'Right from the beginning I told Irene that I would support her netball career; that I would work with her to make her the best player she could be. She had the makings of a top player and I was going to do everything possible to help her reach the pinnacle of her sport.

'Giving her my unqualified support meant that we had to postpone our wedding because the South African netball team was going to England. The wedding eventually took place on December 10, 1994 in Meyerton and I will always remember it as one of the special days of my life. There were 250 guests and Irene was a beautiful bride. The only thing wrong with the day was that it went so quickly; before we knew what was happening it was over. That's the problem with your special days; they don't last long enough; while you enjoy them there isn't enough time to linger over things as you would like to.'

On his wedding day Christie caught a glimpse of what the future held. When the happy couple emerged from the church strangers were waiting to take photographs. Next morning Christie went to a dairy and there on the counter was their wedding photograph on the front page of the Sunday paper.

'That was when I realised that being married to Irene was going to change my life. It wasn't so noticeable in the early months of our marriage but everything started to change after the 1995 world championships, when Irene became known in other parts of the world as well as South Africa. It was as if her becoming popular in other countries made South Africans take more notice of her than they had before.

'I admit that there were some parts of Irene's new-found fame that I didn't handle very well. I would be dishonest if I said that watching guys wanting their photographs taken with her, and asking for a kiss on the cheek while the picture was being taken, was enjoyable. I doubt that any husband would enjoy that situation no matter how long he had been married.

'It is natural to be jealous and that was a very difficult period for me. She was so popular and at times it felt as though I was being left out. It caused a few rows between us early on, but as time went on I learnt to accept what was happening. You grow up. Life is about experiencing things and learning how to handle different situations. Early on I would react and then regret it. Dad used to tell me that if I was having trouble with a particular scenario then I should count to ten. I did eventually, but in the early days I found it hard to get past three.'

While Irene and her team-mates were causing their massive upset in Birmingham, Christie was back home watching the game on television with only a bottle of whisky for company. The closer full-time came, and South Africa were still hanging in against the tournament favourites, the more frequently Christie reached for the bottle, though his hands were beginning to shake so much with the excitement that filling the glass became ever more difficult.

When the final whistle went Christie felt elation and relief in the same moment. He was delighted South Africa had won, but more than anything he was proud of the way his wife had performed, how she had held her nerve under extreme pressure. He couldn't wait for her to get home, but when she arrived he realised things were never going to be the same again.

There was the opportunity to play in Queensland; more tours were being arranged for the Proteas in the wake of their second placing at the world championships; Irene was being asked more and more to do pro-motional work. It was still a far cry from what he would encounter five years later in New Zealand where netball is a major sport, but it was enough to suggest he would be sharing his wife with the public.

'I probably didn't realise just how different things would be. It wasn't too bad in South Africa because netball wasn't so popular. In New Zealand it is far more full on.

'Irene was recognised in South Africa but the people there are differ-ent to New Zealanders in that few have the confidence to come up and talk to her, whereas in New Zealand the people have no such inhibitions. It was a real shock to me to see how popular Irene was in New Zealand; that television crews, newspaper photographers and reporters would be waiting for her at the airport. When I went to Wellington with Irene for the first time I couldn't believe the photographers were at the airport taking my photograph as well.

'By the time we'd settled in New Zealand and Irene was chosen for the Silver Ferns the demands on her time became more and more. Just getting away from the court after a Coca-Cola Cup game took a long time and Irene is invariably the last one to leave because she can't say no to anyone. That part of her personality, which will never change, led to the only disagreements we had in our early days in New Zealand. I would get angry when I had organised something in the evening and Irene would come home and say she had committed either herself or both of us to go elsewhere.

'It is something I have become used to. Irene will use our valuable time to keep someone else happy because she knows I will now try and understand. That's just the way she is.

'Irene being away on tour is the hardest part for me. When I come home at night I love to sit and talk, to discuss what has been happening in both our lives, and to play with Bianca. When Irene is away there is no one to share those sort of things with.

'It has not been easy for me to make friends away from cricket and netball. The culture of New Zealand men is so different to South Africa and it is hard to form relationships. It takes time to build trust when you're in a new country.'

Moving to New Zealand wasn't easy for Christie. For a start he didn't speak the language as well as he would have liked. On his first visit, Capital Shakers' Kathy Doyle and her husband Paddy hosted a barbecue for the couple. While Irene, as usual, was the life and soul of the gathering, Christie was content to spend his time talking mainly to Paddy Doyle and Sir Ron Scott, organiser of the 1974 Commonwealth Games in Christchurch, who was helping find Irene a teaching position.

Christie actually spoke English well enough, though he obviously wasn't at ease with it. Some months later, when he had joined Wellington Cricket, there was a huge smile on his face after he had completed all his reports in English.

As his English improved, so did Christie's demeanour. He became much more at ease around people, which was a good thing as he and Irene get little time to themselves.

'The time we get together we treasure because there isn't a lot of it.

Irene has so many netball commitments there are times when I wonder when we will get time to talk. I take my hat off to her the way she teaches all day and then goes straight off to netball practice. It does take it out of her though because when she gets home she's tired.

'With Irene having netball in winter and cricket being a summer game there is little chance of us being together often. We haven't had a holiday in seven years and there is no sign of that changing in the near future.

'We support each other in everything. I want to be a good cricket coach and would like to referee rugby at Super 12 level. I was an A-grade rugby referee in South Africa and have taken up the whistle again in New Zealand.

'While Irene is away on tours and I am looking after Bianca it is hard. But as Irene points out, one day she will finish playing and I'll still be involved with my cricket coaching and rugby refereeing. Then it will be her turn to stay at home.'

Chapter 16

Touring with the Silver Ferns

THERE IS A TIME-HONOURED TRADITION when sporting teams travel that 'what happens on tour stays on tour.' For those who haven't heard this saying, it means that the lips of those on tour will be sealed about any misbehaviour when the team returns home; that the only people who know what indiscretions occurred, if indeed there were any, will be those who were there. It is a policy that, over the years, has spared countless sportsmen and women embarrassment, not to mention the number of marriages it has kept out of the divorce courts.

Sportsmen, rather than women, have undoubtedly been the ones who have benefited most from this tradition, though some of the mix and matching that goes on in athletes' villages at Commonwealth and Olympic Games means that at times women have also been grateful for the silence of their peers.

Since media intrusion into the private lives of sportspeople and public figures in general has become more prevalent in recent times, the number of potentially embarrassing incidents has declined dramatically; those in the limelight have, for the most part, learned to be more circumspect in their behaviour.

In the case of most women's sports teams, and New Zealand netball teams in particular, unladylike behaviour has never really been an issue. If there was any scandal to be had from overseas or internal tours it has been kept well hidden. If anything, touring with the Silver Ferns appears totally boring to an outsider. It isn't, because the players have a lot of fun amongst themselves. But misbehave? No way. The only thing the Ferns are likely to overindulge in is food! They always seem to be eating. Breakfast before training, then lunch, perhaps a video session, followed by a pre-match or pre-training meal, game or training, then a post-match or post-training meal. Fortunately they work hard or they would pack on the kilos in no time.

Irene van Dyk's first overseas trip with the New Zealand team was when she made her debut in the test against Australia in Newcastle in

June 2000. It was such a short visit that Irene felt like she was on the plane back almost as soon as she had arrived at Sydney's Kingsford Smith Airport. Later that year there was the internal tour, with games against Team Pasifika followed by the series with a World selection, then a visit to South Africa.

In June 2001 Irene again prepared for a trip to Australia where the Silver Ferns were to play in a tri-series with the host country and South Africa. This time she knew the ropes, there were no dramas about visas, and she wasn't surprised by the list of items that had to be packed. Netball New Zealand leave nothing to chance, and the list includes 22 items of clothing or footwear on top of what is provided by the organisation. Players are even reminded to ensure they have an adequate supply of underwear. Then comes a list of other essential items: at the top is the player's passport, but then follows a mug, knife, fork and spoon, and 15 other items before the edict 'please travel light'.

One can imagine the reaction if the All Black or Springbok rugby teams were asked to take along their own crockery and cutlery. There is, however, a logical reason, since they are needed for such things as the pre-match snack, which may not be supplied by the hotel or motel where the players are staying. How, for instance, would they eat noodles if they'd not brought utensils? You have to hand it to women's sporting organisations — they think of everything — though netball has never quite matched the New Zealand Women's Golf Association which at one time included a shopping day within their national championships!

For this tour to Australia the New Zealand players were to assemble on a Friday afternoon and would have three full days together before leaving for Brisbane where warm-up games against the Queensland Firebirds had been arranged. Before meeting up with her team-mates Irene had telephoned Netball New Zealand's Tracey Fear to let her know that she had seen a small news item from a South African newspaper suggesting the Proteas were hopeful that she would play for them at the 2002 Commonwealth Games. Irene wanted to let Netball New Zealand know that there was no chance of that happening; that she was now a New Zealand resident and that the only international team she wished to play for was the Silver Ferns. In the light of what happened while the team was in Australia, it turned out to be a fortuitous telephone call.

The Silver Ferns made their way to Auckland's Allenby Park Motor Inn where they would stay until their Tuesday morning flight to Australia. Dinner was the first thing on the agenda after an afternoon arrival, followed by a team meeting where new Silver Fern Victoria Edward was welcomed on board. There was then the usual chaos as gear was handed out, with many garments often too big, too small or baggy. At least it gave the players plenty to laugh about as they took the mickey out of each other.

At times that evening Irene glanced across at Vicki Edward, knowing how the new cap was feeling. It was only 12 months earlier that Irene had been in the same situation.

There was, however, a big difference. Whereas Irene had previously met her New Zealand team-mates mainly in opposition teams on court, Edward was well acquainted with almost everyone in the team through the years she had spent in the Coca-Cola Cup and playing for national age grade teams. Some, such as Lesley Nicol, Adine Harper and Belinda Colling, were bosom buddies from their days together with the tremendously successful Otago Rebels team.

Despite those advantages, being in a senior New Zealand team for the first time was probably just as nerve-racking for Edward as it would be for any other player. It is, after all, the pinnacle of achievement for any player, and the need to prove themselves worthy of such an accolade is all-consuming.

With assembly formalities completed there was time for everyone to swap gossip from around the traps before turning in for a good night's sleep that would stand them in good stead for the exertions of training the following morning.

On the flight from Wellington to Auckland Irene had thought about the forthcoming tri-nations series and felt very confident about the whole tour. She was sure the Silver Ferns were going to beat arch-rivals Australia again, showing that their win over the world champions in South Africa the previous November hadn't been a fluke.

Those feelings were accentuated by what she heard all around her that first night. It seemed everyone shared her thoughts. There was a different attitude about this team than the one she had joined 12 months earlier, when Irene had been taken aback by the lack of self-belief she sensed among the players. The mood this time was in stark contrast, even though most of the personnel were the same. There was no cockiness, which some observers felt there had been about the New Zealand team that played at the 1999 world tournament in Christchurch. Instead there was a quiet confidence that they were up to the job being asked of them.

It all added up to an atmosphere that was conducive for success and there was a spring in their step as the team headed out to the Manurewa Stadium early on Saturday morning for their first training session. During the session Yvonne Willering concentrated on through court play and Irene breathed a sigh of relief when she found Bernice Mene and Vilimaina Davu were on her team.

Irene has always found Mene and Davu uncompromising opponents, and they don't drop their standards during training. Davu in particular doesn't know how to stop herself challenging for the ball in the same manner she would during a game, and Irene has often returned from a Silver Ferns training session where she has opposed the former Fijian international and ruefully counted the bruises.

Safely through the tour's first training session, which was uneventful apart from Bernice Mene slipping and stretching her leg, though thankfully not seriously, the Ferns headed back to the motel. In the afternoon players and team management got together to spell out the goals of the tour. The management spelt out to the players what was expected of them, and in return the players told management what they wanted to see from them.

'It is not quite as serious as it sounds, and such sessions are really worthwhile because it gives you time to get to know one another again, management and players that is, because you haven't seen them in a touring situation for some time.

'The players get told that they are expected to be on time, dressed neatly and appropriately and that they will give of their best whether it be in training or a game situation. In return the players said the management team should be dressed in matching outfits, though perhaps different to the players, and that they should chill out sometimes and have fun. Those in charge of the team do enjoy themselves even though they have a lot of responsibility. For instance, Ducky [team manager Sheryl Wells] is keen on slices of lemon or chocolate cake, and Yvonne supplies the cake.

'It might sound a little thing, but in a funny way you realise that such things go deeper. The togetherness of it all is setting aims for what lies ahead in the tour. Everything is done with good humour and it really is like being in a family. I bought Yvonne a new blue coffee mug because she had broken the grey one she had always used.

'A cup is essential for Yvonne who seems to exist on coffee. You hardly ever see her eating and I would often ask what she had eaten during the day only to be told, in a nice way, to mind my own business.'

On the Saturday night the Silver Ferns played a game against New Zealand A, winning well, and then took on the same team again on Sunday morning. At various times during the second game Irene played alongside Donna Loffhagen and Belinda Colling, while the feeding was done by Adine Harper, Temepara George and Jenny-May Coffin. She went back to the hotel thinking how well things were coming together, and was also pleased that her Capital Shakers team-mate Jodi Te Huna had done a good job for the New Zealand A team.

There was a third game against New Zealand A on the Sunday night, and while the Ferns won 79–44 Irene felt it wasn't a game that most of the Ferns would want to remember. As she sat and talked to room-mate Adine Harper, Irene decided the reason for the poor performance was that everyone was tired from two days of hard work at the start of camp. It was a different story on the Monday morning when the team went through what Irene remembers as a lovely training session. Irene, Donna and Belinda had a good talking session about what was needed from the different circle combinations before the midcourters worked on getting the ball to the shooters.

The afternoon was set aside for what has now become a prerequisite for New Zealand sporting teams — the photo shoot. Hours spent having photographs taken, autographing balls and posters as well as spending time at the retail outlets of various sponsors are all part and parcel of being an international sportsperson. Some take to such demands like the proverbial duck to water; others do it with a smile through clenched teeth.

Netball New Zealand's main sponsors in recent times have been Fisher and Paykel, who provide the financial backing and support crew for home international series; Coca-Cola, who have the naming rights for the domestic franchise competition; and Vodafone, who sponsor the Silver Ferns. In 2001 those backers were joined by the National Bank which, at a function during the series against England, became netball's 'official bank'.

The Silver Ferns are a sponsor's delight, smiling their way through any function and, when speaking publicly, never forgetting a sponsor's name, whether it be thanking Fisher and Paykel for putting on a series or referring to themselves as the Vodafone Silver Ferns.

The latter habit has led to some barbed media comments that the netballers are programmed — push the right button and out will come 'Vodafone Silver Ferns', even if they are in a one-on-one casual conversation. That doesn't seem to worry the players. They are grateful for the support of all their sponsors, reasoning, correctly, that they would be far worse off without them. Unlike New Zealand rugby players, netballers are not professionals and rely on the support of sponsors for little extras, while the national body is grateful for support that allows them to at least recompense the Silver Ferns for loss of earnings while they are on international duty.

On that particular Monday afternoon in Auckland, the New Zealand players were photographed in their playing uniforms and walk-out number ones. The shoot took four and a half hours — in a swimming pool full of balloons! When it was over the players had a free evening to do as they pleased. The Auckland-based players went home, some went to the movies, and others stayed in the hotel to pack and chill out before the morning flight to Brisbane.

Yvonne Willering had chosen to prepare for the tri-nations series in Brisbane, despite the internationals being played in Melbourne, Canberra and Sydney. This provided an opportunity for two games against the Queensland Firebirds that would help the Ferns adjust to the Australian style of play, which is very different to what they come up against in New Zealand.

New Zealand won both games against the Firebirds convincingly, but they were just the type of workout that Willering was looking for. Between games, which were both played at night, the players got some free time. Irene chose to have a look round Brisbane for an hour before going back to the hotel for an afternoon sleep. Chances to play tourist are rare, but when the opportunity presents itself Irene is as keen as anyone to check out the sights. Shopping expeditions are a different matter entirely.

'Those are planned like a military exercise,' Irene says with a laugh. 'The first time we're let loose in a shopping mall we almost run through the shops seeing what's on offer and making a mental note of which ones we want to buy from later.

'The next day we may get another hour to return and get what we want, because Yvonne never lets us go for two or three hours at a time which would mean we could walk and browse the shops at our leisure.

'Yvonne has got it all sussed and you can understand where she's coming from. If she let us go for two or three hours at a time we would be walking and walking, getting tired. The way she has it organised makes sense. It also means you need a good memory so you can find the shops which have what you want to buy!'

Shopping was the furthest thing from the players' minds next morning when they set out for Melbourne, venue for their first tri-nations game against Australia 36 hours later. At Melbourne's Holiday Inn Irene was to room with Sheryl Clarke, but first they had to find the hotel. No one from Netball Australia met the New Zealanders at the airport, meaning a road map had to be bought so they could negotiate their way to the heart of the city in the mini-vans they would be using for their stay alongside the Yarra River. Was this a cunning plan by the Australians to unsettle the Silver Ferns? Probably not, but the suggestion of such a devious plot made for a bit of lighthearted fun anyway.

Australia and South Africa played the opening game of the competition that night at Melbourne's State Netball Hockey Centre with the hosts, predictably, coasting to a 70–24 win. Watching from the stands Irene felt sorry for South Africa, who were totally outclassed. She also thought the Australians were not on top of their game, despite being far too strong for the country of her birth. The unforced errors the Australians frequently made only reinforced the good feelings Irene had about the upcoming clash between the Silver Ferns and the world champions.

Next morning, seven days after assembling, it was match day at last. A few butterflies fluttering in Irene's stomach was a good sign. It wasn't nerves, more a sense of anticipation, and she couldn't wait to get to the match venue for a light morning training session. As the day progressed and pass-off time grew closer, Irene couldn't help but notice what was going on around her, what everyone was doing in the lead-up to the game, especially Yvonne Willering.

'I had quickly realised how superstitious Yvonne can be. If we do a particular thing before a test and then go out and win with a good performance then you can bet we will have to follow the same routine before the next game.

'I'm not talking about netball things that happen on or around the court, but outside influences. For instance, if we all go out for coffee in the afternoon of a big game and then win . . . hey, I hope the girls like coffee because that's where we will be heading next time. There is nothing wrong with such superstitions. Anything that keeps Yvonne happy is OK with me. A happy coach means happy players!'

Much of the pre-match speculation going into New Zealand's first game in the tri-nations against hosts Australia was about who would partner Irene in the circle. As one writer put it in his preview, two into one doesn't go, no matter which way you look at it. Irene was a certainty to start and that would leave one of the Silver Ferns' other shooting stars, Donna Loffhagen or Belinda Colling, disappointed, he said.

Coach Yvonne Willering described it as the most intense competition for places during her time with the Silver Ferns. It was noted that Belinda Colling is more of a feeding goal attack and had shown in New Zealand's win over Australia late in 2000 that she could combine well with Irene. Loffhagen, however, was perceived as a stronger shooter than Colling, and it was felt that such a potentially potent scoring threat would test the Australian defence. On the debit side of the argument was that the only time Loffhagen and van Dyk had played together was in the heavy defeat at Newcastle 12 months earlier.

Willering opted to partner van Dyk with Colling but then, in a planned move, surprised the Australians by switching at half-time and going with van Dyk and Loffhagen. Rather than upset the rhythm that had put the Silver Ferns 27–23 ahead at half-time, the switch improved the side's attacking momentum.

At the final whistle New Zealand were ahead 55–40 and a raucous capacity crowd that had been chanting 'Ozzie Ozzie Ozzie, oi oi oi' at the outset watched in virtual silence as the Silver Ferns destroyed the world and Commonwealth champions. It was a moment to savour for the New Zealanders, and Yvonne Willering in particular could have been forgiven had she been tempted to gloat. Her team had recorded their first win on Australian soil in 11 years. It was also the first time New Zealand had won successive tests against the old enemy for 19 years.

Rather than get carried away with the moment, Willering, who was aware how quickly fortunes can change in top level sport, accepted the congratulations from all and sundry with humility. It was the same in the dressing room. Delight at turning the tables on the world champions was tempered with the knowledge that they would need to go out and do it again in seven days' time.

It was still nice, however, for the Ferns to sit back and replay in their minds what had just happened. How goalkeep Linda Vagana had set the tone for the game by grabbing an intercept off Australia's centre pass; how the feeding of the shooters by Adine Harper and Temepara George, along with the movement of Colling and van Dyk, had forced Australia into making defensive changes that didn't work; and how, in the second half, Loffhagen's strength and willingness to shoot gave an already stretched Australian defence further problems.

Willering was asked why New Zealand's fortunes had changed so dramatically over their last two games against Australia. The depth of talent now at her disposal was one reason, Willering said; the other was the make-up of the squad.

'There is now harmony within the team, both on and off court,' Willering said. 'That's something I have been striving for.' It was a telling comment given the alleged player revolt that had almost cost Willering her job late the previous year.

For the team there was little time to savour what was being hailed back in New Zealand as a fantastic achievement. A swimming session to ease tired muscles meant it was 1 a.m. before the players got to bed and they had to be up, have breakfast and deliver their bags to the hotel lobby by 7.50 a.m. before taking a 9.30 flight to Canberra where they would meet South Africa three days later.

Manager Sheryl Wells makes sure players do not room with the same team-mate more than once during a tour, and at Rydges Hotel in Canberra Irene's room-mate was to be Donna Loffhagen. Had that happened during Irene's debut trip to Australia 12 months earlier she would have been wary about how she would get on with Donna, considering the comments attributed to her during the debate about whether Irene should be chosen for New Zealand. By this time, however, she felt no trepidation about sharing a room with Donna. The pair were getting on well and the ice, if any still existed, had been well and truly broken a few nights earlier in Melbourne while the team was having dinner.

'Donna was sitting across from me and I said, "You know, I really thought you were a bitch," and before I could add, "but now I know you I think you're really cool," Donna replied, "Most people think that."

'We had a good laugh about it, but that really summed up how I felt. Donna has this persona on court that really winds people up, and because I hadn't had much to do with her till this tour I hadn't got through that outer veneer.

'She had been in the team to Newcastle the previous year but that was only for three days and we worked so hard there was little time to get to know people well. Then she missed the internal tour against Team Pasifika and the World Seven, as well as the end-of-year trip to South Africa, because she opted to concentrate on basketball and the Olympic Games.

'Who could blame her for that? Donna and Belinda are so fortunate to be able to play at international level in both netball and basketball and it shows just how talented they are. There is no doubt that basketball plays a huge role in Donna's life. I found out just how much she loves it when I roomed with her in Canberra.

'Rooming with someone is the best way to get to know them. Once you're back in the room together at night there is nothing else to do but talk. You get to know about your roomie's boyfriend or husband, their thoughts on netball, what their parents are like . . . what they enjoy doing away from netball.

'Not allowing you to be with the same person each time is a great idea. Not only do you get to know your team-mates on a different level, but it stops cliques forming which is always a possibility if the same people are thrown together all the time.

'On the court Donna is amazing to play alongside. From the first moment we were on court together she began encouraging me. If I missed a shot she would tell me not to worry, that we would get the ball back. She would be telling me to breathe deeply, to concentrate. You name it,

Donna would say it. She talks the whole time on court. Belinda is altogether different. She gets the ball to you and then simply gets ready for the next play.

'Later in the tour when Australia got a bit too physical in the second test, Donna was the one who stood up for me after the game, saying it wasn't necessary for the opposition to take me out and that dirty play had no place in netball. It was nice of her to stand up for me, but that's Dons. She says it as it is; that's something you have to appreciate about her.

'Once you get to know her, and find out what she's feeling, Dons is a lovely girl. I really like her, but then I had better not say too much or I will be ruining her reputation as a hard nut!'

After the exciting win over Australia Irene met up with the South African party, but if she was expecting to be greeted enthusiastically she was in for a big disappointment. They didn't seem at all happy to see her. While she knew six of the players well only three — Des Kotze, Leana Du Plooy and Manzo Machoga — would speak to her. Irene had really looked forward to catching up with South African netball gossip. That didn't eventuate and, worse in her eyes, the South Africans not only distanced themselves from Irene, but also from New Zealand as a team.

'They supported the Aussies when we played Australia. To me that was morally and culturally wrong. South Africans had always supported New Zealand teams that were playing Australia, whatever the sport. That's part of our heritage. South Africa and New Zealand have always been close in sport. Perhaps it was because they now had an Australian coach. Whatever it was, I didn't like it.

'Being ignored by most of them hurt. I thought they would have still been friendly, but they didn't even ask about Christie or Bianca. I noticed that Rosina Mogola wasn't with the team but when I asked where she was they said they didn't know. That was rubbish.

'Vlooi [Leana Du Plooy] of course talked to everyone because that's how she is. She had also just spent three months in New Zealand playing for the Southern Sting in the Coca-Cola Cup.

'It was different when I saw the South African management team in the hotel lobby. They were lovely to me and that made me feel so much better. Imagine my thoughts the next morning when I found out that those same people who had been so nice to me the previous day were trying to stop me playing for New Zealand at the 2002 Commonwealth Games. That course of action must have been decided on before I met them. It is unbelievable how low some people can go. How they can turn their backs on someone so quickly.

'I have no doubt Netball Australia stirred the South Africans up about my eligibility for the Commonwealth Games. New Zealand media people who were in Australia have told me that someone from Netball Australia approached them and asked if they were aware that I might not be able to play for the Silver Ferns in Manchester.

'Once people began talking about my eligibility I was so glad I had called Tracey Fear before leaving New Zealand to tell her I was committed to the Silver Ferns and that I wasn't interested in playing for any other country. Why would I play for someone else when Christie and I had bought a house in New Zealand and intend to spend the rest of our lives there? Tracey told me at the time not to get involved, but it became hard not to think about it with people pestering me, wanting to know what I felt about it.

'The first I knew about it was the day following our great win over Australia. Yvonne came to my room and said the bomb had gone off. There was no way Yvonne, who is very protective of her players, was going to let the media ruin what we were doing. I had three interviews that day and Yvonne sat in on all of them. Whenever a reporter brought up the subject of the Commonwealth Games Yvonne would jump in and say we were in Australia for a tri-nations tournament and that's what we would talk about or not talk at all.

'It was something I could have done without at the time. The timing sucked and the whole thing was totally unnecessary, certainly while we were involved in a series. I am positive the timing wasn't a coincidence, coming as it did after we'd just smashed Australia for the second successive time. It looked like the Aussies were fuelling the fire and it smacked of sour grapes.'

With all that going on around her, Irene needed some light relief and she got it the following day when, after a morning training session, the players had the afternoon and evening free to do as they liked. Manager Sheryl Wells made it plain she didn't want them sitting around the hotel all afternoon so Bernice Mene and Linda Vagana went off to find something for everyone to take part in. What they came up with was cycling. Well, sort of cycling. The players had a choice of tandems, double bikes with a roof, scooters, and a lovely lake to ride round.

'It was a fantastic afternoon. Watching Yvonne and Robyn [assistant coach Broughton] on a tandem was hilarious, and Linda and Belinda, who were riding a double bike, almost ended up in the lake. They were heading straight for it but managed to stop just in time. The rest of us thought it would have been perfect had they ended up in the water.

'Apparently the double bikes with a roof were really expensive and I think we blew the entertainment budget in one afternoon, but if we did then it was worth it. It was lovely to get out of the hotel and away from a netball environment for a few hours. Those are the things you remember later on and tell the next newcomer to the team about. "You should have been there the day Yvonne and Robyn were on a tandem" . . . that sort of thing. Being stuck in a team situation can become claustrophobic. Sometimes you need to get out. If you want time on your own Yvonne will try and let you have it. It also works the other way. Yvonne needs time away from us. I remember how it was at the 1995 world championships with South Africa. We weren't allowed to go anywhere on our own. It was so regimented we weren't allowed to take a nap in the afternoon if we felt like it.'

Later it was off to the movies to see *Moulin Rouge*, then out to dinner before returning to the hotel and watching *Chocolat* on video. The rest of the night was spent talking — and laughing. That's the sort of day the players enjoy. Netball? What netball?

The light-hearted day certainly didn't affect the Silver Ferns' performance the following night when they thumped South Africa 74–37. Irene enjoyed that, even though she played only half a game.

Before the Ferns left Canberra for the final leg of the tour in Sydney, Irene watched the hapless South Africans take another battering from Australia. Rather than enjoy their humiliation, which would have been understandable considering their threat to stop her playing at the Commonwealth Games, Irene felt sorry for the South Africans. How different it all was from six years earlier when they'd played Australia in the world championship final.

After a four-and-a-half-hour coach journey from Canberra to Sydney the team checked in at Parramatta's Sebel Hotel. Irene was pleased the evening would be free from team commitments and that she would have time to shop for presents for Christie and Bianca. There was also a one-on-one session with Yvonne Willering and an enjoyable dinner with her team-mates.

The following night New Zealand was to play South Africa. From Irene's point of view it was probably just as well Australia weren't the opposition, given the standard of training on the morning of the game. 'Shocking training. Couldn't do anything right. Hope everything goes well tonight,' Irene wrote in her diary on returning to the hotel. She need not have worried. Again New Zealand were far too strong for South Africa, winning 86–30 and making Irene feel even worse for her former countrywomen, who had no game plan, no consistency and didn't communicate with each other on court.

By now the New Zealanders had been in camp for 15 days. There was one day of the tour left and in the evening they would play the final game of the tournament against an Australian team desperate to avenge the humiliating loss in Melbourne.

Training went well on the morning of the game. Irene felt good about what lay ahead and she also got good vibes from those around her. Once more there was a quiet confidence in the New Zealand camp.

Under the rules for the tri-nations tournament Australia needed to beat New Zealand by 16 goals to lift the trophy. Anything less and, win or lose, New Zealand would be champions. Games between New Zealand and Australia are always hotly contested, but the feeling going into this game was particularly high, with Australia smarting after Melbourne.

Australian coach Jill McIntosh did nothing to lower the temperature when she had a dig at New Zealand's use of imports after the Melbourne loss. That the defeat was just the fourth in 58 tests and seven seasons for McIntosh undoubtedly made it hurt more and it showed in her post-match comments.

'New Zealand played well, but it has taken a few internationals from other countries to do it,' McIntosh said, pointedly referring to New Zealand's acquisition of Irene and back-up defender Vilimaina Davu, a former Fijian international. Asked by a reporter if she could see the irony in a South African playing such a major role in New Zealand's win (van Dyk had missed only 6 of her 50 shots), McIntosh said, 'New Zealand have accepted her into their side, but certainly if you take her out that's a big chunk out of their team, isn't it?'

To add to the tension there was a potentially disastrous incident on the journey from hotel to stadium when one of the rented vans the team was travelling in was involved in an accident.

'A guy drove into the back of our van and we got shaken up a bit. There was silence for a moment or two, but once we realised that everyone was OK the laughter started. I think it was through relief rather than finding the situation funny.

'Before the game we decided that the accident wouldn't be mentioned afterward, especially if we happened to lose the game. We didn't want anyone thinking we were using it as an excuse. It would have been a different story had anyone been hurt because then we couldn't have kept it quiet.'

From the first whistle at Sydney's State Sports Centre, which is part of the magnificent Sydney Olympic Park complex, it was obvious the Australians were hell-bent on revenge. They came out of the blocks firing on all cylinders, to such an extent that Irene says she had never seen an Australian team so desperate. That desperation at times took them over the line of acceptability with some of their challenges bordering on foul play. Besides being more physical, the Australians also played much better than they had seven days earlier and for three-quarters of the game they outplayed the Silver Ferns to such an extent it looked as if they could get the required 16-goal winning margin to win the series as well as the game. That they didn't achieve this was down to New Zealand retaining their composure in a white-hot atmosphere during the last 15 minutes, and having the satisfaction of scoring the last four goals through Irene to leave Australia with a 62–52 winning margin.

Media reviews of the game focused on the physical nature, and one particular incident involving Irene and goalkeep Liz Ellis. It was alleged that Ellis had elbowed Irene in the stomach after Irene had shot a goal.

Irene was surprised by Ellis' action. 'She gave me a shot that was quite unnecessary, but it wasn't just me. I thought everybody had a hard time. We knew the Aussies would come out firing and be physical be-cause they were so desperate after what had happened in Melbourne. But we were not prepared for just how rough they would be. There were things going on that didn't belong on a netball court.'

On the night of the game Loffhagen, shooting straight from the lip, climbed into the way Australia had played the game.

'There are two different sorts of physical tactics,' she said. 'There is the dirty sort and the contesting sort. In the Coca-Cola Cup I like it when it is contested, I like the physical nature of it. I don't like it when you're getting taken out or when people are going for the ball knowing they are not going to get it and don't know when to pull out.'

Of the Ellis–van Dyk incident, Loffhagen said, 'I thought that was very blatant and is uncalled for at this level. She scored a goal and then she got elbowed. It is all the off-the-ball stuff that the umpires don't see.'

Ellis was adamant the incident was unintentional. 'Her and I were both going for the ball a lot and that's just how it ended up. I think at one stage I accidentally got her and she accidentally got me later. So I think the score was one–all.'

Irene would have liked the chance to clear the air with Ellis after the game, but as there was no after-match function the opportunity didn't arise.

'Late in the game I had caught Liz in the eye while we were going for the ball and it would have been nice to be able to say, "Sorry about the eye . . . how many stitches did you need, ha ha," and to talk about what had happened during the game because you can't do that on court. If you do talk at all during a game it is not nice things that are said.

'After-match get-togethers are where you get the chance to mix and find out what the opposition girls are really like. That there were no after-match functions was really disappointing. After all the hard work it would have been nice to enjoy a drink with the Aussie and South African girls on the last night in particular. Some of our girls enjoy the odd wine, while I prefer a beer. Not that anyone touches alcohol during a tour, they are all too responsible to do something like that.

'You don't need to be drinking alcohol to enjoy yourself. Having a juice and a chat would have been good. It isn't only about mixing with the opposition. The after-match gives everyone an opportunity to thank the sponsors and others who have made the game possible. Netball New Zealand do that sort of thing really well, and on all my previous visits to Australia there had been social get-togethers.

'Perhaps it had something to do with the fact that we'd hammered them last time we met in South Africa and they were not as confident as in the past.'

That night Irene wrote in her diary, in capital letters, GOING HOME — CAN'T WAIT. The next morning she and the South Island contingent were out of the hotel by 6.30 a.m. to catch flights to Wellington and Christchurch respectively.

After being professional sportspeople for two weeks it was back to reality. Come Monday morning and Irene would be back in a classroom at Fergusson Intermediate, teaching children rather than taking netball lessons from Yvonne Willering. Still, it wasn't too bad. In a couple of weeks she would be back in camp again for a three-test series against England.

Chapter 17

England Outclassed

NETBALL NEW ZEALAND AND THE New Zealand Rugby Union have a common problem in that it is difficult for either to provide credible opposition for their respective national teams on a regular basis. Only Australia and South Africa, along with France on one of their good days, can extend the rugby All Blacks, especially on New Zealand soil. Netball is even worse off in that, since the massive upset of 1995 when South Africa destroyed the Silver Ferns' world championship dreams, Australia is the only country that can be counted on to give New Zealand a good game. Unfortunately, for several years it always seemed to be the Silver Ferns coming off second best in those trans-Tasman clashes.

Where both codes are fortunate is that New Zealanders don't mind watching one-sided games, providing their team is the one giving the opposition a pasting. They will turn up in the thousands to see the All Blacks post a cricket score against some hapless rugby nation, and it is the same in netball when the Silver Ferns play. Given England's recent record — though to be fair they'd got close to Australia on two occasions during a three-game series in England — no one really expected the Silver Ferns to be extended when England arrived in New Zealand for a three-test Fisher and Paykel series in July 2001. That didn't faze netball fans, and all three games — in Invercargill, Palmerston North and Hamilton — were sold out well in advance.

England were determined they would lack nothing in preparation for the games, spending ten days in Australia where they trained and played warm-up games against various selections, including teams made up of players on the fringe of the Australian national side.

There has been a concerted push in recent times to improve netball in England and the move paid early dividends when they finished third at the 1999 world tournament in Christchurch. Helped by lottery money, All England Netball employed Waimarama Taumaunu, a former Silver Fern who had successfully coached New Zealand club champions Pacific Island Church and provincial side Wellington, as its high performance director. In another innovative move Australian Julie Hoornweg had been given the reins of the national team and was attacking the job with relish.

While staying with her team in the Sydney suburb of Parramatta, Hoornweg was bullish about England's chances in the test series. No, she wasn't predicting they would beat the Silver Ferns, Hoornweg told a New Zealand reporter, but she felt they would give the world's second-best team a run for their money.

Both teams were based in beautiful Queenstown prior to the first test. Stunning scenery provided a dream backdrop as they completed preparations that included games against New Zealand A, and the writing was on the wall for the test outcome when New Zealand's second string beat the tourists. In many ways that was just what Irene and her team-mates didn't want. Once that happened they knew that nothing less than winning by a big margin would satisfy the Silver Ferns' fans.

Irene was looking forward to having Invercargill's notoriously parochial Stadium Southland crowd on her side for a change. She had played in the impressive facility a few weeks earlier for the Capital Shakers against the Southern Sting in a Coca-Cola Cup semi-final. The Shakers losing didn't provide pleasant memories, but the noise of the crowd and the way they roared their team on was especially vivid. That noise was still fresh in Irene's mind and after training at the match venue 24 hours before the game she told reporters how happy she was to be on the home side this time.

Coach Yvonne Willering was more relaxed than normal, even happily accepting that the Silver Ferns would start as hot favourites. England had stated that their visit to New Zealand was part of a long-term objective that included winning the 2003 world championship in Jamaica. Willering wasn't looking that far ahead. She wanted to win the series convincingly, saying the games were not about development and that the public were not concerned about the future, only about how the New Zealand team performed over the next seven days.

One of the biggest problems facing England was the intimidating atmosphere, which would be totally foreign to most of their players. It is an environment that had rattled New Zealand's top players during the past three years when visiting to play against Sting. Even England's final training session had been difficult, Hoornweg admitted, since her players weren't used to the presence of television cameras and press photographers.

Such potentially one-sided situations are difficult for those who are the hot favourites. Players and coaching staff make all the right comments about being just as focused and intense about playing a team such as England as they would be against world champions Australia. They might like to think they are in the same frame of mind but, human nature being what it is, that's extremely difficult to achieve. The two games against Australia in the tri-nations had put the Silver Ferns on a netballing high, both in winning and losing. Such was the intensity and physical nature of those clashes that they really would need to wind themselves up for England.

'I try to treat my preparation for every game with the same intensity, but inevitably there is a different atmosphere around you for certain occasions. Everyone might be laughing and joking on the way to a game, but depending on who you're playing, or the importance of it, there is a different edge to the laughter and banter.

'Going into the England game it was probably more relaxed than if we were up against Australia. That didn't mean we wanted a top performance any less. We were now back on home soil and there is nothing better than producing the goods in front of your own supporters.

'Of course we were confident of winning, but we wanted to play the best netball we could.'

That night in Invercargill the Silver Ferns did themselves proud as they racked up a record score in overwhelming England 78–30, and how the crowd loved it. New Zealand played with flair and speed as they ripped apart an England team that froze like rabbits caught in car headlights. The stars of the show were Donna Loffhagen and Irene van Dyk.

You wouldn't have put money on it 14 months earlier, but that night Loffhagen and van Dyk formed the most potent shooting combination New Zealand netball had seen. Between them the pair missed only eight shots. Irene started a little hesitantly but went on to fire in 51 goals from 55 attempts, while her shooting partner netted 27 from 31. Receiving high-quality passes from not only their traditional feeders such as Adine Harper, Temepara George and Jenny-May Coffin, but also defenders Lesley Nicol and Bernice Mene, the pair sank England with their relentless accuracy.

For 60 minutes the pair ran rampant round the English defensive circle, showing an almost telepathic understanding and amazing athleticism. How different the mood was to the previous year when Loffhagen had cried foul at van Dyk's switch from South Africa to New Zealand. After the mauling of England the pair were sole members of a mutual admiration society as reporters quizzed them about their stunning partnership. Loffhagen commented on how much Irene had improved from when she arrived in New Zealand, and that she was great on court. It made such a difference, she said, to know she could just turn, give Irene the ball and know it would result in a goal. 'I don't know how she shot some of those goals, but she managed it,' Loffhagen said.

She was talking about two amazing third-quarter goals Irene had netted when off-balance, one when she had both feet off the ground and was falling sideways. Those shots had the crowd in raptures, and as she bounded back to her feet after the most spectacular of the two Irene did something she had sworn would never happen on a netball court by giving Donna a high-five. It was a spontaneous gesture between two players who were having a ball.

The speed New Zealand played at completely stunned the English women. England captain Olivia Murphy described it as a shock to the system. Although England had played in Australia during their preparations for the series, Murphy said the speed of movement and the way the New Zealand players hit space was totally different to Australia's way of playing.

Irene understood how the England team were feeling. She had also been stunned by the Silver Ferns' speed when she was first selected for New Zealand and it had taken her time to adjust even in training.

'I'm sure that people, even the most fervent New Zealand supporters, don't realise just what fantastic athletes the Silver Ferns are. What happens on match day is no accident. They work exceptionally hard, not only when they're in camp but while at home.

'Obviously there are times when New Zealand players are training with their Coca-Cola Cup franchise or provincial sides, but even when there is no organised netball they are on programmes provided by the Ferns management that are strictly adhered to.

'It hasn't been easy with me being the only member of the Silver Ferns living in Wellington, but I have Christie for support and he has always been willing to work with me. I think he enjoys making me work hard.'

The second game in the series, at the Manawatu Sports Stadium, was won just as easily by New Zealand. The temperature outside the stadium was around zero, but inside the English found it too hot as the Palmerston North crowd made even more noise than Invercargill had managed four days earlier.

For 15 minutes it seemed as if England had improved dramatically and might even make a game of it. At the end of the first quarter they were level 12–12, but as the game progressed the visitors couldn't maintain the same intensity and gradually they lost their concentration, composure and structure. Yvonne Willering chopped and changed her combinations on court with 11 of the 12 players in the New Zealand squad getting court time, but they were still much too strong for England and at the final whistle had opened up a 65–29 advantage.

As the teams moved on to Hamilton for the final test New Zealand was enjoying a wonderful spell of winter weather that made for freezing night-time temperatures but beautiful cloudless skies during the day. On the morning of the Hamilton test the Silver Ferns were at the Mystery Creek Stadium before nine o'clock and to say they were cold would be an understatement. Despite there being two massive heaters at one end of the court they found it hard to concentrate in the intense cold.

It didn't really matter. The series was won and, barring an upset of Birmingham proportions, New Zealand would complete a whitewash in front of another sell-out crowd. That outcome duly eventuated, but England improved enough to make New Zealand work for their 69–47 win, though there was a feeling that, had it been necessary, the Ferns would have upped the tempo and been more convincing.

Too many cooks, they say, spoil the broth, and that was what happened with the Silver Ferns that night. Yvonne Willering rang the changes throughout the game, getting all 12 players on court, leading to a disjointed effort culminating, unthinkably, in England winning the last quarter 18–12 after being totally outclassed in the previous 11 quarters of the series.

One constant during New Zealand's domination of the series was Temepara George. The diminutive centre had grown in stature during the year with outstanding performances in the tri-nations as well as against England. George was always the smallest player on court, but no player had a bigger heart, greater elevation or more skilful hands.

During the England series New Zealand used three different shooting combinations involving Irene van Dyk, Donna Loffhagen and Belinda Colling, and all were successful thanks to the immaculate service they received from George, Adine Harper and Jenny-May Coffin. Each change of combination in the shooting circle brought new challenges for those charged with getting the ball to them and that was something George enjoyed.

For her part, Irene had never enjoyed such service and that made it easier for her to combine with whoever was her attacking partner. Irene had roomed with Temepara, or Bubbs as she's affectionately known throughout New Zealand netball, at Invercargill's Birchwood Manor motor inn. There is an infectious vitality about both women and plenty of laughing came from Unit 1.

After listening to how George juggles being mother to daughter Jusdean, who was seven at the time, son Erin-Wayne, three, Silver Fern netballer and an office administrator, not to mention planning her wedding to partner Wayne Clark, Irene had a new-found respect for the midcourter.

A footnote to the series came after the Hamilton test with Irene being voted the public's choice as player of the series. Momentarily lost for words when presented with the award, Irene eventually found her voice to thank those who had voted for her and said it made all the controversy she had been through worthwhile.

'That award meant so much to me because it signified the public had accepted me and that they believed I belonged in New Zealand. It made me feel like a real Kiwi girl.'

The award and its booty — a range of home appliances courtesy of sponsors Fisher and Paykel — was timely as Irene and Christie had just bought their first New Zealand home.

Now it was time to again say goodbye to her team-mates and return to Christie and Bianca and the children of Fergusson Intermediate. She would catch up with most of the team in September at the national provincial championships in Invercargill, and in October there was a three-test series against Australia in New Zealand to look forward to.

Chapter 18

Domestic Highs and Lows

NETBALL FOLLOWERS AND MEDIA ALIKE had eagerly anticipated the start of the 2000 Coca-Cola Cup, their appetites whetted by the addition of several world-class overseas players to Netball New Zealand's top domestic competition.

Overseas players were not new to the Coca-Cola Cup. The previous year England's Olivia Murphy and Amanda Newton had played for the Capital Shakers, while their compatriot Helen Lonsdale was in the Bay of Plenty Magic line-up. The trio returned to New Zealand with the England team for the Christchurch world championships later that year, with Murphy and Newton making further visits in 2000 and 2001 with the World Seven and England teams respectively. By 2001 Newton was England's defensive lynchpin and Murphy was captain, but both would admit that their first venture into New Zealand netball with the Shakers was something of a shock to the system.

The game was much faster and more physical than they were accustomed to back home. They knew, however, that the experience they gained in New Zealand would stand them in good stead when they went back to England to prepare for the world championship, and that was borne out by England finishing third in Christchurch.

There was to be a real international flavour to the 2000 Cup. Irene van Dyk had arrived in Wellington from South Africa to play for the Capital Shakers, where she was joined by Lonsdale. An IT consultant with Ernst and Young in London, Lonsdale, who had grown up in the small village of Chester-Le-Street near Newcastle in the north of England, had asked the company to transfer her to Auckland but they insisted she went to Wellington. As it turned out the switch suited Lonsdale just fine.

Auckland had a star import of its own in the form of Jamaica's 1.90 m (6 ft 3 in) goalshoot Elaine Davis, while Bay of Plenty Magic signed South African shooter Michelle Tupper and Canterbury Flames secured the services of Fijian captain and goalkeep Vilimaina Davu. Canterbury also had former Australian Lisa Gregory in midcourt, though Gregory had been in Christchurch since the Cup began and by then had New Zealand residency.

Southern Sting had signed Fiji's Bulou Rabuka. And the Northern Force were going to be coached for the first time by Australian Maria Lynch who brought midcourter Elise Middleton across the Tasman with her.

Davis, like van Dyk, had been one of the individual stars of the Christchurch world tournament. The third most prolific goal scorer at the world championship, Davis had shown she could compete with the toughest defences by being successful with 40 of her 42 goal attempts when up against New Zealand's Bernice Mene and Linda Vagana. Apart from Davis's on-court skills, the Auckland Diamonds franchise were hoping the Jamaican's profile would help swell what had been meagre attendances at home games the previous year.

Diamonds franchise sponsorship manager Julie Coney, who was also a television netball commentator, hoped that Davis' Jamaican flair and the high profile she had achieved after Christchurch would put bums on seats. Another reason for signing Davis was that Diamonds were competing for players with three other teams in their catchment area and shooters in particular were not easy to come by.

At the time Coney commented that the presence of international players gave the competition a boost, but warned that a balance had to be kept when franchises imported players from overseas.

'We need to be careful,' she said. 'The idea of the competition was to foster our players to international level, so we don't want too many from outside. One import per team is probably enough, and we need to ensure that the players we are bringing in are better than the ones already here.'

Not everyone thought overseas stars were a good idea. But of the nine teams in the Cup only the Manawatu–Taranaki based Western Flyers, Counties-Manukau Thames Valley and the Otago Rebels were to field all-New Zealand born teams.

Flyers coach Ivy Topping questioned the impact overseas players would have on New Zealand netball, saying that as she understood it the competition was started so players could be developed for the Silver Ferns. She pointed to the goalshoot position in particular, where van Dyk, Davis and Tupper would play. 'Take one or two goalshoots for the Silver Ferns and one or two for the under-21s and it's not leaving much development for up-and-coming players in that position.'

Those who are sport's lifeblood, the fans, had no such qualms, giving imports the seal of approval by turning up in droves all over the country. Nowhere was that upsurge in interest more apparent than in

Wellington. At the first home game, against Cometz, the organisers had to close the doors while fans were still trying to get inside where all the seats were taken and every bit of standing room used. This despite the fact that the Shakers were playing home games at Taita's Walter Nash Stadium, at the time as unappetising a venue as you could find and 18 kilometres from Wellington's city centre. It was a problem they'd never before encountered, and was reward for the initiative shown by Kathy Doyle and Mary-Anne Edwards in pursuing Irene van Dyk. When the South African star was introduced the crowd almost lifted the roof with their cheers.

For her part, Irene had taken time to come to terms with the training the Shakers underwent, which was in marked contrast to anything she had encountered before. The commitment, quality and intensity of training under Shakers coach Lois Muir, assistant coach Tanya Cox and fitness trainer Barbara Beable took Irene's breath away. The quality of play produced at Shakers training was superior to that displayed during games at South Africa's national championships.

The only hard training Irene had done was with the Proteas and at the Bellerive club in Cape Town. The common denominator in those two was demanding coach Marlene Wagner. In the main, netball training in South Africa had been very low key with no fitness work. There was almost a feeling of 'who wants to get tired practising netball?', so imagine Irene's surprise when she received a telephone call from Lois Muir in December 1999 checking to see if she was following the training programme that had been sent to her.

'I didn't have the guts to tell Lois that I couldn't even understand what the programme was all about. I didn't have a clue what a shuttle was and felt a little ashamed about it. I tried to make up for not doing what I was supposed to by running a lot but I know now it wasn't the same.

'When I got to Shakers training I noticed that some players were questioning Barb about parts of the programme, so I eventually plucked up the courage to tell Barb I didn't understand any of it. She was great and sat down with me to explain what I had to do.'

Watching the skills of those around her, Irene was convinced the Shakers would win the Coca-Cola Cup. Surely there was no better team in the competition? The first hint that Irene was naive in thinking that way came in the Shakers' opening warm-up game against the Western Flyers in Palmerston North. The Shakers sneaked home 73–72 in a 75-minute game, though they were missing key players Amanda Dunlop and Jodi Te Huna.

'That was a wake-up call for me and brought home just what a spread of netball talent there is in New Zealand. I didn't realise the domestic competition would be so intense. For me every game was like a test match. There was the same anxiousness waiting for the game to start as I had felt with South Africa before an international.

'I suppose that's understandable in that when you're playing against Bernice Mene, as I did in my first Coca-Cola Cup game for Shakers, you're up against one of the world's best players. Every week there is a Silver Fern in the opposition. They have great skill and play with such passion.

'I was stunned. It was like "Wow" as I tried to take it all in. No team is a pushover. On any day the supposedly weakest team in the competition can upset the strongest. You have to prepare for every game as if it is the final.

'Making me even more confident about the Shakers' chances before the competition began was having Noels [Noeline Taurua] as our captain. Her leadership was fantastic. There is a calmness about Noels no matter what's happening. Bernie has that same quality when she's captaining New Zealand, always calm and collected, never panicking. That was Noels as well.'

Between the Palmerston North hit out and their opening game, against defending champion Southern Sting in the white-hot atmosphere of Invercargill's Stadium Southland, Irene and her team-mates had a weekend in Auckland where they beat Cometz and Auckland Diamonds despite being described by Muir as 'overwound clockwork toys'. Muir explained that her players had been putting so much effort into training that they were excited at actually playing games, hence the over-eagerness.

Suddenly pre-season was over. The Shakers were on their way to Invercargill for their first Cup game. Irene would have loved to have started her Shakers' career with a win but it wasn't to be, despite a fine shooting performance that saw her sink 48 goals from 51 attempts. Unfortunately for the Shakers, New Zealand goalshoot Donna Loffhagen, playing goal attack, was just as impressive at the other end of the court, netting 30 from 32 and being ably assisted by Janine Topia who scored 35 goals in Sting's 65–56 win.

Next up for Shakers was a home game against Cometz and, thanks to a vintage performance from Noeline Taurua, the Wellington team coasted to a 56–43 win before a delighted capacity crowd. The winning feeling didn't last long as Shakers headed back south to Dunedin five days later where they were beaten 72–68 by Otago Rebels. Two losses from three games meant the Shakers faced a must-win situation against Canterbury Flames at Taita two days later.

Irene was up against a marker of the same height as herself in Vilimaina

Davu and the pair had an absorbing physical battle that moved one spectator to liken it to 'a rumble in the jungle'. At three-quarter time Flames led by three goals, but in the final quarter it was Irene, who had been allowed to put up only six shots in the third quarter, who kept her nerve, while at the other end the Canterbury shooters were losing theirs. It meant the Shakers were able to sneak a 46–44 win.

When North Shore's unbeaten Force arrived at Walter Nash Stadium two weeks later the Shakers were in third place, one spot behind Force, and Irene would be up against an in-form Linda Vagana. The furore over whether she should be chosen to play for New Zealand was just getting into full swing at that stage, but she put that to one side with another top-class shooting display and 45 goals in a 57–51 win that brought the house down. Shakers fans were in no doubt about whether Yvonne Willering should select her.

Two days later the Shakers made it a successful weekend by hammering the Western Flyers 71–49 in New Plymouth with what Muir described as a brilliant performance, and then moved into second place with a hard-fought 55–49 home win over Magic the following weekend.

Looking on track to host a semi-final at Walter Nash, a stadium visiting teams were finding difficult because of its cramped nature and the closeness of the spectators, the Shakers were in a confident mood as they went to Auckland for their final round-robin game against Diamonds. Their confidence was misplaced as the Wellington team turned in a shocker, losing 67–56. Coach Muir said it was a bad day at the office. Captain Taurua said it was awful. Defender Debbie Matoe described it as embarrassing. The Shakers were unfortunate to come up against Diamonds on the night when the Aucklanders finally played to their potential, but they had to admit there was no excuse for some of the sloppy play that led to their downfall.

It had been billed as a battle of the shooters, with Irene at one end of the court and Elaine Davis at the other. On the night Elaine (54 from 58) probably just shaded Irene (40 from 44) with her overall game, but the telling statistic was the 80 shots at goal by Diamonds in comparison with the Shakers' 61. That showed how much possession the Shakers turned over.

The debacle meant the Shakers had to play their semi-final against Canterbury Flames in Christchurch, and they literally threw away their Coca-Cola Cup final chances when they were beaten 50–35 by a fired-up Flames at Cowles Stadium. Such was Canterbury's defensive screen that Irene put up only 30 shots, often having to shoot from the edge of the circle, and, uncharacteristically, she missed 6.

Making the afternoon more miserable was the fact that it was Lois Muir's last game as Shakers' coach and her team had been desperate to ensure she bowed out in a cup final rather than a semi-final.

Southern Sting predictably beat Canterbury Flames in the final, and while it had been disappointing for the Capital Shakers not to be part of the big day, a top-four placing wasn't to be sneezed at. There was also the Smokefree National Provincial Championships at Hamilton's Mystery Creek to look forward to where, hopefully, a good Wellington performance would provide some compensation for not winning the Cup. Irene was looking forward to her first national tournament.

Wellington had performed poorly at the 1999 national tournament in Palmerston North, but there were extenuating circumstances in that the players were devastated by the sudden death early in the tournament of Leilani Read, a former Wellington representative who had originally been chosen for the tournament but had to pull out. Most of those in the 1999 Wellington team had played with the always-smiling Leilani throughout their careers and the tragedy took its toll on them.

There were no such excuses going into the 2000 tournament, with many of those who had performed creditably in the Coca-Cola Cup in the team. They also had a new coach in Kaye Johnson, who had stepped into the representative breech after Lois Muir decided it was time to leave Wellington.

Besides coaching netball, Johnson, a teacher at Wellington Girls' College, has a passion for rugby and she tried to freshen up training sessions by using innovative drills adapted from the oval ball game. At one point Johnson had her players passing the ball with their eyes closed, a technique tried by former All Blacks coach Laurie Mains. The theory, according to Johnson, was that it made the players concentrate. 'And if they can do it with their eyes shut — and they could — then they should be able to do it better with them open.'

Irene and her team-mates were in good heart on their arrival in Hamilton, but it didn't take long for their optimism to be severely tested. Wellington's first-round opponents were strongly fancied Waikato and it wasn't only Wellington's pride that was wounded as they got off to the worst possible start with Waikato giving them a 70–46 hiding.

Captain Pelesa Semu had been under an injury cloud leading up to the tournament after tearing a calf muscle four weeks earlier, and a recurrence of the injury nine minutes into the second quarter meant the skipper wouldn't play again during the championship. Kathy Newman took over the captaincy and the way things were developing you had to feel sorry for her. Nothing was going right, and Wellington's dream of national provincial glory began turning into the nightmare prospect of relegation when they lost their second game 76–64 to Manukau.

There was better news the following day when Wellington, fired up by a newspaper article suggesting the midcourt was the weak link and that the Capital Shakers would need to look elsewhere for talent the following year, scored a 60–57 win over Manawatu. Doom and gloom descended on the camp again the next day with Wellington suffering a humiliating 72–37 loss to Southland that included Irene being subbed for the last 15 minutes when Johnson decided there was no way of pulling back a 17-goal deficit.

If Wellington supporters thought things couldn't get any worse they were wrong. A 61–51 loss to Auckland/Waitakere plunged the team into a relegation play-off with Manawatu on the final day. Cellphones were busy as Wellington netball fans who hadn't made the journey north tried to keep in touch with what was happening in what was arguably the most important game the province had ever played. What they heard wasn't good. Down 6–1 before the crowd had time to settle into their seats, Wellington were always playing catch up. At one point in the second quarter they trailed by 15 goals before showing tremendous character in fighting back to draw level at 57–57 with 20 seconds left and the ball in their possession at an injury break.

With nerves frayed to breaking point, Johnson impressed on her players the need to keep possession but, inevitably given the way the week had gone, it was given away and Manawatu got the two-goal margin extra-time demands.

Perhaps the only time Wellington had cause to smile during the tournament was when Irene dyed her blonde hair purple, and it was soon obvious that it isn't just gentlemen who prefer blondes. It seemed netball watchers do as well. From the moment she walked into the Mystery Creek Stadium she was the topic of conversation, and the focus of cameras. While her new look gained the approval of some, others said they definitely preferred the original, and the change confused one schoolgirl who wanted to know why Irene van Dyk wasn't playing.

'I just wanted to do something outrageous,' Irene told reporters, roaring with laughter. 'I've told Christie that I've coloured my hair. I just haven't told him what colour.' Christie saw a photograph of his new-look wife in the next morning's newspapers and wasn't impressed.

Looking back on the tournament the only word Irene can find to describe it is 'disastrous'. 'There was nothing wrong with the quality of player we took to Hamilton. Most of them were from the Shakers and that team had reached the Coca-Cola Cup semi-finals.

'Right from the start of the tournament there was a flat feeling about the whole thing. There was no intensity and a lack of motivation to make the semi-finals and final our target. It was almost as if we were playing netball for the sake of it. With the Shakers, if we got behind everyone would pull together and get back into the game. That didn't happen with Wellington. We had no guts. We would fall behind and then just let it go.

'I am not going to make excuses for the players; I don't think some of them were honest with themselves. You know when you've had a bad game, though some didn't admit it and neither did those running the team. I would come off court disappointed because I hadn't played well and be told that I did OK. That was a big part of the problem. No one was telling us where we were going wrong so therefore they weren't telling us how to fix it.

'It doesn't matter who you are, there is always room for improvement. If a coach keeps telling you things about your game it makes you think because you don't want to keep making the same mistakes over and over. It is really hard when you know you're doing things wrong and no one is telling you. A player can't pinpoint what is going wrong with her game while playing. You need the coach and your team-mates to be honest and talk about it.

'There was friction between some of the players, coach and manager, which doesn't help, and there seemed to be problems between those running the team and netball officials back in Wellington. That came about after the article that some people said suggested we had a weak midcourt was published in Wellington. Team management should never have made an issue of it. That way the players wouldn't have known anything about it.

'Instead of ignoring it, the article was blown up and pinned on the wall so everyone could read it. That was unnecessary and the midcourters were really upset. No one likes to be told they're not up to it, especially during a tournament.

'I believe the whole thing was taken out of context; that Tanya Cox wasn't saying the players were no good. I tried to ignore it. My attitude was that if we were doing our job it wouldn't have come to that. That's what was most annoying. We had the players, make no mistake, but we weren't turning it on and that comes back to motivation. At least for the relegation game everyone was fired up. The night before everyone decided losing wasn't an option; that wasn't something we were even going to consider. Wellington had never been relegated and we didn't want to be the ones to make that type of history. I suppose having that on our minds made everyone too anxious, too eager.

'It was a terrible feeling at the end. No one knew where to look or what to do. Kaye was more devastated than any of us, if that was possible. There isn't a lot of drinking in netball, but that night there was. We started in the room of Matt Wenham, our physio, because he had a guitar and then everyone went out. There were quite a few sore heads in the morning.'

When the 2001 Coca-Cola Cup came round Irene was more attuned to the New Zealand domestic game, not that the intervening 12 months had made her any less optimistic. Despite the heavy 1999 semi-final loss to Flames, and Wellington's subsequent awful performance at the national provincial championship, Irene still fancied the Shakers' chances of winning the Cup.

Former Silver Fern Tanya Dearns (née Cox) had taken over the coaching reins from Lois Muir and Irene was enjoying the change of style. Playing for Lois Muir had been a tremendous learning experience for Irene and had helped her become a better all-round player than she was while playing for South Africa. Yvonne Willering had also had a big impact on her with the New Zealand team. Now she had another teacher, and Irene loves soaking up the netball knowledge different coaching methods provide.

'Tanya talks less than Auntie Lois. She shows you what she wants rather than tells you. During my first Coca-Cola Cup campaign Tanya was in the background, but she still did a lot of good things and told it as it was, which is one of the things I really admire about her.

'If you're making a mess of something she will tell you in plain language and then help you put it right. I believe Tanya has grown up in her coaching and she did a good job with the Shakers. She's still so young that the players can relate to her, but she manages to divorce herself from the players when it is necessary.'

One of the first things Dearns did was impress on goal attack Jodi Te Huna that she didn't want Irene having to put up all the shots, and the under-21 international responded positively by going away and working on her shooting. The results were evident in an opening game against Otago Rebels, played at the Shakers' new home in Wellington city's modern Queen's Wharf Events Centre, which is as bright and airy as Walter Nash Stadium was dark and dismal.

One of the highlights of that first game was Jodi netting 15 of the team's goals in a 50–44 win and working well in tandem with Irene. A week later the Shakers scraped through 73–71 against Western Flyers in controversial circumstances, with some quick thinking by centre Frances

Solia taking advantage of a hesitant umpire to turn the game the Shakers' way in a frenetic finish.

Next up for the Capital Shakers were the Canterbury Flames, with the game to be played in the same Christchurch stadium where the Shakers had meekly surrendered in the semi-final the previous year. It was much closer this time, 57–55, but the Flames triumphed again.

While there were highs and lows for the Shakers during the campaign, the biggest high was undoubtedly beating defending champions Sting 51–48 at the Events Centre. Roared on by a sell-out crowd of more than three thousand, the Shakers showed what they were capable of with a superb performance to down a Sting team boasting four Silver Ferns and a South African international.

'The atmosphere was as tense as an international and the buzz we got from the game was unbelievable. The Sting are fortunate in that they have great support and a fine stadium in Invercargill, and after what happened that day in Wellington I can understand why they love playing at home so much. Our crowd was worth at least five goals to us. The noise was constant and knowing that they were all cheering for us made it all the more exciting.

'Later on came the low point of the competition when we were beaten by Force, but that's what makes the Coca-Cola Cup so interesting. Nothing can be taken for granted. On any given day any team can win.'

The game against Force was an embarrassing 64–52 loss that meant Shakers had to beat Waikato-Bay of Plenty Magic in Hamilton to reach the semi-finals. That Saturday night in Hamilton provided one of the closest, and most dramatic, finishes of the season as the Shakers edged out Magic 55–54, thanks to the ice-cool nerve of Irene van Dyk.

Trailing for most of the game, at one point by 8 goals and by 6 going into the final quarter, the Shakers turned it around to lead 54–52 in the dying moments. That was when, as had happened several times during the competition, a controversial umpiring decision threatened to decide the game. A Magic goal reduced the deficit to one and umpire Justine Bourne stunned the Shakers by cancelling their centre pass and giving the ball to Magic just outside the circle because of alleged time wasting by Shakers goalkeep Lisa Bogiwalu. Why Bogiwalu would have wanted to waste time when it was her team's centre pass and the opportunity to seal the game with seconds remaining is a mystery.

The decision incensed coach Tanya Dearns, who kicked over a chair after telling the official what she thought. When Magic converted the gift penalty to draw level, the Shakers, who needed a win to progress to the semi-finals, had six seconds to rectify the situation. As Jodi Te Huna lofted a long pass towards Irene from the centre pass everyone in the stadium held their breath and Irene knew what was at stake as the ball flew towards her.

'I thought, "If you miss this ball the season is over," and I was so pleased to get my hands around it and hold on. But then with the crowd going ballistic I couldn't hear what the umpire was saying even though she was right beside me. I didn't know the other umpire was trying to say time was up. When I realised it was a penalty I knew what had to happen and, thankfully, it went in.'

Failure to beat lower-ranked teams by bigger margins cost Shakers any chance they had of finishing higher than fourth, and that meant a semi-final trip to the dreaded Stadium Southland to play top qualifiers and champions, Southern Sting. As had happened the previous year the Shakers froze on the big occasion, going down 60–49 to Sting who went on to again beat Canterbury Flames in the final.

There is little doubt that the intimidating atmosphere got to the Shakers players, with both Irene and coach Tanya Dearns believing the Invercargill crowd was worth ten goals to their team.

Two Coca-Cola Cups had brought two semi-finals for Irene; maybe it would be third time lucky next year. But before that there was the Smokefree national tournament in, of all places, Invercargill, which was definitely not a favourite venue for most New Zealand netballers.

Wellington, relegated 12 months earlier, were back in the first division thanks to a change of format. You will never get netball officials to admit that a different format was adopted to enable Wellington, traditionally one of the strongest netball areas, to bounce back, but many believed that was the case.

Leading into the tournament there was a much better feeling in the Wellington team than there had been 12 months earlier, something Irene put down to new coach Gail Parata and a revamped management team. A gifted player who had only retired after the Shakers' semi-final loss, Parata might have been a newcomer to coaching at representative level but she had been active in a player-coaching role with perennial Wellington champions Pacific Island Church in recent seasons. If Wellington didn't win the national title it wouldn't be for a lack of effort or preparation on Parata's part. Irene, for one, had never worked with a coach who was better prepared.

Once the squad was selected every Wellington player was given an immaculate dossier by Parata detailing every training session and what was expected from them. During the tournament Parata would spend her evenings writing a coaching assessment of each individual, while in turn each player had to record a self-assessment detailing what she felt could have been done better, along with what had been satisfactory.

'Gail put so much into it. No coach will provide better feedback than Gail did. She was never negative, but at the same time she was honest in her assessments. That's something that had been missing the previous year.

'She had also put a top-class management team in place. Our manager, Ngahiwi Meroiti, also umpires and she was invaluable in telling us where we were going wrong when decisions were going against us. Gail's mum Lorna was our cook for the week, and I can assure you we were well looked after.

'Much of the personnel was the same as 12 months earlier and we talked about what had happened then but no one could really explain why things had gone so badly. What we did come up with collectively was that we'd not been hungry enough or focused enough, and there hadn't been a good feel about the team.

'There was no chance of that happening with the team that went to Invercargill. While we concentrated on the job in hand at training and games, we also had great fun. In our free time we would play games such as charades and pass the parcel. There was a treasure hunt with lollies hidden in trees and Jodi [Te Huna] organised a surprise belated party for Froggy [Frances Solia] who had had a birthday the previous week. That might all sound trivial but it meant we didn't waste time being idle and irritating others around us. Having fun makes you play better and we really did feel like a real team this time.

'Unfortunately we didn't do as well as I thought we would by finishing fifth, but it could have been different had we played Waikato and Southland, who we lost to, later in the week instead of early on. Gail was convinced that it would come down to shooting and said that if we had the best shooting stats then we would win. It didn't turn out like that. Against Southland I shot 54 from 55, 98 per cent, while Jodi Te Huna and Jo Haanstra, who shared goal attack, both shot 100 per cent.

'Gail had to reassess her theory because the defenders didn't have enough discipline. They gave the Southland shooters too many second shots through contacts or obstruction. Those unnecessary mistakes meant the shooters had free shots with no defenders closing them down. In saying that I am not having a go at the defenders. We were in it as a team, but Gail was honest in her assessment of why we lost that game because we couldn't have shot any better.

'That wasn't the case against Auckland, even though we won the game comfortably. My shooting percentage was only 89 per cent and I missed too many shots unnecessarily. I was shooting too quickly before getting balanced, or trying to shoot while I was falling out of court, which was silly.

'It was after we beat Auckland that someone began spreading the word that I was off my game, and that I wasn't going to have a good tournament. I don't know why another player would do that, but people were quick to tell me what was being said. I know it only made me more determined to do well and my stats were fine after that. So, to whoever started the rumour — thanks, you helped me get my mind back on the job, though I am sure that wasn't the intention.'

With Stadium Southland sold out for the final, the Wellington players watched Canterbury pip Waikato for the title in a tense finish.

'The final was great. It was one of the most tense netball games I have seen and while my heart was with Waikato, probably because Canterbury had most of the big names, I thoroughly enjoyed it. We had bets among ourselves on who would win and the margin and the noise from our hotel room probably rivalled that at the stadium. Nikki Poka got it spot on by picking Canterbury to win by two.'

That was it for the domestic season, but the biggest test of all was still to come — a three-test Fisher and Paykel series against Australia in New Zealand.

Chapter 19

The Players

IT IS ONLY NATURAL FOR ANY TOP sportsperson to enjoy reading and hearing from media and the public that they are among the top echelon of those who play their chosen code. The most satisfying praise, however, is that which emanates from their peers.

Those who play the game at the highest level are best qualified to judge a player's contribution to the sport, be they team-mates or opponents. They are the ones who look into the eyes of opponents at close quarters in the heat of battle and can judge what they see, or know that the team-mate alongside them has the inner strength, or bottle as some sportspeople prefer to call that indefinable quality, to keep going when they are up against the odds.

In all team sports it is players, not coaches, media or supporters, who recognise those who have the stomach for a fight as well as having the skills that have taken them to the top. There are some flashy players with lovely skills who stand out to those watching from the sideline and stands, but when the going gets tough they, in player's parlance, hide. They are still out there on court or field, but when their team is on the back foot they are no longer demanding the ball or inspiring those alongside to lift their game.

Netball has produced sporting gladiators, the rocks upon which the foundations for successful teams are laid, as much as any other sporting code. Former Silver Fern Sandra Edge, an inspirational captain herself, once said of Australia's Anne Sergeant: 'She had a way of carrying herself, a sort of presence, that ate into your confidence.'

Vicki Wilson took over as Australian intimidator from Sergeant at the attacking end of the court, while Liz Ellis and Kathryn Harby-Williams have carried on from where successful captain and goalkeep Michelle Fielke reigned supreme in defence.

New Zealand has over the years had the likes of Waimarama Taumaunu, Joan Harnett, Lyn Parker, Tracey Fear, Leigh Gibbs, Margharet Matenga, Julie Townsend, Yvonne Willering, and more recently, and from the recent crop of Silver Ferns, captain Bernice Mene leading the charge.

Jamaica has had the threat of goalshoot Patricia McDonald and the leadership of Connie Francis, while no one served England better than Kendra Slawinski, who made her senior England debut against New Zealand in 1982 and was a regular till retiring after the 1995 world championships in Birmingham. A physical education teacher, Slawinski moved into coaching before taking a year off to spend more time with her husband Tim and son Ben.

England was the first country to invite South Africa to visit when they were re-admitted to international play in 1994. With South Africa being off the scene for so long England were expected to be too strong for the visitors, but it didn't work out that way, with South Africa winning the series 5–0 and Slawinski getting her first look at Irene van Dyk.

'I wish she had stayed at home,' Slawinski says with a a laugh as she recalls the series. 'Because South Africa had been out of the mainstream for so long we were probably a bit too confident and they took us by surprise with their fitness and athleticism. They also had Irene who wasn't only very tall, but athletic and had superb hands. Her hands reminded me of Margharet Matenga.

'We were used to coming up against teams with two mobile shooters and now we had a completely different scenario to contend with. The most frustrating part was that we knew where the ball was going but couldn't get it. I think I had a crick in my neck after the first game from turning to watch it sail overhead. Inevitably once the ball landed in Irene's hands she slotted the goal.'

In an effort to negate Irene, England coach Liz Broomhead switched Slawinski from goal defence to goalkeep for the Wembley test, and for a while the tactic worked.

'Liz felt we needed someone to get in Irene's face and put her off. Originally my switch was only going to be for the first 15 minutes but at the end of the first quarter Liz said I was doing so well that we would stay with it.

'It had worked in that we were holding them at 11–11, we were getting some ball and I had managed to force Irene away from the posts. Of course Marlene Wagner was too good a coach to let things go on that way, and Irene knew she had to play differently. She adapted quickly and soon she was slotting the goals again and we were on the way to another loss.

'Irene is so classy. There appears to be an imaginary link between the post and her fingertips, and I can see why teams now have problems containing the Silver Ferns when you have a combination like Donna Loffhagen and Irene in the circle.'

If Irene's athleticism and shooting ability took Slawinski by surprise, so did her on-court demeanour. Like Irene's play, it was something the English defender hadn't encountered before.

'She was so nice you sort of wondered if Irene was for real. She would apologise for bumping into you and would clap when *we* scored a goal. When she scored Irene would immediately turn round and start encouraging her team-mates.

'Irene is for real though, and there is an element about her you can't help but like, even when she's scoring the goals that are beating you. As a defender it helps if you can dislike the player you're marking. With Irene that isn't possible.'

Slawinski is not among those who were against Irene moving to New Zealand and playing for the Silver Ferns — even though it was for lifestyle reasons — because it would weaken South African netball further.

'I am pleased she moved because she has improved so much and added new dimensions to her game. Had she continued to play for South Africa we would have missed the intelligence and flair she now plays with.'

Australian defenders Kathryn Harby-Williams (formerly Kathryn Harby) and Liz Ellis, captain and vice-captain respectively, are two players who have had to contend with the new-look Irene van Dyk since she swapped the dark green uniform for black. Both uncompromising in their approach, Harby-Williams and Ellis are the defensive rocks on which most international attacks have foundered in recent years. Harby-Williams also gives Australia an alternative attacking option with the bullet-like one-arm passes she fires down court at every opportunity.

Harby-Williams was as bemused as Slawinski when she first encountered Irene, looking on in disbelief as the South African shooter applauded goals at both ends of court.

'Irene is such a lovely person, but you just don't do that at international level. I am not surprised that Yvonne Willering has knocked that out of her game since she became a New Zealand player.

'The first time I saw Irene I thought she was an incredible player. She dominated the South African team because most of their players' skills weren't refined; I always felt she would be really outstanding in a better team where the players around her had superior skills to those of the South Africans.

'She's so coordinated for someone so tall. She has an accurate shot, which is her major strength, and movement has been added to her game. When the ball reaches Irene you can usually bet on a goal being scored, but if she does miss then the challenge for a defender is to stop her getting the rebound.'

During the 2001 tri-series in Australia Harby-Williams was caught up in the debate about whether Irene should be allowed to represent New Zealand at the 2002 Commonwealth Games, since it appeared she didn't qualify unless concessions were made. While not wanting to pass the buck, Australian players give the impression that the controversy was fuelled by administrators rather than players. When Irene first moved to New Zealand, Harby-Williams was among those who wished her well and thought the switch would be good for player and country. Acknowledging that she had heard rumours that Irene was going to play for Queensland after the 1995 world championships, Harby-Williams says Australian netball would have been unlikely to turn her away had she made that move and settled in Australia.

As for playing for the Silver Ferns, Harby-Williams says that from a player's point of view it didn't matter who was in the opposition. She was prepared to play New Zealand any time, with or without Irene van Dyk in the line-up.

Liz Ellis wasn't quite as accommodating about the decision to allow Irene to be available for the Kuala Lumpur Games. At one point she described it on Australian television as disgusting.

Ellis stresses this was nothing personal against someone she has a lot of time for and enjoys playing against. In fact, Ellis has said she didn't want Netball Australia to lodge a protest against Irene being allowed to take part in the Commonwealth Games. That's an interesting comment when you consider Netball Australia has always denied they were the ones behind attempts to close the door on Irene, insisting South Africa initiated it.

'What annoyed me most was the ridicule netball attracted through the looseness of its international rules. It would be farcical if Irene ever went back to South Africa and started playing for the Proteas again. I'm not saying that would happen, but under the rules it is a possibility and that can't be right,' Ellis says.

'Irene has perfectly good reasons for making her home in New Zealand and we accepted that she was qualified under international rules to play for the Silver Ferns. However, those rules didn't apply for the Commonwealth Games and I thought it was a shame that the rules were bent.

'The same applied to Vili Davu. Vili was the backbone of the Fijian team before moving to New Zealand for lifestyle opportunities, as Irene did, but it would have been great had she played for Canterbury in the Coca-Cola Cup and gone back to Fiji for international netball. Having said that, you can't blame either player for taking advantage of what are silly rules.'

Ellis first came up against Irene at the beginning of 1995, though she had seen video footage of her playing for South Africa against England the previous year.

'I was impressed with Irene from the start because, without being disrespectful, South Africa weren't quite up to international standard when they came back on the scene. It was like they were in a time warp, but not Irene. The way she played it was like she had been playing elsewhere while South Africa was in isolation.

'At six foot I feel short when it comes to international netball, but Irene was the first really, really tall shooter I had to contend with and had to make up for the height difference with my jumping ability.

'I found Irene incredibly different to other opponents in that she was so sporting. She seemed to spend more time clapping Vicki Wilson's goals for Australia than I did!

'I like to play aggressively and Irene is getting more aggressive all the time since moving to New Zealand. She's a tougher opponent physically than she was when playing for South Africa, and having good players around her has improved her no end. She's now an important part of a team, whereas with South Africa she was the sole focus and you could concentrate on closing her down

'Irene has taken over Vicki Wilson's mantle as the world's best shooter. While I played for Australia alongside Vicki I also played against her in our domestic competition and, as with Irene now, you realise you have to be at your best, both physically and mentally, against either of them or you could end up looking like a dummy.

'While Irene is every goalkeepers' nightmare — a 6 ft 4 in giant who can run and has good hands — I enjoy playing against her because no matter how physical it gets on court she's always ready for a beer and a laugh afterwards.

'I agree with Irene that it is a real shame there are not enough after-match functions these days. I am not advocating players getting over-familiar, but it is enjoyable to spend a few minutes in a social atmosphere with those you have been battling with on court. It gives you an opportunity to meet the person, rather than the player.

'Those who were fortunate enough to be part of the World team that played in New Zealand found that the concept broke down the barriers that existed between players from different countries. For a start the World team girls realised Kathy and I weren't ogres after all!'

Going into the 1995 world championships Australia's Vicki Wilson was undoubtedly the world's top shooter. It was a tragedy for Wilson that she sustained a serious knee injury in the vital game against New

Zealand that not only kept her out of the rest of the tournament, but also meant she was missing from netball for some time. Wilson has vivid memories of South Africa's shock win over New Zealand in Birmingham.

'It was an unbelievable game to watch and we couldn't comprehend what was happening. It meant that the game against New Zealand 24 hours later took on a completely different complexion. Whoever lost that game would be out of the running for a place in the final. Normally we go out for a team dinner before playing the Silver Ferns but that had to go because we had to adjust everything. That almost led to a team blue, but we got the result we needed the next day.'

South Africa beating New Zealand meant they were Australia's final opponents, rather than the Silver Ferns as anticipated, and it turned into a cakewalk for the defending champions.

'South Africa, just back in international netball, didn't know how to utilise Irene,' Wilson says. 'We worked on the theory that the ball would be sprayed if we put them under pressure, and that's what happened.

'When I first saw Irene I thought, "We have got our hands full now." Irene is an ideal spearhead. She's tall, athletic, very accurate and has no fear of the post. The latter is such an important part of a shooter's make-up because when the shooter gets the ball the game stops and all eyes are on her. You're alone with everyone depending on you. That's why you have to focus every second and just try to do your job. Thinking about it too much once the ball is in your hands can paralyse you.

'It can be exceptionally tough, especially at the top level where so much is at stake, but it is character building and that's what makes true champions. Our game plan altered drastically when Irene came into the equation and I don't think anyone has had such an impact before. Our defenders had to have the utmost faith in each other and Simone McKinnis [wing defence] had to work her butt off because we recognised that we had to limit the amount of ball Irene got. Not only is she skilful, she also has the ability to focus for the whole hour. Competing against such a quality player is challenging and exciting.

'It was easier to mark Irene when she was playing for South Africa because a lack of speed within their team meant opposing defences had time to close her down. With the Silver Ferns she's getting good coaching and is surrounded by quality players, which means the ball gets to her much quicker and that makes it hard for defenders.

'When she came onto the international scene there was an innocence about Irene that was quite special and she has never lost it. She's a great role model for young netballers.'

While New Zealand netball fans, particularly those in Wellington, welcomed Irene playing for the Capital Shakers in the Coca-Cola Cup, one person who didn't share their enthusiasm was young Shakers shooter Jodi Te Huna.

Te Huna had been plucked from the obscurity of Wanganui netball by Shakers coach Lois Muir when the Coca-Cola Cup began in 1998 and given the opportunity to play in New Zealand's premier competition. It was a challenge the youngster, who was still at school, relished and she quickly settled into the side. It was a big adventure for Te Huna, who had to move out of the family home and live in Wellington where she enrolled at Newlands College. Making it enjoyable was the fact that in netball everything appeared to be coming easily for her. Then, before the 2000 season, Te Huna heard that Irene van Dyk, the South African super-shooter, was joining the Shakers and she didn't need reminding that the international star played the same position as her.

'It was a bit of a worry all right,' Te Huna says of Irene's pending arrival. 'I didn't play any other position but shooter and that was the only position Irene played. She was the best shooter in the world whereas I was just starting out. It didn't take too much working out who would be starting the games.

'Lois Muir sat me down and talked me through what was happening. She explained to me that I needed to be able to play another position if I wanted to keep progressing and achieve my goal of playing for New Zealand. That was fine, but everything had been going my way since Lois chose me following a Shakers trial. Up to then, everyone had been fitting in with me, but now it was all going to change and I would be warming the bench. I would ask myself why had she chosen to come to the Shakers. If she was coming to New Zealand why couldn't she go to another franchise?

'I was ready not to like her, but once you meet Irene that's impossible because she's such a neat person. That didn't help how I was feeling about my netball though. That first season with Irene in the team was very hard for me. I had been taken out of my comfort zone and I didn't enjoy it. If I'm honest I probably sulked a bit and that didn't help my game.

'Despite all that I'm now proud that I stuck at it. During Irene's second season I was playing goal attack alongside her and loving every minute. When you think about it, how many people get the opportunity to work with the world's best?'

It was in that year that Te Huna, a New Zealand under-21 international, began to really blossom as a goal attack, growing in confidence as the year progressed. The bond between Jodi and Irene was also growing.

For Jodi it was like having a big — very big — sister to talk to about her netball, and there was no one more supportive.

'I remember a team meeting in Invercargill after a game in which we'd been beaten,' Jodi says. 'Looking straight at me, Irene said, "You're a brilliant player, you just have to believe in yourself."

'I took those words away from the meeting and thought about them often, so it was only natural that when I was thinking of leaving Wellington and the Shakers at the end of 2001 I should talk to Irene before making a decision. I had been in Wellington since 1998 and felt I needed a change of environment. I had some good offers from other franchises and one in particular, from the Canterbury Flames, was really tempting. It wasn't money that made me think about moving south, rather the chance to play with someone like Julie Seymour.

'After talking everything over with Irene I decided to stay in Wellington, and one of the things that swayed me was just how much I enjoy playing with her. That was quite a turnaround from someone who didn't want her to come to the Shakers in the first place. Now we do weight training together at Johnsonville on Tuesday and Thursday nights outside the netball season.

'Like all New Zealand netballers I want to get in the Silver Ferns, and I joke with Irene that the only chance I'm going to get is if she breaks a leg.'

Unlike Jodi Te Huna, Donna Loffhagen felt no apprehension about Irene arriving in New Zealand to play for the Shakers. It made no difference to her position at the Southern Sting. That changed, however, when Irene announced she was making New Zealand her permanent home and that she was available for the Silver Ferns. Suddenly Loffhagen's Silver Ferns place could be in jeopardy. It was no surprise that when reporters asked the forthright Loffhagen for her opinion it was forthcoming.

Two years on, Loffhagen made no apologies for anything she said during the controversy about whether Irene should be allowed to play for New Zealand, though she does have some sympathy for what her rival had to endure.

'It was never anything personal against Irene. She's an amazing person. My gripe was with the international rules which I thought were ridiculous. I still feel that way. I said at the time that South Africa were not up to international standard and if their best player was taken out then they would get worse. I think I have been proved right on that score.

'Once the storm blew over and Irene was picked for the Ferns then so far as I was concerned she was a member of the team and would get any help she needed. Any new player coming into the team is looked after by the others and Irene was no different. She had earned the right to be there, but it must have been really tough for her with the pressure she was getting from the media. During the arguments people probably didn't take into account how Irene was feeling. I know now that it was hard for her.

'Not only did she have to handle what was happening in the public arena, she also had to adapt to playing with New Zealand's top netballers. It was never going to be easy for her but she has worked hard and come a long way with her netball. Irene is a very different player now to the one that fronted up in a New Zealand team for the first time.

'Along with the other girls, Irene has played a part in how close the New Zealand team has now become. Over the years there has at times been disharmony within the Silver Ferns, for various reasons, but that has all changed. Netball New Zealand should take some of the credit for that because they were the ones who appointed Yvonne Willering and Robyn Broughton. That has to be one of the best decisions Netball New Zealand has made.'

Another Silver Fern shooter, Tania Dalton (née Nicholson), who took time out from the international scene following the South African trip in late 2000 to give birth to her first child, says it takes a shooter to understand a shooter and the emotions they go through during a game.

'Being a shooter might be glamorous when things are going well, but it can be a lonely spot if you're not quite on song,' Dalton says. 'You're constantly measured by your statistics, so many from so many. Watch a television broadcast of a netball match and that's all you seem to hear.

'Do they measure the percentage of intercepts defenders get from those they attempt? No. But then I suppose that's why we become shooters. Because we enjoy playing under pressure, either being the hero or the villain.

'Irene is able to keep smiling and encourage those around her even after missing a shot, and that's important. If you let it get to you it shows on your face and defenders immediately know your confidence is going. I know that from experience. Playing for New Zealand in 1996 I let it show and it really got me down. It was a hard lesson but I learnt from it.

'I haven't had a lot to do with Irene but when I do see her we connect. I hung out with Irene and Bernie when the Ferns were on tour and we had fun. She wins everyone over, and all that rubbish about her playing for the Ferns would have gone on much longer than it did had Irene had a different nature.'

Former New Zealand captain Bernice Mene and Irene have become firm friends since Irene became a Silver Fern, but the friendship began before that when the pair spent their last night in Kuala Lumpur following the 1998 Commonwealth Games together, despite playing for different countries. Mene says they hit it off because they have the same outlook on life. Both prefer to see the good side of people and situations rather than look for the negative.

Their first meeting took place in an Auckland hotel, at a Netball New Zealand sponsors' lunch to welcome the South Africans on their first visit after being re-admitted to the international netball fraternity.

'Irene sat next to me and, as usual, she was chatting away. It doesn't take her long to make friends.

'From a netball point of view we knew what to expect from Irene. She was obviously South Africa's main weapon and our job was to stop the ball reaching her. We did a reasonable job in that regard in the one-off test in Auckland, but the South Africans, who had lost their three tests against Australia on the way to New Zealand, obviously went away and analysed what had happened on the trip and learned from it for the world championships. The South Africans played a different style of netball that we found tough to combat. They got the ball into Irene well and she did the rest.

'I agree with Irene that everything seemed to go South Africa's way in that world championship game in Birmingham, but that's the way sport is. You can make your own luck but sometimes the ball keeps falling the way of one team.'

In view of the controversy that surrounded Irene's selection for the Silver Ferns, she was delighted to find that Bernice Mene would be by her side for the media duties she had to carry out on the day she was first picked. Mene was happy that she was able to help smooth the path for Irene's initiation into the New Zealand team.

'The day was difficult for Irene. She was so excited at being chosen for the Ferns, yet unsure about how she would be received by those doing the interviews. I'm a bit of a mother sometimes and I like to look after people, so I was comfortable being by her side.

'It was the same when we were in Australia for the tri-nations and the controversy over whether she should be allowed to play in the Commonwealth Games surfaced. The management, including myself as captain, discussed what was happening and decided we would keep the media away from Irene. She was there to play netball, not talk about the Commonwealth Games.

'Irene was really sensitive about what was happening, especially with the South Africans taking part in the same competition. While she might not show it, Irene does worry about things. She puts on the smiley face and everyone thinks she hasn't got any worries. We are the same in that way. Part of a captain's job is being able to read people and I knew Irene needed some reassurance.'

The ability to read people also told Mene that Irene wasn't enjoying herself in training when she first teamed up with the Silver Ferns; that the speed she was receiving the ball at was giving her difficulties after being so used to passes being lobbed into her. That Irene has worked hard to adjust has earned her Mene's respect, but her former skipper is convinced that the best is yet to be seen of Irene.

'Irene still has potential that's not fulfilled. I believe she will become a real game breaker once she begins to combine better with the other players. Her height, agility and sheer athleticism in taking the ball make her difficult to mark. Defenders might think a ball is going out of court when she somehow manages to extend her arms and drag it in.

'Off court Irene's vivacious personality is invaluable. She gives so much of herself, is always happy and really genuine.'

With netball still an amateur sport, or semi-professional at best, players have to juggle their time to fit everything in. By the end of 2001 Mene, who was also a teacher, was feeling drained and looking forward to the school holidays.

'If I'm tired, how does someone like Irene feel? Not only does she have netball and school to worry about, she also has Bianca to organise. I take my hat off to the netballing mothers.'

Chapter 20

The Ultimate Challenge

RARELY, IF EVER, HAS A NETBALL EVENT been so eagerly anticipated as the Fisher and Paykel series between New Zealand and Australia that was played in Wellington, Invercargill and Christchurch in October 2001.

Each country had tasted success over their great rivals during the previous 18 months. Australia had outclassed the Silver Ferns at Newcastle in June 2000. New Zealand had bounced back to win convincingly in the one-off test that was part of a tri-nations series with South Africa in the republic four months later. New Zealand had followed that up with a 15-goal win at Melbourne 12 months after the battering they'd received in Newcastle. It was sweet revenge, but Australia turned the tables seven days later in Sydney where they won by ten. Again those games were part of a tri-series with South Africa, and it was New Zealand who took the trophy home because Australia had needed to win the Sydney game by 16 goals to edge out the Silver Ferns.

There was something unsatisfactory about the outcome of those four games between the netball heavyweights in that there was no clear winner. As the curtain came down in Sydney New Zealand's celebrations at winning the series were tempered by having just lost to Australia by ten goals. It was the same with the Australians. They'd just scored a notable victory but had to watch their rivals lift the trophy.

Everyone agreed that to decide who was current top dog in world netball, even though Australia could of course claim to be world champions at least till 2003, a three-test series was needed. That was about to happen.

Two weeks before arriving in New Zealand, Australian captain Kathryn Harby-Williams said whoever came out on top in what was a true test would have bragging rights and a psychological advantage leading into the 2002 Commonwealth Games in Manchester. Yvonne Willering agreed. Questions remained unanswered when it was a one-off clash. Players on the losing side always felt they could change the outcome given another chance straightaway. This time, that would happen.

The Australians arrived in Wellington on flight NZ142 from Melbourne on a grey, chilly, windy Wednesday afternoon but the warm welcome they received at the airport made up for the inhospitable weather. Australia's international netballers love visiting New Zealand where their sport has a much higher profile than at home, a fact borne out by the television, radio and newspaper reporters waiting for them outside the arrival hall.

While experienced members of the Australian team such as Harby-Williams, Liz Ellis and Sharelle McMahon knew what to expect, those who hadn't been part of a senior tour of New Zealand previously looked a little bemused at all the attention the team was getting. Harby-Williams and Ellis, as captain and vice-captain respectively, along with coach Jill McIntosh, went easily through a series of interviews with various journalists, some they knew well from previous encounters, others they were meeting for the first time. It didn't matter into which category the reporter fitted, they were all given time patiently and with a smile.

It looked as if butter wouldn't melt in the mouths of these attractive young women, but the New Zealand public knew better; they were well aware of how physical the Australians could be on court after watching the Sydney test on television. Consequently many of the questions directed at McIntosh and Harby-Williams focused on how physical — brutal, some said — that clash had been.

McIntosh brushed the accusations aside. Media hype, she said. Her team was here to play netball, just as they'd been in Melbourne and Sydney, and she couldn't believe how incidents from the last time the teams had met had been blown out of proportion. Some of the comments made post-match had been an insult to the umpires who had 'controlled' the game, McIntosh said.

Harby-Williams set the scene for what was to be an enthralling series by describing it as her team's ultimate challenge. There was nothing better, she said, than a three-test netball series between Australia and New Zealand.

Since 1995 Harby-Williams and Ellis have formed a formidable defensive duo that, to opposing teams, must seem like an impregnable barrier in front of goal. If it was possible, Harby-Williams' game seemed to have gone up another notch since she had been made captain following the retirement of Australian shooting legend Vicki Wilson.

You don't need to speak to Harby-Williams to know how proud she is to captain her country's team. The body language says it all. Leading her team on to the court with head held high and shoulders thrown back, Harby-Williams resembles a warrior leading her troops into battle.

The languid walk may suggest all is calm within, but in reality she's a tightly coiled spring ready to explode into action at the first whistle.

As they watched film of the Australians' arrival on the television news in their Wellington hotel that night the Silver Ferns' hearts began beating a little faster. The enemy had arrived in town. Before that the New Zealanders, who had assembled at the Copthorne Plimmer Towers Hotel on Sunday afternoon, had gone about their business and training in a professional manner, but the upcoming tests only became a reality when the Aussies landed.

Sunday had been spent catching up with the latest gossip and trying on the new outfits handed out by manager Sheryl Wells. The major talking point was the birth of Silver Fern Tania Dalton's daughter Tayla, who had made a painful entrance into the world the previous week. Dalton had been on the historic October trip to South Africa, and had played for Northern Force in the 2001 Coca-Cola Cup while pregnant. Imagine that happening these days in Australia!

Dalton was already mapping out her return to netball, hoping to follow in the footsteps of Julie Seymour who was returning to the Silver Ferns for the tests against Australia after giving birth to her first child. Seymour was still breast-feeding her son, Harrison, and Willering had given permission for the baby to come into camp with Julie, who brought her mother along to look after him. That decision raised eyebrows in some quarters but not with the players. Irene says you would never have known there was a baby around.

'Harrison and Julie's mother were on a different floor in the hotel so we didn't see either of them apart from when we were travelling, and then we made a huge fuss over him. There were no problems whatsoever. It was a sensible move. Julie was playing well enough to get back into the team, and as she was still feeding Harrison he needed to be with her.

'It was a home tour, which made things easier, and no one made an issue of it. Sometimes when we were on the way to training someone would ask Jules where Harrison was and she would say her mum had taken him for a walk, or that he was having a rest. Actually it seemed as if Jules had never been away. The only thing different to when she was with the team previously was that this time her baby was sleeping in a room in our hotel.

'These were special circumstances in that she was breast feeding. No one likes leaving their children to go on tour, but you realise it has to happen. Imagine having a team full of mothers all taking their children on tour . . . Of course it wouldn't work, but at times you have to be flexible and this was one of those times. Those who questioned Yvonne's decision were the type who can start an argument in an empty room.'

Preparations for the test series began on the Monday morning, and first up was a session with sports psychologist Greg Kolt. Such sessions are now commonplace in most sports at top level, but it is very much up to the individual what they get out of them. Some find them helpful. Others are sceptical and decide it is not for them.

Irene has always tried to go into psychological sessions with an open mind. She finds them interesting and if she can glean even one small thing from a session then, to her, it will have been worthwhile. For Irene the session with Greg Kolt turned out to be more interesting than usual. Two days later, for the first time during a test match, she consciously used a technique suggested by a sports psychologist.

'From the start there was a good feeling about the session because it was all hands on. We all discussed everything. It wasn't just him standing in front talking blah, blah, blah and us falling asleep.

'Lots of game scenarios were discussed and how people react differently to them and how to help concentration. How do the team know if you as an individual are struggling, and how are they going to lift you? What goals to set and how to achieve them.

'We looked for a word or phrase that could be used on court when things got tough. The golden phrase we settled on, our keyword, was "own it", an anagram of won it. Bernie would shout that if we were going through a rough period and it did help.

'One thing I took personally from the session was to breathe deeply in certain situations. It is the first time I have taken something specific on court from a psychology session and it definitely helped me.

'When the ball was turned over at the other end of court by Bernie or Linda I would take a deep breath and tell myself that I had to score from this move. I had never done that before and I think it worked in helping me stay calm in such a pressure situation. The key to the session was that Greg was so natural. It helped me. Hopefully it helped some of the others as well, but only the individual knows that. It is not something you really talk about once you're out of the session.'

A two-hour afternoon training run and an evening game against players from the Capital Shakers meant everyone was ready for a good night's sleep to prepare for another busy day on Tuesday.

On Tuesday afternoon the players gathered in the team room to watch a video of their 15-goal win over Australia in Melbourne, a game they'd enjoyed so much and had gone away from thinking they'd played brilliantly. No one could blame them for thinking that way. You don't beat the world champions by such a margin without playing brilliantly!

'It was the first time we'd watched it together and when the tape finished we couldn't believe we'd won that test, and won it so well. There were parts where we were so slow, and made so many unforced errors.

'When the video began we were all bright and upbeat, ready to enjoy one of our great moments. As the game progressed everyone got quieter and quieter. There were times when we looked like amateurs.

'Watching our reactions, Yvonne smiled and said she was pleased that we'd seen it for ourselves and recognised it wasn't our best game. She had told us that after the game, but it was only watching it again, removed from the emotion that accompanied the big win, that we realised how right she was and that there was so much work to do.'

That night the Silver Ferns had a game against the New Zealand men's team. It is an exercise that Willering always finds beneficial. The men have excellent skills, great elevation and are strong. Willering will ask them to perform specific tasks, such as throw long passes to tempt the New Zealand defenders into intercepts.

Irene didn't seem her normal self during the game. She was listless and her concentration wavered after only one quarter.

'On our first night in camp I hadn't slept well because I was sweating so much. I got up next morning feeling so tired and drained. I had drunk two bottles of water during the night, which is something I never do. I never, ever wake up for a drink during the night. Yvonne was understandably worried because I couldn't concentrate for two quarters. I would play the first well and then go downhill.

'When I went to bed on Monday it was exactly the same as the previous night. I was sweating so much I was soaking wet and had to get up and change my night clothes. It was so strange. Then something twigged, and I checked the electric blanket. The person who had the room before us must have left it on and I never thought to check. No wonder I couldn't sleep and felt drained in the morning.'

Once that problem had been sorted out Irene began to feel better. So did Willering. Her shooter was back to normal.

The relaxed atmosphere in the camp began to dissipate as the first game drew closer. Nerves tightened as thoughts turned to the task ahead. Being a home series meant that whenever the New Zealand players stepped out of their hotel there were well-wishers urging them to kick some Aussie butt.

Saturday, game day, arrived and Wellington's morning paper, the *Dominion*, led its back page with Silver Ferns captain Bernice Mene saying there was no limit to how far this New Zealand team could go. In what was a refreshing departure from the common practice of players and coaches playing down their own team and boosting the profile of the opposition in case they lose and end up with egg on their face, Mene didn't hold back when talking about her international team-mates.

There were no wild boasts about the likely outcome of the first test. Mene has too much respect for Australia to go down that road, but her demeanour made it plain that there was now more self-belief in the camp than in the past.

'I looked around during training and could tell everyone had worked hard to be at peak for this series. You know they are strong enough to last a full game against Australia which will be played at a fast pace,' Mene said.

'There is huge potential in this team because they are all skilful athletes. It is a very talented group. The balance is right, with experienced players alongside fresh faces that bring an exciting edge to the environment. There is real self-belief, and the consistency and understanding needed at international level is now coming. Everyone has done the work, we all have the same goals and there is a quiet confidence within the team. Really, there is no limit to where we can go with this team.'

Reading those words from the captain on awakening would have done the Ferns' confidence no harm as they went over in their minds what lay ahead, something that's bound to happen given the time players have on their hands on match day.

Night games are the norm in international netball. This means there is a full day to fill in and that's where someone such as Jenny-May Coffin shows she can be just as innovative off court as she is in the midcourt. According to Irene, Jenny-May is one of those people who dream up games and pranks at the drop of a hat.

'Jenny-May has something up her sleeve every day. If we have to wait around at any time she will get a game going straight away to occupy us. Earlier in the week she had everyone in hysterics by hiding under a table in the team room, hidden away by a tablecloth that went down to the ground. We put a whiteboard marker at the far end of the table and when Robyn [Broughton, assistant coach] came in Belinda asked her could she pass the marker to her. "No problem," said Robyn, but as she reached over to get it Jenny-May grabbed her foot from under the table.

'Robyn freaked out, she was running up and down shouting. It was hilarious. Yvonne sat on the side with tears running down her face from laughing so much. When everyone had settled down we noticed that Donna and Linda hadn't arrived so we set it all up again. The question was, which one do we ask to pass the marker? Belinda said it had to be

Linda because if someone asked Donna she would probably tell them to get the marker themselves. So Linda it was, and the joke worked just as well with her as it had with Robyn.

'In the lead-up to our pre-match preparations on the Saturday, Jenny-May split us into threes for a make-up session. One person was to apply the make-up blindfolded, with another the navigator and the third, poor person, the recipient. I was with Donna and Belinda and, thankfully, Belinda was the subject. I had to put on the make-up with Donna guiding me.

'Lipstick, eye-shadow, blush, nail polish . . . it all had to go on. Actually when they took the blindfold off I hadn't done a bad job so Donna must have been spot on with her navigation. The main thing was it helped take our minds off what lay ahead till the time came to focus completely on the game.'

When the team arrived at Wellington's Queen's Wharf Events Centre most of the 3800 crowd were in their seats and the pre-match entertainment was in full swing, making for a carnival atmosphere. The fans raised the roof when the Ferns walked into the stadium for a warm-up, and by the time the teams were introduced individually on to the court the venue was a seething cauldron.

'Once we got to the stadium we were anxious to get out there and start playing. Being the first game in the series meant there were more nerves. The pressure was so great that you could almost touch it. There is always more pressure in a home series but it doesn't just come from the media or public. We put it on ourselves because we expect to win these games and set our goals high.

'We know we have the ability to beat Australia — we'd proved that in recent games — but that doesn't make it any easier. While we were singing the national anthems I looked at the Australians and told myself they were no better than me or the other Ferns. The nerves were jangling so much that I had to take a few deep breaths, but once the game started and I caught the ball for the first time it was sweet.'

Sweet is not a word that can be used to describe the start New Zealand made to that first test match. Within minutes they were 1–7 down and seemingly on the way to a real hiding at the hands of the Australians. The capacity crowd, so vocal minutes earlier, were stunned into comparative silence as the number under Australia's name on the scoreboard clicked over consistently.

Willering had surprised by switching regular wing attack Adine Harper and centre Temepara George; but if she had done it to confuse the Australians it didn't work. The only ones confused in the opening minutes were the Silver Ferns who struggled to find the midcourt cohesion that had been a feature of their recent successes, and by the time the switch was reversed Australia were in charge.

'Before the game Yvonne told me not to lose my smile, whatever was happening. When the girls turned around after an Australian goal she wanted them to see me still upbeat and hoped that would act as a spur.

'After that shocking start Donna turned round to me with those big eyes of hers and said, "F....." I said, "Don't worry, it will be alright," and began shouting at the girls that it would be OK, that we would get it back. Then I looked at the scoreboard and thought they must think I was the biggest idiot around because everyone could see we were six goals down.

'Within minutes, however, we were back on terms with them, which shows you that anything can happen during a minute in netball. Robyn has timed us and we can score a goal in six seconds from the defenders getting the ball to us attackers putting it through the net, and there are a lot of six seconds in an hour-long game.'

Unfortunately for New Zealand, the Australians can score just as quickly and when the first quarter whistle went the world champions were 16–11 ahead. By half-time they led 33–24 after at one point stretching their advantage to 11 goals. By three-quarter time New Zealand had reduced the deficit to four goals at 42–38, and with three minutes to play had got it back to one goal with the ball in hand.

The resolute defence of Harby-Williams, Ellis and Peta Squire held firm, however. They put the New Zealand attack under relentless pressure and Julie Seymour, who made a tremendous difference when she took the court as a second-half substitute, threw a long pass over Irene's head and out of court, while Temepara George strayed offside at a vital moment. At the final whistle Australia were 51–47 ahead and the Silver Ferns could only think about what might have been had they not got off to that horror start.

Australia's defenders double-teamed Irene, who shot 39 from 44, and that left gaps for Donna Loffhagen but the goal attack put up only 10 shots. Loffhagen said it had been difficult as she had been out of the circle feeding, rather than in it complementing her shooter.

'The feeder role isn't my game,' Loffhagen said. 'I felt Irene was on top of Liz Ellis but we have to utilise her height better. At least we showed there is character in the team. We dug deep and it was an awesome second half.'

Awesome second half it might have been but New Zealand were one down and the three-test series would be over as a contest if Australia won again in Invercargill four days later.

New Zealand's players didn't need telling that. They were in sombre mood both in the changing room and back at the hotel, leaving Willering with the job of picking them up and getting them in the right frame of mind for the next game. She wasted no time in doing that.

'Everyone was sad and depressed when Yvonne came in and asked what were all the glum faces about. No one said anything; we all just looked at her so she carried on talking. "OK, you did a few stupid things but we have got time to work it out. Whenever we've lost to Australia in the past you've told me that it would be different if you could just play them again quickly. Well, this is your chance. You will be playing them again. You fought back like hell tonight. It showed me you have got character and that you can dig yourself out of a hole. Get over it. We will work on it tomorrow. You have got another chance, so think about what you've got to do. Don't just go and sulk. That won't get you anywhere. We've lost. It's over. Now we start again."

'Yvonne stopped us feeling sorry for ourselves and made us look ahead, not back.'

The following morning, after a session in the swimming pool to ease tired and bruised bodies, the Silver Ferns headed for Invercargill which has become something of a netball Mecca since Stadium Southland was built. To say that Southlanders are proud of their stadium is an understatement, as a Wellington journalist found out on the way south to cover the game. After changing planes in Christchurch he had just settled into his seat beside a woman he had never seen before when former Australian netball captain Anne Sargeant, who was covering the tour for Australia's ABC television and sitting in the row behind, asked him what Stadium Southland was like.

Just another stadium, was his reply, which brought a sharp retort from the woman in the next seat who let him know in no uncertain terms that it was New Zealand's best. No, she hadn't seen all New Zealand's major stadiums, but the pride in her voice said everything.

There is little to choose between most indoor stadiums in New Zealand. The only real variable is in the fans who fill the seats, and in that regard Southland can claim to have an edge thanks to their fanaticism. The Silver Ferns, especially those who had been part of visiting teams during the Coca-Cola Cup, had found it a welcome change to have the crowd on their side for the England game and knew the noise would go up another notch with their great trans-Tasman rivals the opposition.

While there were some welcome diversions in the deep south, including a birthday party for Temepara George complete with carrot cake,

candles and sparklers, there was a single-mindedness about the New Zealanders as they prepared for the second test. It was very simple. They
told each other that losing this game wasn't an option. They were willing
to do anything to win the test and keep the series alive; to give the fa-
natical fans inside the stadium something to shout about and those
watching on television a game to remember. To achieve those goals they
were even prepared to borrow something from the Australians' make-
up.

'Watching a video of the first test we saw that whenever Australia
did something successfully they would cheer each other on. It would be
very visible, right in our faces as if they were winners and we were
losers. Sharelle McMahon and Eloise Southby were perfect examples. If
they did something well they would clap hands and go through the whole
rigmarole.

'Not only are they building confidence within themselves through
geeing each other up, they are also making the opposition feel as if they
are losers. We decided that's something we would do. We would be there
for one another, visibly cheer each other on, make eye contact whenever
possible — in short, communicate better with each other. Bernie and I
had lots of eye contact during the second test. As we walked to our places
after the anthems we winked at each other and it made me feel so good.'

The body language of the New Zealanders as they walked into Stadium Southland to a rapturous reception gave observers who had watched
the team at close quarters over recent years a good feeling about what
was to come. Nerves that had been so obvious four days earlier had gone.
As they waved to their supporters there was a confidence about the Ferns
that had been missing in Wellington.

Such optimism appeared misplaced as the second test began in the
same vein as the first — with Australia racing to an early 6–1 lead. The
capacity crowd that was still shouting their lungs out could have been
forgiven for a feeling of déjà vu, but on court that was anything but the
feeling.

'It might sound crazy, but I felt we were in control the whole time,
even in those early minutes when we found ourselves behind again. This
was different. We were in synch and our rhythm was smooth.

'In the shooting circle there was a completely different feeling. Part
of the game plan was for Donna to share the shooting duties early on, to
take shots so that the Australian defence had two shooters to take care
of, not one. Donna did that beautifully by putting up seven shots in the
first quarter and scoring with six of them.'

The bad start again left the Silver Ferns with a hill to climb, but rather than let it become a mountain they bounced back with five unanswered goals to level, and then upped the ante by taking a 16–12 first quarter lead. With a foundation laid, New Zealand built upon it with a sound second quarter that gave them a 30–23 half-time lead and from that point they were in control, eventually winning 58–47.

While it was a magnificent all-round team effort, the golden shooting duo of van Dyk and Loffhagen had destroyed the Australians with a precision performance. Irene was at her unflappable best as she used all her athleticism on the way to sinking 45 of her 47 shots, and Donna backed her up with 13 goals from 17 attempts.

At the back Linda Vagana and Bernice Mene not only kept pressure on the Australian attackers who had been so successful in Wellington, but took vital intercepts and rebounds that lifted their team-mates. The midcourt of Temepara George, Julie Seymour and Victoria Edward, along with Jenny-May Coffin, who was thrown into the fray in the last quarter when fresh legs were needed, provided the shooters with a quality of ball that had been missing in the first test.

This time it was the New Zealanders smiling at the final whistle, the Australians heading for the changing rooms with frowns on their faces. Just how much the loss meant to the Australians showed when Sharelle McMahon, a fierce competitor, gave Southland fans a subtle two-fingered salute as she made her way off court. Few people would have seen it, but it probably gave her some satisfaction.

Two days later a reporter who had seen the gesture asked McMahon about it. She denied it had happened, but the blush that spread over her face spoke louder than words. Anyone who thought Australia had allowed New Zealand to level the series to set up a grand finale, and there were some talkback callers and letters-to-the-editor writers who entertained such a ridiculous idea, only needed to see McMahon's gesture to know how far wide of the mark they were.

Afterwards Irene kicked herself for passing up the chance of achieving a lifelong ambition of shooting 100 per cent in a test match. The delight at scoring 45 goals from 47 attempts was tempered by the fact that the two missed were from close range.

'Shocking,' was how Irene described those misses to media after the game. 'The perfect game was there for the taking and I blew it. I wouldn't have minded had the ones I missed been from long range. I could have accepted that. But no, they were two of the easiest ones, thanks to a lapse in concentration.'

She was being harsh on herself, but then shooting 100 per cent really would have capped off what was already a wonderful night.

New Zealand's second-test win set up a mouth-watering series finish at Christchurch's WestpacTrust Centre, a venue that held contrasting memories for Donna Loffhagen and Sharelle McMahon. The pair were central figures in a dramatic finale to the 1999 world championship, with Loffhagen missing a goal in the dying seconds which allowed McMahon to slot the winning goal with the last shot of the tournament.

How much the 11-goal loss in Invercargill had hurt the Australians was obvious from the moment they landed in Christchurch. There was a renewed urgency about their preparations. While as personable as ever, there was a steely look about coach Jill McIntosh that showed she meant business even more than usual.

Australian media officer Kath Keenan was taken by surprise when McIntosh called an extra video session during the first afternoon in Christchurch. Keenan had arranged an interview for captain Harby-Williams but that, rightly, took a back seat to what McIntosh decided, though it was of little consolation to this reporter, kicking his heels in the hotel lobby for a couple of hours.

In another departure from her normal approach, McIntosh decreed that training sessions were closed to the media and public. Why that happened was plain to see later on, when McIntosh named her starting line-up just before the third and deciding test.

There was also a subtle shift of emphasis from the Australians when they were interviewed. On their arrival all the talk was about a three-test series showing which team was top dog in the netball world. After Invercargill, Australia's main focus was on defending their gold medal at the Commonwealth Games. It seemed they were a little apprehensive about the outcome.

Over in the New Zealand camp it couldn't have been an easy time for Loffhagen, returning as she was to the scene of the 1999 disappointment, but she handled it in her usual straightforward way as the media milled around towards the end of the Silver Ferns' Friday training session. As usual manager Sheryl Wells was organised, asking each media representative who they wished to interview at the end of training. Both television stations and the *Dominion* asked for Loffhagen.

As always, television took precedence, so I had to wait while she finished the other two interviews, a period prolonged by the stadium lights being switched off.

Never one to beat around the bush, Loffhagen laughed as she approached me, apologised for keeping me waiting and said: 'Let's get it over with. Everyone wants to interview me because they want to talk about *that* goal, or rather the goal that wasn't. OK I missed that goal, but it was two years ago and people have got to move on. Shooter was a position I chose to play and you take whatever comes with it.'

It wasn't only the media who were reminding Loffhagen about what had happened two years earlier. On the team's first visit to the WestpacTrust Centre Belinda Colling walked to a spot near a goal and asked: 'Is this where you missed from?' Adine Harper helpfully pointed out that it was a little more to the side.

Irene believes that the players were trying to make light of a situation they knew was going to be on Loffhagen's mind, but she still felt compelled to point out that this was a different team and that what had happened two years earlier was irrelevant.

'I told them that I was now in the team and didn't want to hear about 1999. It had been a terrible moment for all those girls who had been a part of such a heart-breaking loss, but it was doing no good going over it again now.

'Donna would have felt it more than anyone because of the way it happened. You don't forget things like that when your whole nation is depending on you, and the media didn't help by bringing it up with her going into the third test. They didn't need to ask her things such as, "Can you still remember it?" — what a dumb question — and "Are you over it?" The media really sucked it out and it was unfair of them, totally unnecessary.

'Of course it was a heaven-sent story for the media with Donna and Sharelle coming together again in that stadium. I can't blame the media for writing it and reminding people about what happened, but to keep reminding Donna about it . . . that was wrong.'

In contrast, the Australians were milking every moment of their return to the place where they'd retained their world title. Newcomers to the team were treated to every detail of that famous victory, especially how they plucked victory from certain defeat in seconds.

McMahon was only too willing to talk about her love of Christchurch and how it felt to be part of such a dramatic finish. 'It was great, but I don't know whether my heart would stand another end like that. I would like a bit of breathing space this time,' the Australian goal attack said.

Fittingly, the biggest crowd to attend a netball game in New Zealand, almost 7000, filled the WestpacTrust Centre for the deciding test, hoping for a reversal of the world championship result. In marked contrast to Invercargill the Silver Ferns appeared tense when they entered the stadium, with Irene the only player to return the fans' waves. The Australians looked no looser, however, and McIntosh was more animated than ever before during her team's warm-up.

The first big surprise of the night came when the teams were introduced and master tactician McIntosh had Jacqui Delaney playing wing attack for Australia. The New Zealanders had expected McIntosh to tinker with her midcourt after losing by 11 goals, but they surely wouldn't have imagined Delaney playing wing attack. Why would they? One of Australia's leading goal attacks, Delaney had played wing attack only twice in her career and admitted she was stunned when McIntosh raised the possibility with her.

'It was a real shock when Jill said it might happen,' Delaney says. 'She put me in the right frame of mind by pointing out that the positions are similar, but at wing attack there is not the pressure of having to shoot the goals as well.

'That made me realise she obviously had faith in my ability. Jill wanted a more patient forward line and bringing me in meant we'd three experienced heads in attack, along with Rebecca [Sanders] at centre.'

The Silver Ferns began where they'd left off in Invercargill by scoring the first two goals. Donna Loffhagen was quickly into the game with a long-range goal from her first shot and Irene began to feel this would again be the Ferns' night. Again, however, first-quarter mistakes cost New Zealand dearly as Australia went on a run that put them out to a 14–11 quarter-time lead that paved the way for a 50–46 win and a 2–1 series success that again left the Silver Ferns wondering where it had all gone wrong.

'Those three first-quarter goals haunted us till the end of the game. We just couldn't break back. At one stage we got back to within one goal, but whenever we got close we lost the plot.'

Once more, in the wake of the loss much was made of the Australians being more physical and tougher than the New Zealanders. That was beginning to wear thin with Irene.

'The Aussies aren't alone in being physical and I think too much is made of that part of their game. Sure, in Sydney earlier in the year, when they were desperate, there was some off-the-ball stuff. But when it comes to straight physical challenges I don't believe we are soft.

'I gave a few knocks to Liz and Kathy. In the heat of the moment you do anything to get the ball. It got physical, but it was both ways. We weren't the little feminine ones hanging on, everyone was getting stuck in. It annoys me when people say we can't handle it. We are strong, hard players who can take knocks but we want to try and use our skill rather than run the opposing player off the court.

'The game in Invercargill was just as physical as the other two tests, but because we won by such a big margin no one talked about that part of the game. No one that night said we were soft and couldn't take the knocks.

'The two teams are so equal it all comes down to what happens on the day. Four goals is two turnovers. A couple of bad bounces can lead to a four-goal loss. That's how close New Zealand and Australia are. In that first test, one pass over the end of court and an offside . . . that was the difference between the teams.'

Inevitably, with New Zealand losing the series, questions were asked about Yvonne Willering's future. Her two-year contract had just ended, the job was to be advertised and she had to decide whether to apply to continue.

Amid the disappointment of losing the third test and the series the Silver Ferns rallied round Willering, saying that to change coach at that point with the Commonwealth Games the following year and world championships in 2003 would be a bad move. On the night Willering refused to talk about her future. She had always told her players never to make career decisions while emotions were running high either in victory or defeat. She was following her own advice.

Two weeks later, having had time to think things over, Willering announced she would again be applying for the position.

'I was so pleased when I heard she had decided to try and retain the coaching job. The players had all told her on that last night in Christchurch that she had to apply. We wanted to win the Commonwealth Games for her. We knew in our hearts that we should have won the series against Australia.

'When I first came to New Zealand there were stories in the newspapers saying that some players wanted Yvonne out. That may have been the case at the time, but since I have been involved with the Silver Ferns there has been no dissension and everyone, players and management, have pulled together for the good of the team.

'Yvonne had a nice way of communicating with the players. There wasn't one player who didn't respect her and that led to a great team spirit. Sometimes there is that something that makes a team special. It doesn't happen very often but all the Silver Ferns thought we had that bit of magic.

'Not for a moment did I think that Yvonne would miss out on the job. It wasn't her who lost the game against Australia, it was the players. Had we followed her game plan we would have won.'

The day before the coach was to be announced I rang Irene to tell her that Yvonne was probably going to be overlooked and Ruth Aitken would get the job. She couldn't believe it.

'I rang Bubby, Bernie and Tania to see if they knew what was happening. Bubby was totally stunned, but I think Bernie had an idea something was wrong. She had been into Netball New Zealand for an interview and it hadn't gone as she thought it would.

'That night I rang Yvonne but she didn't get back to me till the next afternoon when everything was official. She left a message on my phone and I spoke to her in the evening. Of course she was bitterly disappointed, but she had thought it might happen. After her second interview Yvonne feared the worst.'

Those who play sport at an elite level have to be adaptable when it comes to coaches. A coach can be there one minute and gone the next. It is the same with players. From being flavour of the month they can find themselves warming the substitutes bench or out of the team altogether.

'A player can learn from all the coaches she comes in contact with throughout her career. I know I have.

'When you work with a coach for a long period it is easy to get attached. I know I did with Yvonne. I am sure others felt that way when Leigh Gibbs was the coach. Ruth is now the coach and we have to look forward. Everyone will still have the same goal. That's to win a gold medal at the Commonwealth Games and win the world championship the following year.

'It is a fact of life that coaches come and go, especially at international level, but it is never easy when you see someone lose a job you know they love.'

Within days of Willering being replaced as Silver Ferns coach Irene was in Auckland with Christie, who was coaching the Wellington under-19 cricket team at a tournament. It was a perfect opportunity to catch up with Willering.

'We spent a lovely day together and didn't talk much about netball. Yvonne totally spoiled Bianca and gave me the whole touristy bit around Auckland. She showed me where she surfs and took us home to see her animals and cars. There were dogs, cats, rabbits, guinea pigs, chooks . . . the only thing I didn't see were the donkeys.

'She showed me her beach buggy and her pride and joy — a 1976 Corvette Stingray. It is a fabulous car. It was an idyllic day that may never have happened had we stayed player and coach with the Silver Ferns.'

Once she was confirmed as Silver Ferns coach, Ruth Aitken hit the ground running at the beginning of 2002. She was already a national selector and coach of the New Zealand A team that was about to take part in a challenge series with some of Australia's top Commonwealth Bank League teams.

The series was Aitken's swan song as A team coach, and proved to be a successful one, with New Zealand A winning the competition.

It was then time to turn her attention to the Silver Ferns and the tour to Jamaica at the end of February. Apart from the A team's success, it hadn't been plain sailing for the new coach. In fact, she needed to negotiate some stormy seas.

For a start there were suggestions the New Zealand players were upset by Yvonne Willing's removal. That was undoubtedly the case but, as Irene said, coaching changes are a fact of life and players have to move on.

Just prior to Aitken naming her squad for the Jamaican trip, Bernice Mene dropped a bombshell by announcing her retirement from international netball. Mene's announcement came like a bolt from the blue, though there had been a few whispers she wouldn't retain the captaincy under the new coaching regime. Whether that was indeed the case only Aitken knows, but Mene's decision left a hole in the Silver Ferns defence that hadn't been anticipated. A hole that became a chasm when Linda Vagana said she was unavailable for Jamaica.

Julie Seymour was handed the captaincy, a move greeted enthusiastically by players and media alike, and the New Zealand team, with 14 players instead of the usual 12, assembled in Christchurch before setting off for the Caribbean.

Irene didn't have pleasant memories of her previous visit to Jamaica with South Africa in 1998. The Proteas lost all three tests and the trip had been poorly organised. It was totally different going there with the Silver Ferns, thanks to the management team planning everything down to the finest detail, including having a doctor in the party for the first time.

Two warm-up games provided easy wins for New Zealand but if the entrée was tasty, the main course proved hard to swallow and almost became impossible to digest.

The Silver Ferns got Ruth Aitken off to a winning start, but not without some anxious moments and some bizarre decisions from Jamaican official, Dalton Hinds, who was sharing the umpiring duties with New Zealand's Kirsten Lloyd.

New Zealand had to overturn a five-goal deficit in the last quarter to beat a feisty Jamaica 46–44 and the final 15 minutes were nail-biting for the Ferns' bench. The closer New Zealand came to the home side, the more penalties Jamaica received from the male umpire, making calls that had the Ferns shaking their heads in disbelief.

The New Zealand management had covered everything within their control, but could do nothing about what can only be described as biased umpiring. If the Ferns thought Hinds was biased in the first test, they were convinced after the second, which Jamaica won 53-44 to level the series. It was Jamaica's first win over New Zealand.

Aitken saw the series as an opportunity to assess her players with a view to the Commonwealth Games later in the year and the rotation policy she adopted didn't help New Zealand's cause. Dalton Hinds definitely helped Jamaica's.

Nine times in the game, six in the first quarter, Hinds called New Zealand players for stepping. Normally you wouldn't see that number in a three-test series. Hinds appeared to be targeting Irene in particular and it became frustrating for the shooter.

'The signs had been there in the first test that Mr Hinds was going to pose a real problem, so I made a point of going over to him at the final whistle and thanking him for the game. I thought it might help for the next game. It didn't.

'During the second test every time I got the ball in the first few minutes he was pulling me up for stepping, yet I was doing nothing different to what I had been in the first game. Why was he picking on me?

'The way he was interpreting the stepping rule was ridiculous, but there was nothing to be done about it. The answer was in our own hands — or feet to be more precise.

'We had to make the change because if he's got it in his mind, we weren't going to get away with anything. It meant we had to go right back to basics when we landed after taking the ball.

'We couldn't land with a wide base because he had no idea which foot landed first. He obviously wasn't used to umpiring at such a high level. The team didn't play well in the second test, but I think what was happening with Mr Hinds ate away at us and contributed to our overall performance.'

New captain Julie Seymour gave Jamaica credit for their performance, but launched into Hinds' contribution to the game.

'I am quite openly saying the umpire was disgusting. We felt like we were playing against eight players out there,' Seymour said after the game.

Such outbursts are virtually unheard of in netball, but anyone who watched the game live, or on television back in New Zealand, knew where Seymour was coming from. Irene was right behind her.

'Good on Julie for saying what she did. It took a lot of guts, that's for sure. It might have been said in the heat of the moment, but she was speaking on behalf of the whole team.'

Whatever the reason — biased umpiring or a poor performance by

New Zealand — the series was now up for grabs and the situation wasn't lost on Irene or her team-mates.

'It was bad enough that we were the New Zealand team that lost to Jamaica for the first time. Had we gone on to lose the series we would have been crucified.

'I don't think people realise what a bloody good team Jamaica are — they're right up there. At the last world championships the Silver Ferns only beat them by two goals and that was in New Zealand. Australia were beaten there last year — winning a series in Jamaica isn't easy.

'Some people back home made it a bigger issue than it deserved. As we used to say in South Africa, they were pulling the pond from under the duck.'

New Zealand showed commendable composure in winning the deciding test 44–42 to silence the critics back home. Unlike the first two tests, when she used all allowable 12 players, Aitken didn't ring the changes in the third.

The rotation policy didn't go down well with some back in New Zealand. Former assistant coach Robyn Broughton said it was devaluing the Silver Fern bib, while Auckland Diamonds' coach Georgina Salter, who in the past has applied unsuccessfully for the New Zealand coaching job, said the rotation was messing with tradition.

'We knew from the start Ruth would be making lots of changes and the players accepted it,' Irene says.

'Ruth told us at the beginning that would happen, because she wanted to see who could handle change and who was comfortable in what was going to be a hostile atmosphere. She knew there would be flak back home but that was the way she wanted to do things.

'The tour was great for the players as well as Ruth, because it gave us the opportunity of getting to know her and the way she coaches. It takes a while to get used to a new coach because they all have a different perspective of the game and their own way of doing things.

'I'm just pleased we won the series despite all that went on. If we hadn't, I don't think we would have wanted to come home. We would've had to find a deserted island!'

The ultimate challenge Australia presented, the fall-out that followed and the tour to Jamaica completed Irene's first two years in New Zealand, and seven years of international competition. It has been a remarkable journey for a woman who, when first chosen to represent South Africa, could never have imagined where netball would take her.

There have been many highs and a few lows, but overall it has been a journey filled with fun and laughter, and along the way Irene has touched so many more people's lives than would have been the case had she stayed in South Africa. The story is far from finished. Irene has improved markedly as a netballer since moving to New Zealand and her goal is to turn netballing silver into gold for her adopted country.

Twice she has watched the Silver Ferns have world championship glory snatched from their grasp. On the first occasion she was one of the architects of New Zealand's downfall; four years later she was a helpless spectator.

Irene is likely to have an opportunity to help take New Zealand netball back to the top of the world at the 2003 world championships in Jamaica, but first there is the 2002 Commonwealth Games. Such has been the fairytale that is the life of Irene van Dyk, it would be no surprise if she and the Silver Ferns strike gold in Manchester.